# The Adventurer Within

## North to South France

### By a 'Have-a-go' Cycle-tourist

### David Paul Elliott

Copyright © David Paul Elliott 2025
This book is sold subject to the condition that it shall not, by way of trade or otherwise, be lent, resold, hired out, or otherwise circulated without the publisher's prior consent in any form of binding or cover other than that in which it is published and without a similar condition including this condition being imposed on the subsequent publisher.
The moral right of David Paul Elliott has been asserted.
ISBN: 9798336514766

*To my family and for my late parents Beryl & Paul, and for Eileen & Alf, who would all have loved to hear of my little adventure.*

# CONTENTS

AUTHOR'S NOTE ................................................................................................. i

BEGINNINGS ..................................................................................................... 1

OVERVIEW OF THE ROUTE ........................................................................ 4

WEEK ONE ........................................................................................................ 6
*Travels from North Devon to Dover via London. The channel crossing to Pas-de-Calais then cycling south and then east through the departments of Picardy, Somme, Oise & Aisne.*

WEEK TWO ..................................................................................................... 72
*South east through Ile-de-France and Burgundy via the departments of Aisne, Seine-et-Marne, Yonne, & Cote-d-Or.*

WEEK THREE ............................................................................................... 135
*Continuing through Burgundy into Auvergne-Rhone-Alps and visiting the departments of Cote-d'Or, Soane-et-Loire, Ain, Isere, & Drome.*

WEEK FOUR .................................................................................................. 221
*The south of France now as Provence is reached and with it the departments of Drome, Vancluse, Gard, & Bouches-du-Rhone.*

WEEK FIVE .................................................................................................... 270
*Bouches-du-Rhone & Herault followed by the Mediterranean coast and peddling across the Camargue into Occitaine. Return to Calais, then home to Devon via Dover & London.*

# Author's Note

Kindness was offered to me frequently on my little adventure by people I met along the way. Many of these chance encounters were fleeting moments with someone who was generous of spirit but whose name I never learned. Others shared personal details with me. Either way, the time taken to complete this book prevents me from seeking consent to mention these people in my story. To overcome this and preserve individual privacy, I've changed a few names and in one case the location. At the end of each day's journey I wrote contemporaneous notes, one hundred and eighty-one pages of notes in fact, which, together with well over a thousand photographs taken on my trip, have proved invaluable in supporting my recollections.

# Beginnings

I am standing in the living room of our North Devon home looking down at the absurdly long map that's rolled out across the old wooden floor. I cobbled the map together using ten pages from a large-scale European road atlas and a roll of Sellotape; a few days from now the map will prove its worth when I set off to cycle the length of France. I should probably mention that I rarely use a bicycle from one year to the next, I never have; nor have I pedalled a bike with a load, not once. I have a car so what's the point? I should also say that I haven't camped for decades because as we grow older it's traditional and sensible to break free from the naivety of youth that makes sleeping on the cold earth, miles from a toilet, a bit of a wheeze, when let's be honest, as anyone with an ounce of common sense knows, nothing, absolutely nothing, could be further from the truth.

Today is Thursday, it is just after lunchtime, and the sun is casting a pleasingly warm beam of light through the sash window next to me – last week was March so it's no surprise that it's a bit parky outside. Later this afternoon I shall furl my long skinny map and pack it into one of two hefty pannier bags that are destined to hang either side of the rear wheel of my bicycle. Other bits and bobs including my tent will be strapped on top of the panniers. I practised loading the bike a few days ago and I have to say it looks quite the sight, although it may well be that I am carrying too much and to be quite honest, that could be understating it because my bike looks rather overwhelmed by the luggage. I have never tried this cycle-camping lark before so I'm adopting a 'better-safe-than-sorry' approach to what I am taking with me, and you never know what you will need, do you? Well, I certainly don't, so taking most of what I can think of seems the prudent approach to me. Tomorrow morning, whatever the weather, I shall cycle the eighteen miles from this house to

Barnstaple, North Devon. It is a modest distance, I know, but eighteen miles will be a bit further than the longest cycle ride I've ever done, and that was years ago. Then, from Barnstaple, a series of trains will take me and the bike to Exeter, then to London, and finally to Dover for a night in lodgings. The next day I shall pedal down to the docks for the Saturday morning ferry to France.

Self-propelled across France, north to south, coast to coast, a solo trip on a *'velo'* laden with all the accoutrements required to camp, cook, and maintain myself and the bike – how exciting!

I've packed some food, clothes for all weathers, washing gear, a wind-up torch, a first-aid kit, maps – lots of maps, spare parts, perhaps too many, and innertubes of course, several innertubes in fact, plus a few tools, and a paperback – *'One thousand helpful tips to fix your bike when it all goes belly up'* sort of a book, you get the idea. Anyway, there you have it: an exceedingly cumbersome bike, a ridiculously small tent, a crazy-looking map, a camping cooker bought in 1969 and not used for decades, some euros, and a hundred words of the French language if I'm lucky. It all sounds like a bit of an adventure to me!

How can anyone about to embark upon such travels not be filled with enthusiasm? I know I am. Imagine: out in the open air, traversing a foreign country, close to nature on near-silent transport, self-reliance; it's just these facts that attracted me to the idea of a long bike trip and allowed me to ride roughshod over any suggestion that lack of experience is any impediment to such a glorious endeavour. A human-powered journey of roughly a thousand miles and stretched over thirty-plus days – surely having no previous experience just adds spice to the enterprise. Perhaps I should point out that by way of forcing myself to actually go ahead with this little escapade I bought myself a brand-new bike, then I boxed myself well and truly into a corner by telling people my idea was to cycle across France.

I can ride a bicycle, you know, at least I could the last time I gave it a go. After all, it's *'like riding a bike'*, they say. You never forget, apparently – let's hope not because in spite of all my best intentions the only cycling practice I've done for this journey was earlier today. This came about when I was momentarily slapped by a pang of timidity about just how the next few weeks may pan out. My concern was accompanied by a feeling of regret because I haven't even tried my equipment out yet. I do hope this doesn't end up being one of those 'all the gear – no idea' situations.

Anyway, as there is no point whingeing at this late stage, I overcame the unsettling realisation of being totally unprepared by loading both port and starboard panniers onto the bike. This was about an hour ago, before I pootled six hundred yards down the lane and then back to my house. You will be delighted to know that I didn't topple into a nettle-filled ditch, nor did a pedal shear off and catapult me into a hedge. In fact, no problems occurred whatsoever, not one, so I am now emboldened, which is just as well because as I mentioned, my departure is tomorrow morning so I'll just have to train on the job.

Back indoors after my little practice, I roll out the map once again. I find it oddly reassuring to gaze over my intended route; the map reminds me of the many hours I have spent planning exactly which roads are most suited to a would-be cycle-tourist. I think this may be a good time to describe my do-it-yourself cartographic oddity: Unrolled, my map is eleven feet long and just over a foot across. There's an extra-wide bit Sellotaped to the bottom. The overall shape of this whole map caboodle is roughly that of an inverted flagpole with the flag hoisted. Ordinarily the map lives an isolated existence inside a black plastic tube where until a few hours ago it had been left undisturbed for some months – but now, with departure almost upon me I need to refresh my memory as to where I am going and the route I intend to follow. At first my long skinny map is a little strange to gaze upon, but I would ask anyone doing so to put the visual oddness aside for a moment and consider that I have invested copious time and much thought into finalising my route. I really have planned my route to the $n^{th}$ degree and hopefully I have designed out most of the more predictable problems a have-a-go cycle-tourist such as myself would wish to avoid: Congested cities, mountains, arterial roads, that sort of thing. I reckon my map will prove to be invaluable in the coming weeks and I am actually rather proud of it. That isn't a bit sad, is it?

Next, I shall provide you with a short synopsis of my intended journey. It will bring this introduction to a conclusion and give you some idea if pressing on with this book beyond these first few pages is likely to be a complete waste of your valuable time or not.

## Overview Of The Route

Assuming I get as far as France, my first two days beyond Calais will be spent pedalling south through the rolling farmlands of Picardy – nothing too challenging by way of navigation or landscape to start with. Then I'll turn southeast and traverse the battlefields and water meadows of the Somme valley. Next, I'll pedal due east to give Paris a wide berth; delightful though the city is I have absolutely no desire to become entangled with the capital or its traffic.

Once beyond the catchment area of Paris the bike and I will slingshot ninety degrees to our right, head south, and enter the department of Seine-et-Marne before pressing on through the rolling plains and vineyards of the Champagne region. Further south is the department of Yonne and beyond that the tranquil canals of Burgundy. The route from Calais to this point is clear cut, but midway through Burgundy I've pencilled in a choice of two routes. If I am feeling up to it, I shall leave the Canal de Bourgogne towpath and set off over the Morvan Mountains. The mountain route will save me a good forty miles but it's the steeper of the two options. Alternatively, if I am not feeling up to tackling mountains I shall remain on the level canal towpath as far as Dijon, a beautiful medieval city that marks the halfway point of my journey. Next, the undulating lanes criss-crossing upland France-Comte will give me a taste of the more challenging heights of Auvergne-Rhône-Alps. Beyond France-Comte I shall potter down the Rhône-Saône valley, making sure to stay clear of the busy city of Lyon.

Next, Avignon, Orange, and Arles, and then, doubtless encouraged by the heady whiff of wild lavender and thyme I will ease my way into Provence before pedalling across the mysteriously flat and salty world that makes up the Camargue. My objective is the coastal village of Saintes-Maries-de-la-Mer, which sits on the shores of the Mediterranean Sea midway between Marseille and Montpellier. From Saintes-Maries-de-la-Mer two more days on the bike will see me to Montpellier for my transport back to England. So, there we have it, right across France under my own steam, north to south, North Sea to Mediterranean Sea, job done, unless my legs give up the ghost before I exit Pas-de-Calais, of course.

Following the route marked in fluorescent yellow marker pen on my long map will allow me to experience the very best of rural France. It's not the most direct route as planning has been very much focussed on seeking out quiet rural lanes, canal towpaths, and the quietest of byways. Small campsites, out of season, will be my accommodation of choice with wild camping as my backup. I feel that resorting to bed and breakfast is a bit of a cop-out so it is absolutely not on my agenda, not under any circumstances... unless I must!

# WEEK ONE

## Day 1 – Friday 16th April

## ENGLAND:

## From Home in North Devon to Dover, Kent

The Victorian clock in our living room strikes a single chime as it does on the half-hour. The only exception to this is when the clock has an age-related strop and decides not to function. The older I become, the more sympathetic I am to the attitude of our belligerent marble timepiece. Like our house, the clock is a hundred and fifty years old or thereabouts. The clock's 'listen-to-me' chime has always been far too loud; we're used to its noisy reverberating tone, but it's guaranteed to wake up guests. Anyway, the clock has just announced, in no uncertain fashion I should point out, that it is exactly nine-thirty, and as this is not a clock to be ignored, I open the front door and step outside promptly as it commands.

My bike is propped against the right-hand stanchion of a wooden pergola that I built years ago to span the garden path. The path bisects our front garden before terminating at a large wooden gate, which in turn opens onto a short lane that links our house and the neighbouring farm with the village road. It's a bright sunny morning and the hilltop village I live in is silent, as it usually is. The air temperature, in low single figures I imagine, chills my nose as I breathe in.

You know the feeling when you've waited for something for ages and anticipation has built over time? Well, for me, such an occasion has just arrived. *'Today's the day,'* as they say, and I am excited and nervous in equal measure. I am about to set off and have a go at what, for me at least, is a first. To be honest I have doubts about my own abilities because in all truth I might not be up to this, and because I have been idle or unfocused or both I have not prepared, this total lack of cycle training is gnawing a little. But it's far too late for last-minute regrets and self-admonishments so I cast doubts aside for the time being. I know I can ride a bike after all, and surely this is the only skill I need. I may not have used my new micro tent or my vintage cooker but I have checked them out visually and they look fit for purpose. Am I fit for purpose, is the real question. No more dithering, it's time to find out if I'm up to it.

As I stand astride the bike's crossbar the view immediately in front of me is of a detachable black bag secured to the handlebars and equidistant between the brake levers. The bag is the size of a small shoebox, it is waterproof and contains the items I cannot afford to lose: passport, money, train tickets, camera, and two lenses. There is no other luggage on the front of the bike as I decided to go for a pair of rear pannier bags, which, as I sit on the bike are positioned slightly behind me, one either side of the rear wheel. On top of the panniers and secured with bungee cords is my little tent, all brand new and wrapped up in its shiny nylon drawstring bag. I put the tent up in the garden a few days ago: it looked very small and I've not slept in its like for forty years, perhaps more. I was more supple in those days of course, but it should be fine and if it's not I will find out tomorrow night in Northern France, somewhere south of Calais. Hopefully my peapod tent will prove less flimsy than it appears, and nowhere near as primitive and claustrophobic as it undoubtedly looks.

Stashed side by side with the tent and on top of the panniers is a self-inflating mattress. The mattress is also rolled up and held in place with bungee cord. A self-inflating mattress! Who'd have thought? Such items didn't exist last time I camped anywhere; an airbed was the alternative in those far-off days. Airbeds were made of the most slippery plastic known to man and guaranteed to go flat in the night. Invariably they lived up to expectations, which was especially annoying if you were the person who had invested two hours of valuable holiday time on your knees puffing the thing up, only to lose fifty cubic feet of precious air as soon as you start the race against time to insert the rubber bung to keep the thing airtight. (I really should get over that experience.)

I won't need my long map until I reach Calais so I have rolled all eleven feet of it up to fit snugly into its black plastic tube. The tube in question is waterproof, robust, two inches in diameter and fifteen inches long. When rolled up the map has a hollow centre which I am using to store a few spare spokes in, I'm not sure why I am taking them as my bike is new and shouldn't need any, also I've never replaced a spoke on a bike and have absolutely no idea how I would go about it. Nevertheless, I feel I should have a couple with me. Failing to prepare is preparing to fail and all that.

Beyond our garden gate the cars that park in the lane to deposit children at the little Victorian primary school have all gone. This is the critical moment I have been waiting for, because if you inhabit the world of novices, as I now do, you will know that the last thing I need is an audience when I cycle out of the village.

I settle the nerves by having a final pre-departure glance over the splendour of my majestic gleaming white velocipede before departure. It truly looks a beast of burden; do I really need to take that much? As I settle onto the saddle a heady mix of anticipation and trepidation returns. My right foot rests on the pedal; once I exert pressure, momentum will follow naturally and there will be no turning back. Cometh the moment, cometh the man and all that.

Pedals Away! – Departure coincides with a few photographs and unspoken thoughts from family and neighbours who have come out to watch – along the lines of, *Just what does he think he's doing?* which is not at all unreasonable. The first few hundred yards generate a mixture of feelings, excitement mainly, although I can't deny there's a whiff of uncertainty. Fifty yards on I want to look back but if I try to turn around my balance will go and I shall probably fall off, so I wave to those watching with the back of my hand held above my head.

At long last I am setting off on an adventure long in the planning and even longer in my mind. Both tyres are checked and fully inflated, I've made sure the rear panniers are secure and their contents checked and rechecked against my list, the bike seat seems to be in a comfortable position. I squeeze the levers for the first time and feel the brakes bite effectively. Well, they do on the level lane leading out of the village – it's a promising start. All my important possessions are in the handlebar bag, I'm sure they are. My passport, euros and sterling, train tickets and camera, everything has been checked and checked and checked again.

Two hundred yards from home and just out of sight of the onlookers the lane turns sharp left and I can't help but smile as I think to myself, *The bike and I have just passed the wobble test. We are as one, man and machine, ideal!* Passing the last few houses in the village, I'm buzzing with anticipation of the journey ahead, and I know I am very fortunate to have an exceptional wife who doesn't object to my solo cycle trip.

Once clear of the village the road falls away gradually and then more steeply, and for a moment I can feel the weight of the bike under me as I freewheel downhill. In near silence, the bike glides through the woodland and into the cold wind generated by the momentum. I need to be cautious now and allow myself time to become accustomed to the weight of the load. I decide to take downhills slowly as the bike hints at being able to run away with itself. I've factored in more than enough time to reach Barnstaple for the late morning train so I can afford to cycle steadily now in order to gain confidence in the bike's ability to handle a load, and more critically in my ability to handle the bike.

This downhill section, not fifteen minutes' walk from my home, is through mixed woodland. The trees, close together and spindly here, are banked high to my left where they're silhouetted against the bright sun. This natural ancient woodland is quite beautiful, especially so on this early April morning when millions of new leaves high in the trees are backlit by shafts of spring sunlight. The scene is complimented by the sound of birdsong, what a joyful and uplifting start.

As the road levels out the air is cooler and damp in the shaded hollow and I catch the scent of wild garlic from the woodland floor: ramson, bear leak, wood garlic, different names but all the same plant, a member of the Allium family. Wild garlic flourishes here in amazing quantities; if I were to walk half a mile into the wood to my left, on a shady north-facing glade I would come to several acres of wild garlic. It pervades the woodland floor to the exclusion of all else, tens of thousands of garlic plants, and on this delightful spring morning they will all be in bloom with their clusters of star-shaped white flowers and heady, musky aroma. This little-visited and more secretive part of the wood also provides a home for native mammals and when our children were younger, my wife and I would walk with them deep into the woods at dusk. Our reward for standing silently was often limited to the flashing white rump of a roe deer as it bounded away through the undergrowth; nevertheless, it was a walk always worth doing.

Three miles on and now that I've exchanged the tarmacked road for the Tarka Trail, I pause to check the tension of the bungee cords, both tyres, and the load – all seems well and I'm probably being over cautious. The Tarka Trail follows the route of a disused railway, it's level for much of its way and as I'm heading towards the coast, I benefit from an almost imperceptible downhill slope, which allows me to cycle with very little effort for much of the next four miles. As it follows the River Torridge valley the trail traverses beautiful quintessentially English scenery, or more precisely Devonian; the landscape is rolling rather than spectacular here. As I pedal close to the freshwater River Torridge, home to otters, salmon, and kingfishers, the scenery flattens out and in time it will give way to the tidal estuary, a land of curlews, dunlin, and very occasionally a seal coming to feed on fish and shellfish. Here, perhaps four miles from the salty ebb and flow of the sea, is the fictional home of Henry Williamson's Tarka the Otter. Nowadays the river is still home to otters but you have to be determined and fortunate to spot one; I have seen just two in twenty years. Grey herons, on the other hand, are a regular sight. Statuesque, silent, and motionless, they are often seen along the Torridge where they wait in the eddies looking for prey, indeed as I approach Landcross I know that if I peer down the steep bank into the trees below the trail I will be able to look into nests at the heronry, but only at this time of year because it will be all but invisible when the foliage is fully out in a month or so.

I am not yet five miles into the day but already I am warming to the bike and to the act of cycling. It's reassuring how well the bike performs; it's a relaxing mode of transport, and so peaceful. Thankfully the bike is much lighter on its wheels than its bulky appearance would suggest.

I cycle with the salt marsh to my left as I come into the ancient seafaring town of Bideford. The salt marsh covers several acres of intertidal mud flats, most of which is hidden from view by reeds, six to eight feet high with wispy tops that have been turned into golden quills by the bright sunlight. Bideford was already an important port by the thirteenth century, some say its name derives from its location *'by-the-ford'*. As I approach the town from the south an impressive stone bridge spans the river to my left. First built of wood in 1286, the stone replacement standing today was first constructed in 1474 and at 677 feet is one of the longest surviving medieval bridges in England. Paying attention to the bridge, careful observers will notice that the twenty-four stone arches of the 'long bridge' are neither identical in size nor equidistant. At first glance this appears to be an architectural *faux pas* but not so: it's believed that the original stone bridge was funded by local businessmen and the width of each arch reflects the size of the financial contribution made. The bridge provided the only connection between Bideford town and East-the-Water for over five hundred years except for a time in 1968 when, following heavy rain, the westernmost arch collapsed into the river. Thirty years later a modern bridge, more suitable to the size and volume of today's traffic, was built high above the river a mile downstream from here.

Between Bideford and the next coastal village, the Tarka Trail offers unrestricted waterside views as the funnel of the estuary opens up. This is glorious cycling, especially today with the sun sparkling over the water only a few feet to my left. Three miles on and I come to Instow, a pretty and very desirable place to live that lies at the confluence of the Rivers Torridge and Taw. A quite charming little place, Instow's popularity owes much to its safe beach, a yacht club, and a view across the estuary to the quaint and ancient fishing village of Appledore. The Taw and Torridge Rivers merge at Instow before flowing into Bideford Bay and then the Bristol Channel. Situated within a few miles of each other Bideford, Westward Ho! Northam, Instow, and Appledore are all attractive coastal towns much reliant on tourists, but it wasn't always so and local place names such as Bloody Corner and Bone Hill give a clue: imagine the terror you would have felt had you been here in 878 and watched as Hubba the Dane *(Ubba Ragnarsson)* led his Viking army in a fleet of seventy longships up this very estuary. Bloody Corner, marked nowadays by a cast-iron plaque on the roadside between Northam and Appledore, claims to have been the site of the battle King Hubba didn't survive. Bone Hill, a high point in Northam with the whole of the estuary laid out before it, is testament to the same battle.

Once clear of the sand dunes that span the low headland between Instow village and the River Taw, I turn east and with my back to the sea I follow the river upstream towards Barnstaple. Here the Tarka Trail is completely level and virtually straight, it hugs the estuary for miles and the route must have been a magnificent train journey before Doctor Beacham wielded his axe to this and so many other rural branch lines over fifty years ago. Ordinarily this part of the trail must make for easy pedalling but to my considerable dismay my first-day cycling euphoria is dampened somewhat as I find myself pedalling against the strong headwind funnelling down the Taw estuary towards me. North Devon is normally a land of westerlies, winds that blow in over Bideford Bay after a journey across the Atlantic Ocean uninterrupted by land. Not so today and I am amazed by the strength of this unexpected challenge. My discomfort is compounded as the temperature has fallen markedly even though the sun is still blazing. This headwind is a stark reality check as I find myself having to drop several gears just to counter its force. I don my fleece to keep out the cold although in reality the chill is inconvenient but no more. The real impact is the surprising ability of this formidable wind to reduce my progress; double the effort for half the speed! I hope headwinds aren't experienced too regularly. The flip side of this windy challenge is that I have only just started my cycling experience, I am only just out of the traps and my legs have barely warmed up; wind and hills are going to be a struggle at first but I will get better at such things with practice. Keep calm and carry on.

The wind has robbed me of what I honestly thought was a generous amount of spare time to cycle from my home to Barnstaple. In the event, I am here just on time as my arrival in Barnstaple coincides perfectly with the departure of the cross-country train to Exeter. My carriage pulls into Devon's premier city just over an hour later and a full ninety minutes before the connecting train to London Waterloo. An hour and a half is far too long to loiter at a railway station when a riverside pub is only a mile away. Such a quandary needs no further thought so I head off to enjoy a pint in the riverside beer garden. I am very tempted by a pub lunch and at a push could convince myself I have earned it, but instead I save the money and opt for a packet of shortbread biscuits from my pannier bag. I have read somewhere that shortbread is favoured by cyclists as a quick energy boost so I am carrying two packets, not that I qualify for the title of cyclist just yet. The pub is very quiet and I am amazed when John, whom I worked with several years ago, comes into the pub garden. As we are both forty miles from home this is quite a coincidence. It is good to catch up and during our chat I discover that John cycled through France as a young man; he advises me that cars sounding their horns at cyclists in France are not doing so out of irritation as may be the case here, but because they are acknowledging a favoured national sport and offering encouragement. He also said that in his experience, albeit many years ago, cyclists are invariably met with kindness and that I shouldn't be surprised if a local farmer helps me out by offering wild camping or *'aux sauvage'* in a field if I am unable to find a campsite. The opportunity to hear such positive comments about cycling in France is very welcome. Our time together passes quickly and all too soon it is time to say goodbye and for me to cycle back to the station.

Infrequent rail travel over the years has left me with the impression that going anywhere by train is inherently pleasing, quick, and relaxing. Today I am taking a heavy bike onto a train and I am most impressed, amazed even, that there is no additional charge for the carriage of my bicycle for two hundred miles, and I am pleased to find a seat just a few feet from my bike, which allows me to keep an eye on my belongings: however unlikely, it wouldn't do to have anything go amiss on the inaugural day of my adventure.

Some hours later we pull into Waterloo Station, London. My next port of call is Charing Cross Station on the north bank of the Thames and a little more than a mile from Waterloo. I have allowed myself just over an hour to push the bike between stations, in the event the task proves more difficult than expected as I appear to be the only person in the whole of central London who is trying to walk against the relentless flow of people scurrying out of the city after a day at work. Commuters, thousands of them, like a plague of locusts are exiting the city centre; many are on autopilot so they can devote time to their mobile phones, walking at speed with their heads down. How do they even do that without tripping over? It's never like this in rural Devon. It soon becomes very clear to me that I should have allowed more time to pile-drive my cumbersome bike through the crowds; taking no account of rush hour in London was foolish of me. Fortunately I have pre-booked my seat and a bike space on the next train. This is just as well because every bike space is booked on all other trains to Dover this evening.

I arrive at Charing Cross at seven o'clock on the dot and with just two minutes to spare I board the train, a bit out of breath and somewhat flustered but I have done it and after the adrenaline rush of the capital subsides a relaxing and uneventful two-hour journey to Dover is just what is needed.

It is a short ten-minute bike ride from Dover Priory Station to the front door of my guest house, it's an establishment that I find has much to commend it: the proprietor makes a great impression by offering me a pot of tea within minutes of my arrival even though it is approaching ten at night. I booked this homely and welcoming place by searching the internet a few months ago, it had plenty of positive comments from previous guests and it is a list I shall add too when I return to Devon.

Today feels like it has been a very long day indeed. This morning I got on the bike rather gingerly and cycled out of the village. Downhill through the woods I went and along the Tarka Trail to the coast, then I almost missed my train from Barnstaple because the wind wanted to teach me who was the boss. The second battle of the day was against the commuters and it was another I nearly lost. But in all truth, I wasn't sure what to expect on day one and in reality, I think the day went rather well and here I am in Dover, just a hop, skip, and a jump from France. If I'm honest I am rather tired after twelve hours by bike and train. I forgot to take note of how far I cycled today and I can't be bothered going back down to the bike to find out now. I reckon if I add the distance from my home to Barnstaple with a mile each way to the pub and a couple to the B&B I must have cycled getting on for twenty miles, add another few for the headwind and some more for the luggage, and that's why I've had enough, but you know what, it has been a good day, an interesting day, and a rewarding day. Perhaps the best reward is the proper pot of tea that has just arrived at my room. Just the ticket before bed.

# Day 2 – Saturday 17th April

## Department Pas-de-Calais:

## From Dover, England to Licques, France

This morning my home and family are three hundred miles to the west and I am about to cycle down to Dover docks, catch the ferry, and watch England fade into the distance. Arriving in France later this morning will be exciting of course but also bittersweet as we always travel together as a family and today I am alone. Our family look forward to the ferry crossing – the ferry rather than the tunnel, mind you. We have done it many times and like all families have our little holiday traditions, like enjoying the little fruit tarts they sell on the ship as we cross the Channel, and then, on arrival, me saying, *'Quiet, please – I have to concentrate and get used to driving on the wrong side of the road.'* I do the driving in Europe and my wife keeps us out of trouble as she navigates using a paper map. None of this electronic satnav nonsense, she reads all the signs because her French is far better than mine. We make a good team, but today it is just me, which is rather sad. It doesn't feel right, to be honest.

I have just enjoyed a 'Full English' breakfast and carried my bags out of the B&B into a warm sunny morning. The host wishes me well as I prepare to set off by clipping both pannier bags onto the bike. Fortunately I spot that a screw has sheared on the left pannier; inconvenient, yes, but I am glad to have seen the fault now because without the screw the bag is only held in place by two plastic lugs that don't really look up to the job. Good fortune is with me because I spot a Halfords superstore out of the dining room window. How lucky is that? So, after thanking my hosts for a splendid overnight stay I pedal away and arrive at Halfords just as the staff are opening up the shop. I find the bolt needed and buy a couple just to be safe. The tool required to tighten the bolt costs eight pounds of my rather meagre twenty pounds a day budget. *C'est la vie!*

As a car driver I have taken the ferry across the English Channel many times in the last four decades, but this morning is a first for me crossing as a cyclist and I am surprised to discover that scrutiny of my documents is far more thorough than whenever I have travelled by car. That said, the embarkation staff were extremely helpful considering that I was running later than planned after my Halfords visit, and they allowed me to board the ferry after everyone else with only a few minutes to spare. Almost being late seems to be a developing theme, I hope not.

Crossing the Strait of Dover is a joy. The sea is silvery graphite-grey, its surface is shiny and mirror-like, the sky is cloudless, and not a puff of wind disturbs the water, which sparkles in the bright sunlight. Looking astern I cast my eyes beyond the rolling wake of the ferry to the whispery haze that stretches the full length of the horizon. The opaque, mesmerising line is actually the white cliffs of Dover and the haze makes them look particularly light and airy today, an ethereal and peaceful view that is strikingly beautiful and could easily be a painting by the romantic English watercolourist J.M.W. Turner. After several minutes I draw myself away from this magical last view of England and stroll along the deck towards the bow of the ship. My view along the French coast is clear as far as the twin Belgian ports of Gravelines and Dunkerque to the east. To the west I can see the headland of Cap Nez Blanc, and beyond it, in the distance, I can just make out the pale silhouette of Cap Gris. The world before me looks tranquil and perfect in all directions although I know that hidden from view, between here and the first headland, is Sangatte, the vast migrant camp otherwise known as the jungle. I am relieved to be here and not in that infamous and hostile-sounding place.

Fifteen minutes later the Sea France ferry ties alongside and its vehicle ramp is hydraulically lowered and secured to the quay. Three flights of metal stairs later and I am in the bowels of the vessel, standing in a vast car deck with two other cyclists. We wait together for the other vehicles to disembark. Allowing the cars, lorries, and camper vans to drive off first allows me to experience a completely empty car deck, not a familiar sight but it makes me appreciate just how spacious these roll-on-roll-off ships really are.

Always a feverishly busy place, Calais has been a major port since the Middle Ages. The city was controlled by England for two hundred years from 1347, during which time it was referred to as the jewel in the English crown. Today, Calais has a population of over 120,000 and of course there are tens of thousands more who transit the port daily. The bag of valuables that I took onto the ferry is clipped back into its position on the handlebars and the security cable used to ensure the bike didn't move at sea is unshackled from the ferry bulkhead. Then, after cycling down the vehicle ramp, I pull into a layby on one of the many dock access roads to check my map. The other two cyclists do the same: Chris and Helen are heading to nearby Belgium to enjoy a cycling weekend to celebrate their wedding anniversary; we chat briefly about our respective trips before bidding each other good luck.

The zipped top of my handlebar bag is made up of a durable fold-over transparent lid, which holds my map, enabling me to look at the route ahead as I cycle. It is a novel thought that the sea is now behind me and the next coast I shall see on the map will be the Mediterranean a thousand miles from here, but that is thirty days away and now I must concentrate on extracting myself from the confusion that is Calais docks.

Once I have cleared Calais my intention is to head south and camp at Licques, a small village around fifteen miles – or now that I am in France, twenty-four kilometres – south of here. My cunning plan for escaping the hubbub of Calais and reaching Licques by the easiest possible route is to follow any road sign I see that points to 'Centre Ville' and then as soon as I come to the Canal de Calais, I shall simply exchange the road for the towpath and follow the canal out of town thus avoiding the traffic and arterial roads that home in on the port. Not only that, I have a choice of canals: nearest is the Canal de Calais, which, once it clears of the city turns east and heads off towards

Belgium, less than twenty miles from here; alternatively and in the opposite direction is the Canal des Pierrettes. Either canal will do me nicely, I'm not fussy either way.

Half an hour later, when canals and signposts to 'Centre Ville' have eluded me I find myself quite unintentionally in a residential area. I feel and probably look out of place but fortunately for me an elderly gentleman is tending his front garden so I stop and ask for directions, a rather bold move by me as I cannot speak French. I know some words and a few phrases but I am quite uneducated in the language, a fact that may well prove to be something of an Achilles heel. I get away with it this time and the man tells me not to follow the canal as it is industrialised. His advice takes me through an adjoining residential area and out of town on the most minor of lanes. Soon the little road weaves its way beyond built-up Calais and deposits me, quite suddenly, into open farmland. Prior to resuming his gardening, the man thoughtfully asked if I had sufficient water for my journey, a modest gesture perhaps but one that gladdened my heart.

Once clear of the city I cycle over a large flat plain of open farmland. It is a relief to have left Calais behind and to enjoy the relaxation that comes with pedalling slowly and steadily to get into the swing of things. It is quite cold and windy now but the sun is out and I think how fortunate I am to be experiencing such weather; only two weeks ago it was March and it could well be raining or even snowing here today.

Open countryside, this is more like it! I can hear the faint rhythmic sound of the wheels, just a quiet whirring as the bike rolls along the rural lane, no car radio, no other traffic, how joyous this is. The little road wends its way between fields of mustard; the crop is already in flower and birds, skylarks probably, are singing high above. Other than birdsong and the whirr of my wheels this is an envelope of silence.

The view across what is a rather featureless yet pleasant landscape is broken by the sight of a female mallard tending no fewer than thirteen ducklings in the narrow water-filled ditch dividing the road from the edge of the mustard field. It is a wildlife sighting I would surely have missed had I been in a car and seeing the family of waterfowl gives me an early indication that cycling in a near-silent fashion, at around eight miles per hour, is going to be a delightful way to travel. I guess this is how I envisaged cycle touring would be, certainly it is what I hoped for and I am warming to it very quickly.

A couple of hours into France and the cycling could hardly be easier: no rain, no hills, and although it is early days the weight in my bulky panniers, at least when I am cycling on the flat, is proving entirely manageable. It is a novel experience to be observing the French countryside perched high on my saddle without the distractions of car instruments and the like, and I have to say it's a most liberating feeling to realise that my daily commitments are now distilled down to the simplest of objectives. One: Travel from A to B under my own steam. Two: Find something to eat and drink from shops along the way. Three: Keep myself warm and dry if at all possible. Four: Locate somewhere to place my small tent at the end of each day, ideally at a campsite and better still, one with a shower. Even getting lost doesn't really matter a jot when I think about it.

Ten miles are under my belt now and the rural lane changes from being dead flat to undulating, just a little. The lane is sufficient up and down to add interest but not enough for me to have to struggle up hills, neither, of course, do I benefit from freewheeling downhill. Thankfully the fresh wind that was noticeable if not particularly troubling earlier has now disappeared. Millenia ago the landscape through which I am cycling was carved into a flat shallow bowl shape. On the rim at the far side of this bowl a swaying row of poplar trees tells me that the wind still blows in the distance, but here in the hollow the bike and I are sheltered, and now that the breeze has gone it is surprisingly warm as I wheel into the first village on my French trip.

Campagne-les-Guines is a small, quiet place, insignificant even, hardly worth a second glance many may think, but this has not always been the case. Four hundred and fifty years ago, in a field near here, King Henry VIII came for a meeting with the French King, Francis the First, in what was later called 'the field of the cloth of gold', so named because both put on a great display of wealth. Here they signed the

'Treaty of Ardres', an agreement whereby the English evacuated Boulogne and returned it to France in exchange for two million crowns, which was a colossal sum of money for the British monarch. Regrettably I can find no information on display that records this place in history, but it is a pretty enough village and I am glad to have savoured its past.

Once Campagne-des-Guines is behind me a steep incline forces me to dismount and push the bike uphill for the first time. Pushing feels an ignoble way to proceed, wimpish even, and on a point of national pride I am mightily relieved that no Union Jack flutters aloft from my rear pannier. Hopefully this lack of identity will allow me to hide my discomfort behind some form of stateless anonymity. France is the land of cyclists, after all, and I don't imagine for one minute that anyone would suspect a French national would stoop, head bowed, and reduce themselves to pushing their *'velo'*. If I am lucky any local who spots me will assume me to be Belgian, especially as the Belgium/France border is just a few miles away, and the Belgians are the great cycling rivals of the French. How remiss, I could have brought a Belgian flag for just such a moment.

Having pushed the bike up the long and somewhat tedious hill I reach a modest summit where a viewpoint offers a panoramic outlook over miles and miles of level farmland. Laid before me this agrarian land is dotted with small farmsteads interspersed with the occasional hamlet, a pleasing and mellow scene indeed.

During family holidays stretched over many years and over countless miles of driving across France I have often witnessed the unseemly sight of some French bloke standing at the roadside facing the verge having a wee. Naturally, being from the other side of the English Channel I have never stooped to such a base level of behaviour, and as an Englishman, I am of the firm belief that to act in such a fashion is simply primitive, an uncivilised way to conduct oneself, you may say. I am discovering, however, and to my eternal shame I should reassure you, that such basic matters take on a quite different perspective when one is on a bicycle and twenty miles from campsite facilities. Once the large hill is behind me, the land has plateaued out, and my heaving chest has stabilised, I prop my bike against the concrete plinth on top of the viewpoint to rest a while and take in the pastoral scene before me. After several minutes at the viewpoint and doubtless aggravated by generous swigs from my water bottle it is apparent that being miles and miles from campsite facilities is becoming problematic, especially as France is renowned, internationally if I may say so, for the rarity of its public conveniences. My conflicting thoughts on this increasingly pressing matter are rationalised when I remember that vehicles and people are just as rare as public toilets in rural France and so the likelihood of being spotted, should I have to act in an ungentlemanly fashion, is as rare as hens' teeth.

Eventually I succumb to the inevitable and adopt the 'When in Rome approach' of facing away from the road. Please note that unlike your average Frenchman out for a day on his slick racing bike I am not wearing some body-hugging spray-on Lycra cycling top. I am English and I have a cumbersome touring bike, which is resplendent and quite unmissable with its massive bright yellow panniers: for colour co-ordination I am wearing a brand new and thus blindingly fluorescent dayglow-yellow top, and so it is at this precise moment when the only car for many miles pulls to a halt at the viewpoint, scattering gravel as it does. To ensure my embarrassment is complete the Citroën 2CV or whatever it is, is fully laden with ladies of a certain age. I believe *'merde'* is the appropriate local vernacular for such occasions. Almost as soon as it arrives the car drives away from the viewpoint and I am left to resume my composure and having done so, my travels. Note to self: Buy a beret and a string of onions to blend in.

The road to Hermelinghem is flat for the most part until I near the village where I am pleased to say that I am gifted the exhilaration of cycling down the first substantial hill of my adventure. I have pedalled getting on for thirty miles since yesterday and my confidence is growing with this cycling-tourist malarky. Even so, I cadence brake as I freewheel to limit the risk of the bike snaking downhill due to the disproportionate weight at the rear. Overcautious, perhaps, but I have no idea how a bike pushed from behind by its own weight will react should I let the reins go. Anyway this is not a race and it is very pleasant indeed to enjoy freewheeling, at a fair lick I may add, for what seems like ages. As the bike and I glide down the long gradient I feel genuine sympathy for a fellow cyclist as he cycles towards me, his heaving lungs struggling to climb the long hill. I can see that he is finding the hill hard work even though he is about half my age and unburdened by any luggage.

It is mightily disheartening, let me tell you, when I look down at the map and realise that I am on the wrong road! Now, I cannot honestly claim to have sensed the acrid whiff of burning rubber but let's say the brakes were applied with vigour. Prior to this exact moment I was developing a considerable amount of enthusiasm for the bike as a mode of transport but to be honest, this feeling diminishes just a tad when I start to push my bike up the hill, retracing the exact route of the puffing cyclist who passed me a few minutes earlier.

I discover that the symptoms that result from having to push a grossly overweight bike up a prolonged and steep incline in the sunshine are most unpleasant, think: dry throat, thumping chest, burning legs particularly the calf muscles, and then, after fifteen minutes (it seemed like an hour at least) of breathless huffing and puffing, under the sun I should point out again in case you missed it, a sense of despair creeps up as the reality hits me. This incline will be one of many, probably dozens, maybe hundreds, between here and the Mediterranean. Doubtless I shall report further on the topic of hills depending on which of the following outcomes occur: (1) I become more accomplished and take them in my stride, (2) I remain unfit, become steadily more disheartened as time goes on and resign myself to the pain and torment that pushing a very heavy bike uphill can inflict, (3) I am hospitalised or worse.

Why am I even thinking like this when I am well aware that most setbacks are temporary? As if to prove the point, once the physical discomfort of climbing the hill is overcome my heart lifts immediately because not only has the hill been conquered but the view ahead encourages me with that most wondrous of natural features: a long downhill road sweeping gracefully into the distance and out of sight. Good fortune is indeed with me for the slope leads all the way into the little town of Alembon and then to the hamlet of Sanghen before terminating in the village of Licques, which is exactly where I intend to spend tonight.

Whilst planning the route I spent countless hours poring over guidebooks and maps, researching the availability of campsites. As my departure was prior to the Easter holidays, I knew that many sites would not yet be open for the season, so it was prudent for me to have a note of the location of those campsites, albeit few and far between, which were definitely open and taking in visitors. Licques is the first of these sites and I have indicated its position on my map with a small white sticker. There are over thirty such campsites indicated and the wavy column of little white squares runs like vertebrae the full eleven feet length of my long, thin map. Each sticker is about four inches from the next, which equates to roughly a day's cycling. Several alternative backup sites are marked in the same way; hopefully this attention to detail at the planning stage will prove invaluable in the weeks ahead.

I enter Licques towards the end of the afternoon along the Rue Antoine de Lumbres. Flanking either side of the road is a row of solid two-storey houses. The dwellings are interspersed with the occasional commercial premise, one of which is a particularly ornate bread shop. *'Pains – Founil de Licques'* is written above the shop in antique blue and white porcelain tiles. Pillars of similarly ornate tiles form four vertical panels, two being either side of the Boulangerie entrance; each panel depicts an agricultural scene: firstly, a farmer sowing wheat, the second illustrates harvesting the grain, next, the baker is making dough, and finally, on the fourth panel, the scene is of bread being taken from the oven. It is a visually stunning shop front, historically fascinating, very traditional, and extremely French, so I stop and take some photographs. Next, I come across *'Le Pommiers-des-Trois-Pays'* campsite. *'The apple trees of the three regions'* proves to be the ideal port of call for my first night in a tent.

The campsite is divided into neat grassy sections each large enough for several tents. Individual pitches are separated by low hedging, which gives the place a cosy feel with some privacy. Wooden chalets are placed around the perimeter of the site beyond which trees grow in abundance. Having booked in for the night I cycle around the site a couple of times seeking a stout tree to secure the bike to. Unfortunately no such trees exist but all the pitches are level and dry, which is rather more important. The owners inform me later that, *'Security pas problem,'* and the fact that my bike is not secured does not matter as crime simply does not occur in the village of Liques.

On my circumnavigation of the campsite, I cannot fail to notice the complete absence of tents, caravans, or motor homes; a number of chalets are occupied but it appears that I am the sole travelling guest. I select a pitch situated roughly midway between the washing facility and the campsite restaurant, which seems a convenient sort of location to me. Selecting a pitch is one thing but setting up the tent is quite another when you are inexperienced, and right now I am very glad that I practised putting the tent up last week in the garden, even though I only did it twice.

Although I say so myself, today's tent erecting exercise goes rather well. Picture the scene if you will: an English bloke, not as young as he once was, arrives at his chosen campsite blissfully happy that he has ended the first day in France without falling off the bike or getting too lost. On arrival he discovers he is the only camper, it is late afternoon and the air is becoming chilly under an increasingly overcast sky, there is a hint of drizzle in the air and frost is expected overnight. Other residents are now peering out from the heated comfort of the chalets that overlook the camping field. I suspect at least some of them have resorted to wine because they are mentally numbed by the lack of interest offered by a day spent gazing at grass. The last great event of the day was probably the arrival of the mobile bread van; this would have been many hours earlier and all these people want now is for something, anything, to entertain them until they can venture out from the cosy fug of their chalets and hobble to the bar a few hours from now.

Then, as if by command, some fluorescent foreign wonder arrives on a grossly overladen bike. Lace curtains at chalet windows are repositioned and wine glasses are replenished to make the best of this unexpected but welcome opportunity. The chalet dwellers watch spellbound as the cyclist freewheels onto the site. Unbeknown to him, the audience scrutinise his every move as he examines and finally selects a specific pitch. Slowly raising a glass to their lips, they consider the cyclist's age and take note of the effortless skill he applies to selecting precisely the right bit of field for his needs. The onlookers form the opinion that years of cycle touring have given this bloke a mental checklist of just what constitutes a good pitch, but best of all he has selected one immediately in front of their window, good fortune is theirs, entertainment more exciting than grass has arrived!

Given the size of the panniers this cyclist is probably several years into a trans-world challenge and by the look of him, global circumnavigation is something of a lifestyle choice. Any hopes the curtain twitchers have of an entertaining mishap are reduced by the apparent expertise on display, nevertheless they continue to sip chilled chardonnay and watch closely just in case of an entertaining slip-up. What they really hope for, naturally, is a full-blown calamity, but gazing upon the honed skill before them it is abundantly clear that real misfortune is unlikely. Thank goodness their disappointment can be eased by the quaffing of more wine. The final act of the globe-trotting bike man before them, in his yellow Day-Glo tabard, is to unfurl a minute tent from its cylindrical bag, a tent he then proceeds to make habitable using a flurry of evidently well-practised and slick manoeuvres. If only they knew.

My perspective is quite different as I am acutely aware that absolutely everything can and probably will go wrong, perhaps very wrong. My panniers and hi-vis jacket are dayglow yellow and clearly brand new; how can anyone not notice this fact? My bike is not muddy, it is pristine, the paintwork is unscratched, even the panniers look unused. Surely this newness is glaringly obvious to everyone, in my eyes everything about me screams 'NOVICE'. Novice is exactly what I am and it is a fact I am acutely aware of. The chalet dwellers may not know this but the simple fact is that I scanned the pitches not so much with a mental checklist of exacting requirements but simply to avoid obvious problems like pitching on soggy or uneven ground or camping within range of a pack of feral children. In truth, I am pleased to have avoided the embarrassment of having to reposition the tent because I have unwittingly placed it on top of a pothole or some protruding rock.

While putting up the tent I am very aware that I am now on foreign soil, and being a proud Briton, it is a matter of national pride that my tent is not erected inside out, and it absolutely must not collapse as soon as I take up occupancy. Disconcertingly for me, I notice that nearly all of the registration plates on the cars parked outside the chalets are from the Netherlands. This increases the pressure on me exponentially because as everyone knows, the Dutch are a nation of serial campers; without exception they are competent and I couldn't bear the shame if everything were to go tits up. Fortunately, it is only me who knows that disaster did not come my way because I winged it successfully. None of the onlookers are any the wiser that this is my first night in a peapod tent for getting on for fifty years. Anyway, job done, no shame for me and no exciting entertainment for my fellow campsite residents, long may this trend continue.

Having pegged down the groundsheet and secured the guy ropes I place both panniers inside the tent. Unfortunately for me, I discover at this rather late stage I would like to add, that this unavoidable act reduces the area for me to live in by more than half. The tent is snug when empty and the panniers change snug into cramped but there is no sensible alternative as both panniers and my handlebar bag need to be with me, partly for security, partly to keep them out of the weather, and partly in case I need anything from them during the night. After all, the panniers contain my worldly possessions for this journey so they should be at hand. I cannot believe how much the size of my little house has been reduced and alongside the realisation that I never gave this any thought despite what I thought was thorough planning, the failure makes me wonder what else I have omitted. Had the prospect of sharing the tent with my colossal luggage come to mind I may well have bought a bigger tent. *'It is what it is,'* as they say.

The little campsite shop sells matches by the box, which is handy as I have forgotten to pack any. This is the second error to come to light in as many minutes, hopefully not a sign of things to come. Unfortunately for me, most visitors to campsites live in campervans, caravans, or on-site chalets, none of which have storage limitations as such. The only matches for sale at the campsite come in a box roughly the size of half a house brick. Cumbersome, yes, but I have to buy a box in order to prepare meals on my Trangia storm cooker. Tomorrow is Sunday so the shops will certainly be closed, so with that in mind I decide to conserve my food supplies and eat in the campsite café this evening.

What a splendid little venue the campsite café proves to be. The small rectangular eatery has space for six or so tables and a small bar at one end; its pine ceiling and walls are hung with local pictures, which makes for a homely and warm interior. As soon as I enter, I am enthusiastically welcomed by a small but very jolly group of Belgians, by the owners behind the bar, and a few of the chalet residents. The atmosphere is very friendly indeed and as I walk through the door it is apparent that my arrival is anticipated. It seems to have something to do with the fact that I turned up on a pushbike and I am camping so early in the year when it is clearly far too cold for such foolhardy endeavours. The restaurant goers put this down to me being English and although they cannot understand why anyone would wish to sleep in a microscopic tent on a frosty night (no-one warned me it may be frosty), they applaud me for doing so. To emphasise their approval a Belgian couple buy me a beer before I have even sat down. This has all the makings of a great evening.

I order a hamburger, and what a hamburger it turns out to be. Homemade from quality meat and beautifully seasoned, it is an injustice to list it as a hamburger; really, there must be a better name for food as tasty as this. My tip-top burger, chips, and salad are washed down with a large beer and then another. *'Pression'* rather than bottled beer, naturally. I had the forethought to bring my notebook to the café for the first of what I intend to become a nightly habit of writing up my progress. The spiral A5 book will record the events of each day together with the distance covered, and my running expenses. At the conclusion of day one I have cycled twenty-seven miles against an expected distance of twenty-one miles and I have spent forty-two euros. The exchange rate is very low so this equates to thirty-eight pounds, which far exceeds my daily budget of twenty pounds. Twenty pounds is meagre, I know, but it should be achievable. That said, I am not going to allow a self-imposed limit to cause hardship and I am not overly concerned by today's overspend because ten euros of the total was spent to replace the pannier bolt in Dover, the campsite cost me another ten, and I have just spent twenty-one euros on food and beer. Let's just say it is easy to see where efficiencies can be made.

After three hours in the restaurant, it is time to leave. Outside the bitter chill hits me immediately; it is surprisingly cold even with the false inner warmth provided by local ale. A thick mist has come down with the cold air and hangs like a wispy shawl over the campsite. Thankfully I thought to carry my torch to the café so locating the zip on the tent door poses no problem. Use of hands and knees is necessary to clamber inside the little tent, which looks very much smaller (how can that even be possible?) now that it is dark. Oh yes, the panniers, I'd forgotten just how much floorspace they occupy, and on the opposite side of the tent sundry items take up a six-inch strip against the opposite wall. Between these bits and bobs and the panniers is a narrow channel for me to sleep. I clamber into the sleeping bag and use the dim cone of light from my wind-up torch to illuminate the compact space that surrounds me. I never thought my little home would prove to be this small but I'll get used to it, I have to. I settle down thinking about how cold it is outside; far, far, colder than I expected. It feels no warmer inside the tent of course and the temperature plays on my mind, but before I know it, sleep arrives aided by alcohol, good exercise, and a tasty meal.

Imprisoned in a silent pitch-black void I am awoken violently in the depths of the night by a searing vice-like pain in my right calf. Half asleep and hampered by luggage, a low roof, and unfamiliar surroundings I rummage around in a confused state feeling for my torch. I have experienced leg cramps for years on and off but only periodically and although painful, it is hardly a great problem, and it is usually alleviated pretty quickly by hobbling around and putting weight onto the affected limb. To my considerable anguish I discover that dealing with tonight's bout is not so simple: I am zipped up to my neck in a sleeping bag, the bag is tight because I am wearing all my clothes to keep the frost at bay, so escaping from the cocoon with the haste required is no easy task. Just to make the situation worse, I am halfway out of the sleeping bag and fiddling for the door zip when cramp grips my other leg. Cramp in two legs simultaneously must be new to science and for this to occur inside a micro tent in the middle of the night is just not funny. Bent in two under the low nylon roof I pause momentarily to unzip the tent door. Once open, the cold air and freezing rain hit me as I crawl onto the wet grass on all fours. Thankfully, as expected, putting weight on my legs and leaping from leg to leg in an ungainly fashion brings respite from the cramp quite quickly.

In the final analysis I have just exchanged a rude awakening from deep sleep with pain in my lower legs for being wide awake with two cold and soaking wet feet – you've got to smile, haven't you!

A few minutes later and I am back inside the tent, the towel sorts out my wet feet and I return to my sleeping bag in minutes. How warm and snug it feels. On reflection I am not surprised to have had cramp, my muscles have cycled what is a long way for a novice, but as exercise that is unfamiliar now becomes a daily routine, I will get used to it and better at it. I don't expect cramp to become a regular feature of the journey, I hope not anyway. It's 4.30 a.m. I hope the rain stops before dawn.

# Day 3 – Sunday 18th April

## Department Pas-de-Calais Picardy:

## From Licques to Montreuil-sur-Mer

Awake! Immediately the contrast between the warm sleeping bag and the envelope of cold air within the tent strikes me. The temperature is invigorating, shall we say, so my limbs are going to remain inside the sleeping bag while I muster the courage to expose them to the cold. I take a few minutes to lie perfectly still and absorb the unfamiliar surroundings of my new home. If I were to stretch my arms out I could touch both sides of my little nylon tent, so how about I describe it to you? I shall start at the lowest part of the tent interior where the sidewall is fused to the ground sheet. Here a strip of material extends horizontally around three sides, that is to say behind my head and to my left and right, but not across the entrance in front of me as that is the door. This three-sided orange fabric strip contains several open-topped pockets in which I store my torch or whatever overnight. The roof above me is green and steeply sloping – pale lime green, I would say – and the inner door near my feet is a muted red. It all sounds rather gaudy but the colours are pastel and pale and not at all harsh on the eye.

Undoubtedly last night was very cold, colder than I expected, to be frank, and although the temperature was not ideal or in any way comfortable, more of the same should be manageable, if unpleasant. This morning's bright sunshine brings a cheerful hue to the interior of the tent. Sunlight transforms the fabric into panels of bright ecclesiastical stained glass. It is very different to yesterday evening when the overcast sky made the inside dull and cheerless. Three feet above my head beads of condensation cling to the tent roof; my warm breath, the source of these water droplets, rises like steam from a kettle. If I were to sit up now, there would be a couple of inches of clearance between my head and the wet tent roof. The apex is directly above me and naturally it is the point from which the roof slopes down – because the tent is *bijou* the roof falls sharply on all sides, thus the only place I can sit upright is small and precise and offers little opportunity for movement side to side or back to front. Towards my feet the roof is lower than the apex, about six inches lower, I would say. This is where the roof meets the entrance at the top of the door.

Only careful and considered movements are possible if I am to avoid brushing my body against the wet backdrop of tent fabric. I'd quite forgotten that this is what life is like in a small tent and it is a surreal experience that takes me back in time to my youth. I allow myself a few more minutes to gaze around the tent before clambering out of my cosy three-season sleeping bag into the chilly damp air. Because the tent is compact and lacking in height, I discover that the easiest way to extricate myself is by reversing out of the zipped door on all fours, so, in my enthusiasm for keeping my knees away from the saturated cold grass I emerge bum high, as it were, an inelegant way to greet any passing Frenchman but fortunately this embarrassment is avoided as I am the first to arise. The curtain twitchers still slumber in their fuggy chalet interiors.

The grass is sodden, and large patches of the ground are white with frost. Not only that, the still air hanging over the campsite is very much colder than the air inside the tent; I can feel its sharp serrated edges with each breath. The penetrating chill certainly makes an impression but it pales compared to the beauty around me where beams of early morning sunlight slice through the dawn mist that hugs the surrounding countryside. Thankfully there is not a breath of wind and in spite of the bitter air the clear morning sky hints of better weather to come. Today is my first full day in France, the morning feels full of promise, and I am brimming with gleeful anticipation of the road ahead.

Prior to leaving *Pommiers-des-trois-pays* there are tasks to be completed, the start of a daily routine perhaps. First a shower, which warms me up greatly, then, because I am keen to make progress, I reject the time-consuming cooked breakfast option. Today is Sunday so no 'Full English' is bordering on self-neglect, I should point out. Anyway, I settle for black tea (because I have no milk) six fig biscuits, and a quarter packet of dried apricots. A few feet clear of the tent door my faithful Trangia storm cooker heats water and generates puffs of steam as it works its magic. The steam is accompanied by a slight aroma of meths and within minutes ferocious boiling creates the only sound on this otherwise silent morning.

It surprises me that I feel nostalgic about brewing tea: I bought the Trangia in 1969 when it was the pinnacle of cooker reliability for anyone wishing to heat food outdoors. The cooker is compact and works in all weathers and I have used it many times in the English Lake District, the Highlands of Scotland, and in Europe while hitch-hiking country to country as a young man. It was a pricey bit of kit in its day and after more than forty years without use I have just discovered that the Trangia has sentimental value, which is a bit odd, really, because when all is said and done it is just a metal camping cooker. The parts of the storm cooker are made from aluminium to make it lightweight, it is circular in shape and measures about ten inches across by six inches high, it comprises two bowl-shaped wind shields, which, when assembled, fit on top of each other like a letter 'U' on top of an upside-down letter 'U' – once together they form a shape similar to an egg cup. Two small pans come as standard together with a miniature one-cup kettle with a fold-flat handle. The pan, or the kettle, sits in the hollow of the upper 'U' and is thus sheltered from the weather on all sides; the lower 'U' cradles the meths burner. When deconstructed this whole ingenious ensemble fits together along the lines of a set of Russian dolls. The smallest component is the small meths burner, fuel reservoir, and wick, which form a single unit stored inside the kettle when not in use, the other bits and pieces just fit into each other.

This morning, I am just making tea, but when I cook a meal on the Trangia this evening, that will be the first time the cooker has seen action in over four decades. Nevertheless, I have absolute confidence that it will function faultlessly whatever the weather.

I am far later setting off than I wish to be and will need to be a lot snappier in the days ahead. The unfamiliar process of collapsing and packing the tent and then tightly rolling the sleeping bag so that it fits into its compression bag, while keeping everything off the wet ground, all takes time. I then discover that loading the panniers takes longer than anticipated, as much as anything because I am not yet familiar with the best way to organise the contents. No matter, I am confident the process will speed up with practice. It is ten-thirty when I eventually begin my first full day of cycling in France. After clipping the panniers on and drying the seat and handlebars I climb onto the bike and glide silently out of Licques. I have yet to see another human being today.

The world beyond the campsite is deserted but then it is Sunday morning so I figure the villagers may be in church. Visibility improves gradually over the next hour as the sun works its magic except in the landscape hollows where the mist clings stubbornly in place. The road gently weaves left and right and up and down but nothing too challenging, thankfully; there is no need for me to change gear or huff and puff, which is a good thing because it is too soon in the day for too much effort. The little country road takes me between pastures on my left and small woods to the right. Frost remains in thick white lines in the shade of hedgerows and under trees so I must stay alert for shadows crossing the road where frost or even ice may linger; it wouldn't do for me or the bike to slip and come a cropper so early in the trip.

My face is numbed by the sharp breeze generated as I pedal along and even with gloves on my hands are cold, but it is the serenity of rural France rather than the chill that makes the greatest impression on me as the miles steadily clock up during the first hour of pedalling. It surprises me that I have yet to see a single person or even a vehicle moving, indeed all that exists in the world beyond the lane, hedges, and farmland, are a row of tree tops protruding above the mist at the end of the valley and half a dozen black and white cattle. What a sight, and what a lovely way to ease into the morning.

France is subdivided into administrative areas called *'Departments'*. Eighty-three departments were created in 1790, ten years later this increased, and now stands at ninety-five. Each department has a name and a number –I am now in Pays-de-Calais, which is number sixty-two. There are about fifteen other departments on my route between here and the coastline of southern France. Department eighty, Somme, is the next I shall visit, probably the day after tomorrow.

This morning the terrain started as rolling farmland but within the hour minor undulations in the route increase in size as the road starts to negotiate small hills, and in just a few miles my route has changed from 'easy-to-cycle' and more or less level, into a 'push-the-bike' route with regular hills. I had not planned on having to gasp so early in the day and having to do so is not even remotely funny. I do not have the legs of a cyclist yet. This is some consolation for my inability to pedal up hills, of course, and a bit of an excuse for my lamentable performance. That said, at the back of my mind is a niggling thought that developing the limbs required to cycle the uplands south of Burgundy, just three weeks from now, may be a bit optimistic. Time will tell!

The next few miles are ticked off more easily and by the time I reach the next village I can quietly rejoice that the hills seem to be behind me. Devres is a pleasant little place and home to around five thousand people; it is known locally for its pottery but there is nothing to tempt me to stop here on a quiet Sunday morning so I end up leaving Devres almost as soon as I arrive. Beyond the village the little road follows the valley of the River Course. In front of me, the polythene window on my handlebar bag displays all of today's route as I cycle along. Before I left Devon, I marked the whole of my intended route from Calais to the south of France with a bright green fluorescent line, and looking down I see that today's route is more or less a straight line on the map, one o'clock to seven o'clock you could say, from NNE to SSW.

The D127 is a minor road linking fifteen rural hamlets like a string of beads. Devres is roughly halfway to my overnight stop near the town of Montreuil. After Devres I pass Auberge d'Inxent where several generations ago the Duke of Windsor, after his abdication as King, visited his mistress Wallis Simpson far from prying eyes in England. This historical snippet aside, notable features are few until quite without warning, as I am silently freewheeling through the village of Courset, I am treated to the sight of a weasel as it flies out from the verge and scuttles across the road just a few yards in front of me. It is travelling far too fast for the size of its legs and defying all laws of motion. The dawn mist that so restricted views at the start of today has vanished now, allowing me to enjoy the unspectacular beauty of Picardy. In every direction I am treated to rolling scenery that is mellow and easy on the eye and not at all unlike the chalk downs of southern England.

A small picnic area set in woodland next to the road makes an ideal place for me to stop for a snack. Propping my bike against a sturdy tree I notice that a lone motorcyclist is doing the same. We chat about the weather and our respective modes of transport, but unfortunately our conversation is very limited and for the third time in twenty-four hours it is clear to me that I really should have put more effort into learning the French language. Suddenly our attempts at conversation are halted when we are both taken aback by a cyclist who whizzes past at incredible speed. Neither hand is on the handlebars as he is waving both arms above his head and shouting loudly in French. This continues until he rounds a corner and disappears out of sight, 'How strange!' I blurt out in English and to our mutual surprise and hilarity the motorcyclist and I discover that we are both in fact from England. The motorcyclist works in finance in 'the city' and had popped over from Kent to enjoy the empty roads of northern France for a day. Lunch finishes a short while later and we part company with a 'cheerio' rather than an *'au revoir'*!

Early afternoon is sunny and it is warmer now, ten to twelve degrees, I would think, so not only are the gloves packed away but I am now down to a tee-shirt and a dayglow tabard as I pedal along the little country road running parallel to the River Course. The river here is just a minor chalk stream, barely five feet wide and very similar in appearance to the infant River Test in Hampshire. The gin-clear river gurgles encouragingly beside me and the narrow grass verge that separates the road from the river is generously carpeted with small wildflowers. The white and yellow blooms provide a welcome hint of spring and are in stark contrast to a row of trees on the far horizon that look very wintery indeed, with their stark silhouetted forms and leafless branches. Nearer, another row of trees grows on the far side of the river. These trees have all been pollarded quite harshly; squat trunks and stumpy branches are all that remains. The trees look rather sad, to be honest, it is as if their bare branches are reaching desperately towards the sky hoping to grasp any passing breeze-blown leaf.

Several farm buildings sit close to the road here, they look centuries old and have absurdly pitched rooves with ridges bowed by age. Each roof is completely out of proportion with the rest of the building; they look quaint and quirky. Whitewashed walls make up just a third of each building's height, the upper two thirds being the tiled roof. With some imagination these ancient farm buildings look like pixie dwellings from a distance.

A few miles on I come to a farmstead entrance with a large blue and white dovecote positioned near the road. Daffodils are in full bloom around the base and the dovecote looks to be inhabited by several pigeons. A cat is climbing up the support post just below the birds but as I cycle closer to it, I can see that the birds and predator are all ceramic. The deception and humour bring a smile to my face; it is a detail I would likely have missed had I been travelling in a car.

Although today has been a day of almost constant pedalling my progress has been steady rather than spectacular and by mid-afternoon a gnawing hunger reminds me that I have not had enough food to fuel a day on the bike. Breakfast was speedy rather than nutritious and lunch was limited to shortbread biscuits and water. Fortunately for me and with perfect timing, I come across a few food vendors operating café vans from an edge-of-town car park as I enter Montreuil. The princely sum of one and a half euros buys me a very tasty and surprisingly large portion of *pommes frites*, which I enjoy outdoors at one of the pretty table-chair-parasol combinations. The seats here are all brightly coloured and they lift the otherwise rather glum industrial appearance of the area, giving it a happy and inviting look.

Montreuil or Montreuil-sur-Mer to name the town accurately, was once situated next to the sea, but the coastline has receded over the last thousand years and now the town lies over a mile from the coast. In the tenth century Montreuil was the main sea port for this area and famous for its cloth trade. It was an industry that endured here for the next two hundred years until the estuary silted up and the cloth trade left with the tide.

Near to the centre of Montreuil the massive brick ramparts, constructed after the destruction of the town by the Habsburg emperor Charles V, glower down at me as I cycle closer to them. Formidable, impregnable and menacing, the ramparts add real atmosphere to the town. Three hundred years after they were built, in the post-Napoleonic era of the early eighteen hundreds, Jean Valjean was the mayor of Montreuil in the enduring epic tale of Les Misérables written by Victor Hugo. Montreuil oozes history and as I cycle closer to the old part of town, I feel a sense of going back in time. I have to push the bike now but this has nothing to do with hills, it is because the narrow old-town streets are congested with people; some young, some old, whole families out together for the afternoon. Many of the people are bartering for goods at an outdoor market. The jostling is good humoured and noisy as buyers rummage eagerly for overlooked treasures in the pop-up outdoor *brocante*. The flea market completely fills several of the quaint narrow streets that huddle below the looming ramparts. Pushing the bike is a slow and careful process but after an almost people-free day I find this heady mix of humanity, chatter, and activity both invigorating and very welcome.

Having enjoyed a taste of what Montreuil has to offer I press on out of town in a westerly direction towards the coast. I am setting off on the final leg of today for my pre-planned campsite, marked by a little white square on the map. The site is only a short distance beyond Montreuil, which is a good thing as when I arrive at the site entrance it doesn't look at all inviting. There are some chalets that seem to be habited but other than that, the site looks closed to passing visitors so I give up on it and return to Montreuil.

Camping Fontain-des-Clercs is conveniently placed just a short stroll from Montreuil's fortress walls. Having pitched my tent and still full of calories from my outdoor chip feast I venture into town on foot to take some photos. Remarkably all signs of the earlier outdoor market have vanished and exploring the now empty cobbled streets, with a little imagination, takes me back to earlier centuries. Several of the older houses have been constructed using the half-timbered method popular in medieval times. On some of the buildings the original wooden studs, cross beams, and braces are all visible on the outside walls. The ancient look of the place is enhanced with bygone-looking street lamps that hang from wrought iron hooks fixed high on the house walls.

By climbing between and then above the medieval buildings I come to a path that leads me to the rim of the ramparts. Here I am rewarded with a panoramic view over the little town. It was a bit of a slog to get here after a day on the bike but well worth doing. Beyond Montreuil a seemingly endless patchwork of fields is set out before me – yellow, green and light brown, the fields sweep to the horizon to be met by a blue sky peppered with fluffy clouds. What a sight this is from the elevated and well-positioned wooden bench I have come across. What could be better than resting my legs and having my fill of this glorious scene? Talking of legs, after a couple of hours of trekking round the town I realise that mine have had more than enough exercise. They have put in a good shift today so I give up on my walk and return to the site to cook a meal and write up my notes.

After eating, I record some of the sights of today and note a few statistics for future reference. I am pleased that after yesterday's excess today has been a very frugal day and I have spent a total of just nine and a half euros on chips and campsite fees. I have pedalled for three hours and forty-two minutes since setting off this morning. Liques is now thirty-two miles away but it feels like more and I am more than satisfied with today's mileage. Thirty-two miles is a modest distance, I know, but it is still further than I've ever cycled in my life. My speed seems to be averaging out at around eight miles an hour, which suits me just fine; three times walking speed seems the perfect pace at which to enjoy the countryside of rural France, if you ask me.

I have cycled a total of seventy-eight miles on my sparkling new bike since leaving home three days ago and tomorrow my grand total will be over a hundred miles, which I will consider a worthy milestone for a novice. My final thoughts before sleep comes my way are of the sudden realisation that I no longer feel pangs of self-doubt about my lack of cycling experience or ability. If nothing else I seem to be taking this in my stride. I've not fallen off and I've not seized up. Admittedly I've yet to convince myself that I haven't taken on more than I can manage, but once I get a big-mileage day in and crack a few challenging hills, both of which are inevitable sooner or later, I think my confidence will grow. In the meantime I'm just going along for the ride. Literally.

*Day 4 — Monday 19th April*

*Department Pay-de-Calais:*

*From Montreuil-sur-Mer to Auxi-le-Chateau*

After writing five pages of notes in my journal last night I thought listening to the radio would be a pleasant way to pass the time. I have a Nokia phone and if I put both my thumbs together, they are the same size as its flip-open screen. I can text and make calls but that's all as my phone has no internet capacity, or much else for that matter. So last night after my notes were written up I scanned the MP3 player I bought specifically for this journey, in the hope that I would be able to comprehend the general idea, if not the detail, behind the news headlines as broadcast on French radio. In the event, the quest for world news outwitted me last night and all I found to listen to was a selection of rather odd Eurovision genre music of the sort that seems so popular on the continent — naturally I gave up and went to sleep early. Amazingly, the sound of Euro-music before dozing off did not disturb my sleep pattern or give me nightmares.

I woke up at nine o'clock this morning after twelve hours of uninterrupted sleep, unbelievable! Last night the peapod tent was chilly even inside the sleeping bag, and my sleep was interrupted by an owl that screeched loudly in the depths of the night. Nevertheless, I must have been far more tired than I realised to have needed such a long time asleep.

Montreuil is frost-free this morning, although the town is wrapped in what northerners would call 'murky weather', and there's a definite chill in the air. The lightest of winds, a grey overcast sky, and a slowly swirling fog give Victor Hugo's town a rather sombre winter's day feel to it; even the massive ramparts look mysterious and other-worldly through the grey foggy filter. This is not the sort of weather I would have wished for but I have to admit that Montreuil looks atmospheric and eerie this morning and it is a sight well worth experiencing.

Today's cycle ride begins only a few miles from the sea, after breakfast and loading up the bike I shall travel eastwards and inland and it won't surprise me one bit if this early sea-fret lifts as the morning progresses. An optimistic view, perhaps, but nevertheless I push my luck and exchange shoes for sandals and my coat for a jumper. The change to lighter clothing is in hope rather than expectation and I know that my choice may prove to be folly, especially as the temperature is still only in single figures.

I am only a few days into my travels and I have already fallen into the trap, two mornings in a row I should say, of writing my journal while eating breakfast. This is not good use of time at the start of the day when there is so much else to do and it is a habit that needs nipping in the bud. Talking of breakfast – it is now time to flash up the storm cooker. I reconfigure the Russian-doll parts so that the meths burner sits in the upper 'U' ready for action. As expected, the cooker lights with the first match. This morning, breakfast is a family-sized can of ravioli, which is an odd start to the day I know, but whichever way you look at it the meal will be quick to make and filling. Storm cookers are simple things with no temperature control whatsoever, so unless I am very careful the ravioli will be blasted to oblivion and possibly beyond. I'm not sure that I fancy a huge mound of ravioli this early in the day, or at any other time if I'm honest. Pragmatic and speedy, yes. Calorific, most certainly. The best breakfast? Perhaps not.

By ten-fifteen I have eaten more than my fill and packed the panniers, but the tent is still up and the bike has yet to be loaded. My change into lighter clothing feels a little premature now; let's just say I am encouraged to step it up a bit by the cold air.

By half-ten I leave town through the same streets that hosted yesterday's outdoor market before heading out of Montreuil in a southeasterly direction. The first few miles of the day are through undulating but rather featureless farmland as the little country road weaves its way through the settlements of Boisjean and then Roussent where I meet up with the Authie valley.

The River Authie flows just sixty-four miles from its inland source to the point where it enters the sea at Berck, a beachside town on the Opal Coast. The origins of the name 'Authie' are uncertain but may well originate from the pre-Celtic word '*atur*', which means river. The valley is pleasingly French in appearance, peppered with a mixture of proudly kept rural homes and the occasional tumbledown chateau. All is peaceful here and traffic is a rare sight even though it is the start of the working week. The murky weather has cleared in places, allowing me glimpses of the landscape that lies on either side of the D119 road. I note that many of the fields are edged with long strands of poplar trees. This early in the year the trees are pencil thin and leafless, although pompoms of parasitic mistletoe add unexpected interest to virtually every tree.

Glancing down at the map, I see that I am now on the opposite side of the River Authie to Valloires, a Cistercian abbey dating to 1226. A century or so after its construction the abbey was used as a hospital to treat sword and arrow injuries. The arrows in question rained down from English longbows; at the time this was a new and terrifying adaptation of warfare the like of which the French had never faced until the nearby battle of Crecy in 1346.

Near the hamlet of Douriez I stop at the gated entrance of a once-grand house for a drink from my water bottle. The closed gates I am leaning over mark the start of a long private lane to the Manoir-des-Templares, which is a majestic fourteenth-century building set back from the road. Viewed through its pillared entrance the building looks sad and unused; undoubtedly once a lovely structure, it has been abandoned and left to decay.

While stopped at the chateau gates I fiddle with the bike for no particular reason and discover, better late than never, you may reasonably think, that raising the seat pillar by just half an inch makes a far more comfortable position for pedalling. Not only that, but by adjusting, or to be more accurate forcing the rear panniers an inch further back, more clearance is created between the revolving pedals and the panniers. This simple alteration prevents my heels from occasionally brushing against the forward corners of the pannier bags as I cycle along, something that has irritated me for a bit. I cannot explain why but it is fair to say I am disproportionately gleeful at the outcome of this bike fiddling, which should add both comfort and efficiency to my cycling.

Talking of efficiency, it appears to me from the few occasions that I have witnessed it so far, that French cyclists do not favour changing gears as they approach a hill, they prefer to stand up in the seat and power up the incline by leaning forward and shifting their torso and centre of gravity towards the handlebars. Good for the French, I say, but I am not convinced the technique is for me; my journey is not a gallop so I will doggedly continue to tackle hills by changing gear, applying brute force, and pushing if needs must.

I glide into the town of Auxi-le-Chateau in the middle of the afternoon after covering the twenty-nine miles since leaving Montreuil. This relatively untaxing distance has taken me three and a half hours, although this includes stops to drink water, take photos, or just to admire the view such as at the Manoir-des-Templares. Fortunately I just about got away with my change to lighter clothing, although it's only brightened up in the last hour or so. As soon as I arrive at Camping Municipal des Peupliers I decide to take advantage of the weak afternoon sunshine and light breeze to dry my tent and some clothes. The wet items are hung between two conveniently placed poplar, or *'peuplier'* trees. At under five euros a night this municipal site is very reasonably priced, it is also well laid out, clean and tidy, and has a ready supply of warm water: I can ask for no more.

My travels today have been conservative in both speed and distance. Even so, I feel that a hearty evening meal has been earned and with this in mind I visit the large Aldi shop just five minutes down the road. Barring a bowl of takeaway chips at Montreuil and the meal at Licques campsite I have eaten only the food that I carried with me from England, so now seems as good a time as any to replenish my supplies. The total cost of my supermarket purchases pleases me no end: Ten eggs, two packets of *lardon fumes* (smoked bacon pieces) a small tub of margarine, a large baguette, four crème deserts, and a litre carton of *melange jus-de-fruits*. All this for only four and a half euros, enough for two hearty meals – bargain!

Naturally, it would have been mightily remiss of me not to visit the supermarket's wine selection. My last visit to France was three years ago and I had heard that wine prices had increased considerably since then. I am pleased to report that this did not prove to be the case, at least not at the less prestigious end of the wine display, which to be honest is where I feel more at home. For example, a 75cl bottle of Côtes du Rhône (*appellation contrôlée*, no less) for just over one euro; Medoc (also A.O.C.) costs two and a half euros; even Bordeaux, although probably far from the best, is just over a euro; even a full bottle of upmarket St-Émilion Grand Cru would only set me back nine euros.

Back at the campsite I overload on calories and decide to have another early night. It feels very much colder than a few hours ago so it makes sense to retain body heat in the sleeping bag. My late father's multi-function watch has been a very useful companion on my trip. He used it for weather predictions, and to assist him with navigation and waymark information when sailing. Barometric pressure is one of its useful functions and as the reading is now 1,033 millibars I should be able to look forward to a pleasant day tomorrow.

Prior to settling in for what may well prove to be a rather cold night I try for a second evening to tune in to the French news on the MP3 player. Unfortunately it is beyond me to find any radio stations and I have no idea if this is because reception is poor here, or because I am a Luddite and find the device quite unfathomable. Anyway, I end up listening to Carole King's acclaimed album 'Tapestry', which I preloaded before setting off. The music is a joy. I switch the device off after half an hour and allow the distant calls of a cuckoo and some nearby woodpeckers to lull me to sleep.

# Day 5 – Tuesday 20th April

## Departments of Pas-de-Calais and Somme: From Auxi-le-Chateau to Frise

There is no logical reason for this but I have woken up full of enthusiasm for a day on the bike, which is a bit odd as today's roads are likely to be the most challenging so far. It's not even as if the sun is out, nor is it warm, and if I had any sense at all I would stay put and savour the comfort of my sleeping bag. Instead, I am raring to go. Once out of the tent I ignite the cooker with a match from my brick-sized box and the day begins with culinary vigour as I whack the full contents of a packet of smoked lardons into the small Trangia frying pan, along with some butter. The pan is balanced atop the storm cooker and in less than three minutes this one-temperature-fits-all blast machine ensures the lardons are ready. Stage one done, next I crack five eggs into this sizzling and gloriously aromatic bacon and butter mix along with a bit of salt and a twist of freshly cracked black pepper (I may be cycle touring but there is absolutely no need to be uncivilised). A couple of minutes later my breakfast is ready and what a breakfast it is! Tasty? I should say so. Not only that but my breakfast is exactly the same eggy-bacony feast that I enjoyed for last night's evening meal – ten eggs in twelve hours – cracking! The storm cooker frying pan doubles up as a plate, which reduces washing up but even so, it takes me longer to clean the pan than it did to cook and eat the meal. *C'est la vie!* It was worth every minute.

After packing up my worldly possessions I pedal off to add to the hundred miles I have covered on the bike since leaving Devon. I set off under an overcast and grey morning with none of the clear sky the high barometric pressure led me to anticipate. As a result I cycle out of Auxi-le-Chateau into a surprisingly cold and very glum morning. The unwelcome weather causes me to don my fleece and gloves, which, believe it or not, I end up wearing until well after lunch.

Before leaving Auxi-le-Chateau behind, and rather oddly, you may think, I stop to buy sun cream but worry not, this is future-proofing for the south of France and not because of any likelihood it will be needed any time soon. Naturally the three bars of chocolate I bought at the same shop were my real reason for stopping. Chocolate adds negligible weight but packs a tasty and high-calorie punch whenever I need it.

The more I think about the day ahead, the more daunted I am at the prospect of having to pedal forty miles to the next campsite and tackle the biggest hills so far. With this in mind buying chocolate was both tactical and motivational, and whatever effect the chocolate may or may not have on my ability to manage hills, an interesting test of both my ability and my stamina lies ahead.

Auxi-le-Chateau straddles the River Authie, a waterway that once marked the boundary between the departments of Pays-de-Calais and Somme. Not many miles beyond Auxi I come upon a British cemetery dating to the great war: Wavans cemetery is very small, it has just four and a half rows of headstones. Each of these very short rows is beautifully cared for by the Commonwealth War Graves Commission. The cemetery is surrounded by a low stone wall and the headstones within are set on a chalky hillside overlooking the vast rolling fields above Noeus-les-Auxi. This morning the cemetery is shrouded in mist, the daylight is muted and dull, essentially it is a monochrome scene before me and you would be excused for thinking that it would look bleak here on such a morning, but it does not, it actually looks very serene. A very fitting location for the forty-four graves here.

Forgive me if I single out just two of those who are laid to rest; all made the same sacrifice but of all these brave men, two stand out for me. The first is Major J.T. Byford-McCudden, a WW1 flying ace who was awarded the Victoria Cross. This, the ultimate recognition for military bravery, was in addition to his Distinguished Service Order and

Bar, the Military Cross and Bar, and the Military Medal. It is simply astonishing that this young man, just twenty-three when he died, had earned six gallantry medals. How could anyone so young be so very brave so very often? Placed next to the flowers carefully laid against the Major's headstone are two documents, both sealed against the elements in transparent plastic covers. One is entitled *Casualty Details* and is largely devoted to replicating the citation written for the award of his Victoria Cross as published in the *London Gazette* on the 29th of March 1918. The document states that both his brothers fell in combat during the Great War. The other document is a photograph of Major Byford-McCudden in uniform. These personal details are incredibly touching, and here, at this most intimate and moving of places I look out on this overcast morning, where absolutely nothing is out of place. I gaze beyond the headstones to the rolling plains of the Somme that surround Wavans. Standing alone in contemplative silence, I feel very humble and immensely sorry.

At the furthest point from Wavans cemetery entrance I come to the shortest row of headstones. Just four graves are positioned side by side here; one of these is the other memorial I felt drawn to. Otto Wolter's headstone is inscribed with a carved cross in the German military style together with 1.M.E.K.J.R.83, and 10.9.18. Until this moment I was quite unaware that those who were once foes shared such places after death. Otto Wolter had of course made the same terrible sacrifice and it made me think that although these men were once foes, being buried together here after the hostilities are over is perhaps where forgiveness starts and secure futures begin. Wavans is unbelievably poignant and for some time after leaving this little parcel of land I cycle in silent contemplation, acutely aware that I have given just a few moments for reflection, whereas the forty-four servicemen buried at Wavans have given their forevers. If you ever visit the memorials of northern France you will be struck, as I was, by how immaculate and manicured these war memorials are kept. We have much to thank the War Graves Commission for.

Picardie lies immediately south of Pays-de-Calais and taken together this combined landmass makes up the prominent northeastern tip of

France. Picardie has three departments – Aisne, Oise, and Somme – and shortly after crossing into Somme, I pass a large sign on the verge, which reads *Par la Picardie et le people Français votez Front National*. This bold encouragement to vote for the far right makes quite an impact on me coming so soon after the poignancy of Wavans and I find myself considering the obvious contrasts between the two sights, but such thoughts and the big questions they create do not sit easy in the mind, so I allow myself to be absorbed into the landscape that surrounds me here. Immense fields, rows of statuesque poplar trees, and the vast blue skies that have at last arrived are all much less challenging than thinking of past wars and extreme political views.

The unimaginable scale of conflict across this whole area, and just how pivotal the region was to the future of human history is reinforced when I come across another resting place from the First World War: *Tombes de Guerre du Commonwealth Louvencourt Military Cemetery*. Louvencourt is another British war cemetery situated ten miles from 'Albert', a town that was at the hub of relentless wretched combat. I cannot stop at all war cemeteries but it feels wrong not to pause here, even if it is just for a short time.

Near the entrance and set into the neat drystone wall that surrounds the cemetery is a small, ornate bronze door about fifteen inches by ten inches in size. I open the door and find a square metal-lined cavity that contains a book. The book lists the name and location of every individual grave. There is a second book together with a pen for visitors to record their comments and thoughts. After a short contemplative walk around just a small section of this large and pristine cemetery I return to the bike and continue my journey towards Albert. The enormity of past conflict remains a prominent feature of today, and as I wheel into the town of Doullens I spot a roadside plinth in the form of a substantial granite block. The stone is engraved with the words '*Aux Picardie Martyrs de la Resistance 1940-1945*'. Two signs in the last hour, one to the far right and one to the French resistance; both signs have, in very different ways, made me stop and think.

The D938 road is straight, flat, and rural, and after two and a half hours of easy cycling twenty miles of road lie behind me and the town of Albert appears ahead. The town is visible from a long way off because of the enormous golden dome that towers above all other buildings. It is by far the most prominent feature on the skyline and I am intrigued by the sight of such grand architecture in a modest town. When planning the trip Albert was on my shortlist of overnight camping stops. Thinking there was little of interest here, I had planned to travel beyond the town to today's campsite but the sight of the golden dome makes me think this may have been the wrong decision.

Freewheeling into town I find Albert benefits from an uncluttered main street, which has a generous selection of independent shops. Albert is a busy and cheerful little place that I warm to immediately. Towering over all before it is the quite magnificent basilica of Notre-Dame de Brebières. I am tempted to spend the night in the town just so I can explore the basilica; the choice is entirely mine, of course, as my daily itinerary can flex, but in the end, I decide to be more pragmatic and get a few more miles under my belt, especially as my legs are okay to carry on.

I leave Albert along the D329, which is another long straight road with a smooth surface that does all it can to assist me in making good progress. Some miles beyond Albert the large 'Aerolia' factory and its adjoining airfield dominate the view from the road. Judging from the bold artwork on the factory wall the company has been involved in aeronautics since the birth of human flight. Everyone is familiar with the line drawing that depicts the evolution of man from a crawling ape to standing *Homo sapiens*, here that same format is used to depict a series of aircraft from the earliest triplanes progressing through turbo-props to modern airliners, including the superb but ultimately ill-fated Concorde. The linear mural ends with more recent workhorses such as the Airbus A320 and A380.

Beyond the aeronautical factory the land dips into a shallow valley where the scenery becomes more colourful as the road winds its way between fields of bright yellow mustard. Next, I come to Bray-sur-

Somme village, the location of Bray Hill cemetery. I pause long enough to pay my respects and write a brief entry in the visitors' book; being an ex-serviceman, this feels the right thing to do. Two miles further on and after what has been a fulfilling and interesting day on the bike I cycle into the hamlet of Cappy. It is precisely 4 p.m.

I am disappointed to discover that Municipal-les-Charnilles campsite is closed and for a man heading south this is bad news indeed because the nearest alternative campsite would involve me backtracking northwest to Albert. This is absolutely not what I wish to do as the very idea of going back over ground already cycled seems anathema. Of course, I could wild camp at the side of the river, nobody is around and even if they were I doubt they would object, but wild camping doesn't appeal to me today. I think it is something I will have to be in the mood for and right now, I'm not. I have cycled a long way since leaving Auxi-le-Chateau this morning and ending today with a shower, some facilities, and a beer is firmly in my sights.

One of the little white labels on my map shows me that the hamlet of Frise is the location of a backup campsite, which I hope will be open. The few miles to Frise are done in quick order and I arrive in the hamlet to discover it is set amid a very watery landscape indeed. The lane into Frise is particularly picturesque with its abundance of blackthorn bushes, all of which are covered in a veil of white blossom. The hamlet overlooks the River Somme and is encircled by lush watermeadows interspersed with small lakes for as far as the eye can see. Since the Middle Ages residents of this area have made a good living harvesting peat from the land and fish from the waters.

Dusk comes early in April and today its arrival is accompanied by the most exquisite light, and as I pedal ever so slowly along the right bank of the Somme I can't help but feel how fortunate I am to be here at this moment, for this is one of those infrequent, magical, and fleeting times that occur when good fortune puts you in precisely the right place at exactly the right time. To my left is the unhurried River Somme, its clear waters flowing with just enough power to create a languid swaying movement in the vivid green weed that flourishes in the slower waters either side of midstream. The surface water sparkles with dappled sunlight, while four feet or so below the surface the river bed is made up of small coloured pebbles and pieces of white chalk. This wondrous light with hints of pale tangerine has given the river a special luminosity. To my right the weathered rockface of the chalk escarpment above the blackthorn bushes has been transformed to the colour of rose-madder. Photographers refer to this natural light, which occurs mostly at dusk and dawn, as the golden hour. Today I am blessed with a truly wonderful example.

I have seen no people for several hours, nobody since leaving Albert, in fact. None at the aircraft factory, no-one in the villages of Bray, or Cappy, neither is there any traffic, absolutely none. To be honest it feels a bit odd, yet there is a magical quality that I rather relish about cycling along in virtual silence with the extraordinary beauties of the natural world as my sole distraction. Suddenly a sharp gust of wind arrives from nowhere and creates a brief blizzard as thousands upon thousands of white petals are blown free from the blossom in the blackthorn bushes. The petals scamper and tumble across the deserted lane in front of me; the sight is accompanied by the warbling melody of little birds that are hidden in the nearby bushes and the willow trees that edge the river. A grey heron fifty yards ahead of me is wonderfully photogenic but I am not nearly quick enough to capture a shot of the statuesque bird. It takes to the air with a series of improbably slow wing-flaps before landing well ahead of me to continue its hunt for supper in the slow eddies at the edge of the meandering river.

The C7 road guides me into Frise; it is really a lane rather than a road and as the hamlet comes into view I glance down to the cyclometer and see I have notched up forty-nine miles since this morning. This is by far the longest distance I have ever cycled in a single day and surprisingly I am not the least bit tired, although I will admit to feeling more than a little smug.

The first human I have encountered in ages informs me that Frise campsite doesn't accept passing trade at this time of year as out of season it is restricted to those who stay in permanent chalets to make use of its fishing many lakes, my lingering smugness is erased in an instant as the spectre of wild camping reappears on my agenda.

I enquire in the village about alternative campsites and I am told of a place called Feuilleres. Unfortunately its campsite may also be closed until next month and in light of this information I am reluctant to press on. Perhaps triggered by my expression of disappointment the villager suggests that I visit the doctor who lives five hundred metres down the lane as she owns *Camping de la Pointe*. It turns out that this is the very site I was told is closed except for resident anglers. Not so, the doctor tells me; her campsite is very much open and I am welcome to use any pitch I like, and if I would like to go and settle in she will arrive at half past six to collect my fee. Adding certainty to my overnight whereabouts is a happy turn of events, something of a relief, and just what the doctor ordered.

A few minutes later I find *Camping de la Pointe* to be very much to my liking: It is a tidy, well-maintained site and I soon find a pitch surrounded by neat hedging, which gives a sense of privacy and some protection should the weather unexpectedly deteriorate. This will be my fourth night in a tent and slowly but surely the rudiments of a system for setting up camp are developing. Right on cue the doctor pulls up near the tent in her Mercedes and I pay the fee for the night. She tells me that the showers function but with cold water only at this time of year as tent dwellers are not expected this early, and those who visit in April do so in motorhomes or caravans with a self-contained hot water supply. Cold water has no appeal whatsoever but whichever way you look at it, fifty miles of pedalling a loaded bike, even on pretty flat roads, requires a shower, cold or otherwise. Half an hour later I can report that the showers at *Camping de la Pointe* are very bracing indeed. The water is just about on the right side of painful, I would say. Obviously, such torment must be rewarded so I decree to indulge myself with three large Bratwurst sausages and a baguette for dinner. Once dinner and all tent-keeping tasks are done I ride the short distance to Frise to seek out the pub I spotted on the way in. It was closed earlier but two hours have passed and I am very much looking forward to writing up my journal over a beer or two.

'*La Sarcelles*' is a small traditional pub overlooking the river but as it is still early evening its customers can be counted on one hand. Inside, my eyes are drawn to a very large wall map of the Somme battlefields and an outrageously large artificial wisteria. The interior of La Sarcelles is very quirky and very homely in an authentic French bygone-era sort of way. In addition to what I take to be local beers on tap and a small selection of spirits, an extensive selection of tobacco products is offered for sale together with a range of angling necessities – hooks, bait, line, and floats of every colour. I ask the barman who tells me that a '*sarcelle*' is a small duck from the Paris region.

I spend the next two hours sat next to the window overlooking the Somme at what I suspect was once an old kitchen table. The table's large size is just perfect for me to unroll a few feet of the map in front of me, with plenty of space left for my journal and a beer.

This evening written words do not flow at all well, but the beer does, and as beer is a well-known and certain cure for writer's block, I order additional supplies, and in no time at all the efficacious qualities of local ale have the required effect and consequently I finish six pages of notes just before nine p.m. Before leaving the pub, I ponder tomorrow's route by unfurling the whole map across two large tables; as much as anything this allows me to put the distance already covered in context, and compare it visually to what lies ahead. I can see that Frise lies around five miles from the junction of the Canal de la Somme and the Canal du Nord. Both canals merge roughly ten miles south of here near the town of Peronne, and whilst that would not be the most direct route for me to take, going via Peronne would provide me with the opportunity to cycle on canal towpaths for the first time since arriving in France. The idea rather appeals to me but I shall decide in the morning.

As I pedal back to the campsite the outside air feels sharp and uncomfortable on my face and hands, a clear sign that it is going to be a bit chilly tonight and a prompt for me to wrap up well. The short trip from the campsite to the pub and back has pushed up today's distance to just over 50 miles. I have actually proved to myself that I can cycle fifty miles in a day, and more remarkable still I've done it without discomfort or seizing up. It's a surprise that brings a smile to my face, but more than anything else it is a reassuring fact to have in my back pocket in case I need to pedal fifty miles another day.

The total silence during the short ride from La Sarcelles back to the campsite is interrupted only by the background whisper of the river as it flows next to the lane and the eerie sound of an owl hunting. At the campsite the only signs of life are a few lights on in some of the riverside chalets that I pedal past on my way to my pitch, otherwise nothing stirs in the cold night air. A few hours ago, my travels ended with a magical lightshow as dusk descended over the Somme valley, a trio of pints in La Sarcelles rounded off today with a warm glow, and now my dad's barometric watch shows one thousand and thirty-six millibars. It looks very much like a fine day is coming my way tomorrow. To cap it all I have spent twenty-one euros, which is bang on my daily budget. What a day!

# Day 6 – Wednesday 21st April

## Departments of Somme and Oise:

## From Frise to Carlepont

The still world beyond my peapod tent is cold, it is bitterly cold. The nylon fabric is designed to protect me from wind and rain but the material is gossamer thin and did little to keep me warm overnight. The freezing temperature has just catapulted me from fitful sleep into the uncomfortable state of being awake. The cold is painful. Temperatures tumbled overnight to at least minus five, but that's just a guess so quite possibly it was colder. What I know for certain is that last night was well below anything I had anticipated or planned for. My three-season sleeping bag is accurately described; it performed well but it is a full season short of what's needed. Sleep was intermittent and several times I had to respond to the dire need to add more clothing. Each time I did so the benefit seemed minimal. It was cold when I went to bed, so to maintain core body heat I began the night wearing a tee-shirt and a thick fleece jumper. Later I added a fleece jacket; later still, when the cold was boring painfully into my bones, I put on my Gore-Tex jacket as a fourth layer. Below the waist I wore shorts, thick trousers, and two pairs of socks. Not only was I fully clothed and cocooned in my sleeping bag I had the benefit of lying on top of the self-inflating mattress, and although it is only half an inch thick it punches well above its weight by creating a barrier between me and the frozen earth I was lying on.

To be honest I spent the night bound like a nineteenth-century Japanese foot and I have absolutely no idea how I would have escaped from the tent had another bout of cramp come my way. Right now, my natural reaction is to remain perfectly still so as not to disturb the meagre warmth in my sleeping bag.

Beyond feeling sorry for myself the main focus of the morning so far is watching the condensation inside the tent as it rises with each breath I take. Even in my semi-numbed state I realise that being this cold is not healthy and quite possibly unsafe. The effects that the cold is having on me right now are difficult to explain, although I think that's as much as anything because my whole system has slowed down, including my ability to think. Shivering is the obvious visible sign of how the temperature is affecting me, although I'm pretty sure that I wouldn't be able to speak clearly if there was anyone to talk to because my face has no feeling. On top of that I don't think my mouth works as it should. I can't feel much below my ankles and the cold has penetrated deep into my hands; my finger joints are stiff, painful, and uncoordinated when I try to use them. But on the plus side I am alert enough to know that getting my circulation going must be my number one priority above all else.

Somewhat reluctantly I leave the tent whereupon I'm immediately punched hard in the chest as the icy outside air violently assaults my lungs. It is far colder outside the tent so it seems that the thin fabric did a good job after all. The two water bottles that I left outside in their bike frame cradles are covered in ice crystals – hoar frost, I suppose; both bottles are frozen solid, and the plastic has swollen and distorted where the water has expanded into ice. All around me the grass is white and frozen and crisp and brittle. A wintry haze hangs just above the campsite, it looks just like a thin silk blanket held aloft by the treetops. Soft puffs of wind blow the haze aside occasionally and I get a glimpse of the watery blue sky above. Optimistically I take this to mean that the morning will pick up as the temperature rises. I have a strong desire to get my body moving quickly, in as much as I can move quickly, that is, so I start packing away my camping equipment as best as I can, but movement comes slowly and reluctant fingers hamper whatever I try to do. There is no finesse in my packing today, and I have to settle for stuffing items in rather than folding them. My reward will be to get back on the bike; surely cycling will thaw me out when I get going. Breakfast can come later.

A short row of poplar trees edges the far side of the campsite where a dozen or more golden blades of sunlight peek through the narrow gaps between the trunks. The sun shines brilliantly towards me, leaving the trees silhouetted and floating in the sea of haze that hangs low over the site. The intense sun makes this beautiful haze sparkle; the effect is simply wonderful and quite a sight. A dozen or so beautifully made wooden chalets surround the central camping field. Without exception each is kept very tidy by proud but unseen owners. A few select chalets form a neat row that abuts the river and I can see warmth escaping from heater vents on a couple of the chalets. *Lucky residents*, I think to myself. What wouldn't I give for some of that heat? Fortunately for me I have taken to keeping a water bottle inside the tent stored inside a pannier, that water didn't freeze overnight so I can at least have a drink – a very cold drink, of course, but a drink nonetheless.

The first stage of packing has warmed me up a little. I still have to collapse the wet tent and roll it up but for now at least some feeling has returned to my fingers so I reverse my initial idea of setting off immediately. After a bit of cack-handed fiddling about I manage to get the Trangia going and it sets to work blasting the three remaining Bratwurst sausages, which will set me up well until lunchtime. Cooking today's breakfast has used virtually all my methylated spirits so I make a mental note to replenish the fuel as soon as possible.

After breakfast I shake the tent and pack it away. I have to do so with bare hands as I need to keep the gloves dry for cycling. My fingers had started to warm up a little but after rolling up the icy wet tent I am back to square one as my hands are now colder than when I got up, my finger dexterity has all but gone, and my hands feel stiff and awkward. Hopefully when I get on the bike my gloves will restore enough warmth for me to operate the brakes. A dull pain drills into my hands and ears and I am reminded that I cannot feel my feet. How I wish the sun would get to work.

Panniers are clicked onto the bike frame and I glance over my pitch for any forgotten items. This morning, I can't be bothered to look over the tyres, the brakes, or the load, it is too cold for that, it's too cold for anything really. Ordinarily I would refill my bottles with fresh water before setting off but they are still frozen so that won't happen today. It has taken me until ten o'clock to be in a position to set off, which is a great deal longer than anticipated. All around, it is frosty; the icy covering is especially thick in the shadows where it has accumulated like a thin layer of snow. Thankfully there is no wind and the morning has started bright and sunny. There may even be the faintest hint that the temperature is lifting. I'm sure the day will pick up as the sun rises.

By necessity my upper body is still layered up with the four items of clothing I wore overnight. Fleece gloves and hat are added to combat the gentle breeze on the bike, even at the slow pace I usually set. Thankfully the gravel track that surrounds the central pitching area provides good traction so there is little risk of the wheels slipping on the ice and frost as I head for the exit to explore more of the Somme.

As I near the riverside chalets I spot a man in his front garden leaning against a white picket fence smoking a cigarette. He beckons me over. Not only is he the first human I have seen today but he invites me into his chalet for a coffee. What a fantastic stroke of luck! I may be running late but it would be rude not to accept this stranger's kind offer and I like the idea of some conversation over a warm drink very much; in fact there is little that appeals more right now.

I learn that the man is rather ill and recuperating in his riverside chalet whilst his wife is at home. A shoebox three-quarters full of medications rests on the small wooden kitchen table we are seated at as testament to his ailments. He asks what I am doing and why am I camping on such a cold night. I explain that I retired last year and show him my route-map through France, which we chat about for a while. The man's passion is fishing and he shows me a photograph of himself holding an enormous pike that he caught in the adjacent lake. Apparently the pike here are particularly large, large enough to eat ducks, in fact, something he has witnessed on more than one occasion.

The man points out that he is much slimmer now than when the photo was taken, twenty-five kilograms lighter, he tells me, on the instructions of his doctor to help with his condition. We chat about France and England and fishing as the mug transfers its delicious warmth to my hands. The coffee is very dark and strong, but above all else it is extremely warming. *Le monsieur* then rolls yet another cigarette, heartily inhales and immediately suffers a ferocious bout of coughing. I feel for him, trapped as he is in a lifetime of tobacco addiction and the debilitating illnesses it has doubtless caused. I hope he goes on to catch more monster pike.

'*Bon courage,*' he says as I leave.

'*Bonne chance avec la pêche,*' I call to him as I pedal away from the site.

On leaving the village of Frise the road immediately climbs a long steady hill. I would have preferred a few miles on the flat just to loosen up but it is not to be and on a positive note, I am very much warmer by the time I arrive at the top. Coffee and hills are the way to go when you wake up to a bitterly cold morning, it seems. Four layers of clothes are reduced to two and by now my fingers are working pretty well as they should. This is progress indeed.

The *'Frise Belvedere'* rewards me handsomely with an elevated and panoramic view over the meandering River Somme. A large notice board (thankfully written in English) explains that the habitat here, a myriad of water meadows and small lakes, is protected as a home for rare plants and butterflies. Incongruously, this beautiful and peaceful place is part of what was once the vast and horrific battlefields of the Somme. Shortly after leaving the viewpoint behind, I pause briefly at Herbecourt British Cemetery where by chance I come across the headstone of Private Fontana. His memorial is carved with the words 'Aust. Cyclist Corps'. I was totally unaware that cyclists had performed any kind of military role in WW1 and I cannot imagine how difficult cycling must have been on primitive heavy bicycles along very muddy tracks in the middle of a warzone. Later research informed me that the cyclists were involved in recognisance, patrolling, and despatch riding, and in total over a thousand soldiers were members of the cyclist corps.

# THE ADVENTURER WITHIN

A few miles further on, a bridge carries my little country road over the top of the E15 Paris to Lille autoroute. The sight of the endless stream of vehicles hurrying below me makes me extremely grateful to be on a quiet county byway.

Due south from here I continue through a landscape that is archetypical northern France with its immense flat fields, poplar trees in sentinel rows, pretty villages and small hamlets that are all linked by near traffic-free roads; what an ideal place this is for my kind of travelling. The bright sun has raised the temperature a few degrees by the time I come to the Canal du Nord. The canal is a relatively short waterway that connects the Canal Latéral à l'Oise, at Pont-l'Évêque, with the Sensée Canal at Arleux. The village of Arleux lies fifty-nine miles from here along the towpath.

Construction of the Canal du Nord started before WW1. Initially works were funded by the French government as a way to help the local coal industry, but the canal was heavily damaged during the 1914-1918 war and the final five-year phase of construction didn't recommence until 1960. This rather delayed resurgence in the fortunes of the Canal du Nord was prompted by an increase in bulk transport being carried on barges between the Seine basin and the north of France.

With a distance of twenty feet or thereabouts between its banks the Canal du Nord is roughly the same width as its towpath, and although pedalling beside the canal makes a novel change there is little joy in cycling next to the grimy warehouses and dilapidated concrete buildings that line the bumpy gravel towpath. This is far from the picturesque canalside journey I had looked forward to. Several commercial barges glide past me; they look disproportionately long and are fully loaded, literally to the gunnels. In fact they are so laden that the deck and cargo hold hatches are barely a foot clear of the water. These purely functional boats lack the charm of those vessels which started life as working boats but have since been lovingly restored and converted into floating homes.

I cycle past a succession of grimy canalside enterprises on the towpath including a surprising number of stone-crushing plants. Without exception they are unappealing structures set amid a gloomy world of dirt and dust; there is nothing that pleases the eye here and when the gravel track becomes deeply rutted, I exit the towpath at the first opportunity. There will be more scenic canals on the journey, I'm sure.

It's a few hours into the day now and the temperature no longer causes me physical discomfort. The air is still fresh, of course, but it's warming up gradually, which is just fine by me now that the breeze has lost its bite. Back on a tarmac surface the bike wheels spin effortlessly as we scurry down the country lane between fields that look to have been recently ploughed and seeded. A few miles further on, the unattractive sight of industry blights the horizon as cooling towers and chimneys discharging goodness knows what into the atmosphere come into view. It is a sight I did not expect on this part of the journey.

I skirt around the industrial area pausing only to freewheel onto a garage forecourt in my search for cooker fuel. Unfortunately I do not know the French word for methylated spirits (let's be honest, who would?) so my attempts to buy meths rely on trying to describe its colour, which is blue, and trying to tell the garage proprietor that it is used for outdoor cooking. Unfortunately my best efforts confuse everyone and quite reasonably the staff think I need Camping Gaz, especially as *'Blu'* is the brand name of a readily available camping gas in France. Eventually we all admit defeat, call it a draw and I leave empty handed. I probably have insufficient fuel left to heat a meal so obtaining meths in case there is no restaurant near tonight's campsite is near the top of my list of 'must-do' things for today.

I potter along for the next few minutes considering just how I could describe meths better, until, that is, in a surprising moment of tactical brilliance a solution comes to me – I shall find a supermarket and buy a veggie ready meal, problem solved in an instant: 'Sod's Law' guarantees that my fuel will run out at precisely the most inopportune moment, i.e. part-way through cooking a meal, but if I am cooking a veggie meal rather than one with meat no mortal illness will befall me should I be forced to eat it part cooked and tepid. What a plan! Using this logic, I buy a can of potato dauphinoise together with six bars of cooking chocolate because I am quickly learning that on a trip such as this, chocolate, even cooking chocolate, ticks all the boxes. Cheap to buy, small and light to carry, full of calories, readily available, and tasty – even cooking chocolate tastes good after a day on a bike. I believe I prove my case: *Ipso facto.*

Leaving the localised squalor of heavy industry behind me I press on along a series of quiet roads. Navigation here is on a wing and a prayer as there are no road signs and high thick hedges obstruct any view, until by some good fortune I catch sight of a wooden fingerboard partly obscured by foliage. The long-forgotten sign bears the indistinct name of a village in flaking paint. The place name cannot be made out, but as the sign is at least a clue to something or somewhere I follow the hint it offers, blindly for several miles, it has to be said, until I come across a signpost pointing clearly to Cressy-Omercourt, Ercheu, and Chevilly, all of which not only feature on my map but are pedalled through in quick succession as I head towards Noyon.

Noyon has shops and shops may have fuel, so I keep my eyes open for likely retailers. I try a couple of places but difficulties are of my own making yet again as my verbal quest for fuel makes no sense to anyone listening and I am left wondering why I didn't think to carry an English-French dictionary with me. After all, there are some things in life you just cannot wing and conversing in a foreign language is one of them.

As soon as I leave Noyon I find myself cycling through the Forêt d'Ourscamp. The busy road through this beautiful forest is arrow straight, a fact that may well be contributing to the number of drivers going faster than I have encountered elsewhere. Fortunately for me and without exception the drivers are considerate and give me a wide berth as they overtake, which is a great relief. That being said, this is the first time on the journey that I have felt some benefit from wearing my fluorescent yellow top. Clear of the forest, I arrive in the town of Carlepont where I shall spend tonight.

First impressions of Camping Araucarias are that it will be very much to my liking, and after giving the site a quick visual once-over I pitch my tent amid a cluster of fir trees, which stand out from the many others because of their long silvery-blue needles. The site is very attractive visually, it is also quiet and private, and once the bike is unloaded and my tent is prepared for the night, I set off to find the campsite shop, which seems my best bet for meths replenishment. My hopes are short lived when the proprietor explains that they don't have a shop on site. Then, magician-like, he reaches down and produces a half-full bottle of *alcool à brûler* from under the reception desk and hands it to me without charge. *Alcool à brûler* – so that's what methylated spirits are called. I am set fair now because not only can I cook a hot meal, future replenishment should be less challenging now I know what to ask for.

On a pitch near my tent, James and Betty who hail from Berkshire are on a five-week caravan tour of Europe. After brief introductions they invite me to join them later for an evening drink, which is very kind of them both and something I will look forward to. A hot shower before dinner is especially welcome after a day of pedalling, but it is only as I finish that I discover my towel has been left in the tent; it somewhat defeats the objective of a shower if you end up drying yourself with the clothes you have just cycled forty-three miles in. Back at the tent the can of veggie potato gratin proves to be excellent and I'm sure it is better for being piping hot rather than tepid thanks to the generosity of the campsite owner.

The thickly padded seats inside the windowed awning of James and Betty's caravan make a very comfy place to get together, especially as the early evening temperature is falling outside. I have a mug of tea in preference to wine; it is my first tea in almost a week and it is an absolute joy, so much so that I empty three mugs over the next couple of hours while the four of us sit together and chat about families back in England and our previous travels. We had a lovely time making each other's acquaintance and exchanging news and stories.

Back in the tent my notes are written up and I record that today's efforts have taken me forty-three miles further into France. My total is now two hundred, which feels very satisfying to a novice. I am chuffed, to say the least. My journal is put away at nine because it is too dark to write more. Sleep arrives soon after.

# Day 7 – Thursday 22nd April

## Departments of Oise and Aisne:

## From Carlepont to Ciry-Salsogne

Another dry day greets me as I climb out of the tent. I'll take it while it comes but surely this weather cannot last. A rainless week in April, how fortunate is that?

My last task before leaving Araucarias campsite is to fill my water bottles, which, unlike yesterday, are not frozen solid. As I am filling the bottles from an outdoor tap near the site entrance a man comes up to me and hands me a packet of *Lieken Urkorn Feines Vollkorn*. The packet name is undecipherable but I recognise the contents as the nut brown and very dense bread that is so popular in Germany. The absence of a shared language prevents us from having a conversation but I try my best to convey my appreciation to him. Whilst standing with the man I can't help but think to myself: *What does this kind stranger think about me to have gifted me some food? Do I look malnourished? Does he think I am homeless? Or do I look like a fugitive on the run?* These thoughts are quickly expunged as I use virtually all of the German words I know to thank him, wish him a good day and shake his hand. The label on the bread states (in English, thankfully) that there are 1,950 calories in every six slices, which sounds just the job, so, a few minutes later, with the *Vollkornbrot* stashed safely in a pannier bag I climb over the crossbar and glide through the open gates of the campsite with a smile on my face.

As I leave Les Araucarias behind me, I reflect that in this one small campsite I have encountered only four people – the owner, James and Betty, and the German man. The owner gave me fuel, the couple gave me hospitality, and the German gave me food. None of these people know me from Adam, I have met none of them before, and our paths will never pass again. What an uplifting example of human kindness. It's not such a bad old world, is it, not when you think about it.

Wednesday has started with a nip in the air. Low clouds in every direction look a touch threatening although to be fair, there are no signs that it has rained overnight. Looking up, I think it is probably touch and go if it will stay dry today. The road from Carlepont to Vic-sur-Aisne climbs steadily for the first mile crossing open farmland as it does so. I find it extremely satisfying that once I am in the lowest gear I can manage the long hill out of Carlepont without once getting off the bike, although to give you an idea of the full picture I should say that the effort of pedalling to the top gets my heart and lungs going ten to the dozen. That said, only a week ago there is no doubt I would have had no option but to push the bike up the hill. Workouts, callisthenics, training regimes, call them what you will, they are all topics I know nothing of. I don't go to the gym, I never have, it's not my sort of thing – at least I don't think it is – so I marvel at how my body is adapting to the demands now being made of it after only six days of on-the-job training.

The low summit rewards me with the beautiful sight of a level road cutting its way between arable fields into the far distance. Can there be a more pleasing sight for a man on a heavily laden bike? Infrequent traffic and an easy-to-cycle road encourage me to step up the pace. Unfortunately my hopes of being able to crack on a bit and put the miles behind me on this next stretch are tempered because here on the exposed open road I no longer benefit from the shelter of the hill, and a strong crosswind forces gear changes on the bike and a great deal more effort from me. The sensation takes me back to day one on the Tarka Trail when I had my first taste of pedalling into a headwind as I cycled up the estuary towards Barnstaple.

After several miles of cycling with the wind against me, the open road descends into a sheltered valley and follows the River Aisne a short distance to the small town of Vic-sur-Aisne, where I pause in the large cobbled square to look at the map and admire the Donjon de Vic-sur-Aisne. The stone medieval *donjon* is made up of three towers; each tower is four storeys high and topped with a pointed conical roof. Viewed from above the towers must form a triangular shape but from here at ground level my view of this trio reminds me of the mighty Saturn Five rocket with its massive tube-shaped main body and cylindrical fuel boosters attached to each side. As a clue to the *donjon's* more sinister history I notice that windows are only built into the upper three floors, and I'm guessing this was done to prevent escapes from the ground floor.

The area surrounding the Aisne valley, including the historical cities of Soissons and Compiegne, is a part of northeastern France that our family have visited several times over the years. In the summer of 2000 three generations of our extended family came here for a holiday. It was great fun being together and happy memories from that visit prompt me to stop at the entrance to Berny Riviere campsite. I take a photograph for old time's sake as it was here that we all stayed for a week in a couple of static caravans.

Half a mile on and a familiar stone building in the hamlet of Berny-Rivière comes into view: *'Chez Michelin'* is still a place of fond memories for our family, although it is now years since we last visited. This morning *'Monsieur le Patron'* is outside his café as I slowly cycle by. I smile to myself and wonder if they still serve the delicious and outrageously alcoholic rum baba that we still talk about whenever past holidays become the topic of conversation. On our last visit ten of us had a meal in *Chez Michelin*. After a delicious main course myself and several others were unable to resist a rum baba; it was so good we had a second and I can recommend them highly. But a word of warning: if you're ever in the area and find yourself tempted with a brace of these wonderful desserts, make sure you have someone else to drive you back to the campsite. *Monsieur le Patron* has just gone back inside his quaint pub-cum-restaurant-cum-shop and stopping for a coffee, just for old time's sake crosses my mind, but pedalling into the sidewind has robbed me of time so it is with some regret that I feel I should put temptation aside and press on.

An hour and a half later the warm sun and a conveniently placed bench set back from the road under some trees prompt me to stop for an early lunch in the hamlet of Osly-Courtil. Sitting on the bench, my view is of two long rows of flowering cherry trees, one on either side of the street. The trees are in full bloom, making the village centre extremely picturesque. Fallen deep pink petals cover the road and verges, in fact there are petals as far as I can see and not just a scattering, in places the petals are piled half an inch deep. A sharp breeze encourages even more to cascade down whilst I am enjoying my lunch – it's a magical sight.

'*Vollkornbrot*' is an intensely dark, nutty brown bread that is absolutely crammed with seeds. It is dense in texture and very heavy as bread goes, and it has a pleasant earthy flavour that makes for a chewy and tasty lunch. Using the village bench as my kitchen worktop I lather the bread with tinned mackerel in tomato sauce. A generous wedge of smoky French cheese complements it very well although I don't have any wine with me, which is very remiss, but even without wine, my tasty lunch puts a spring into my pedalling that keeps me going all the way from Osly-Courtil to the city of Soissons.

It is mid-afternoon now and even though I have enjoyed near continual sunshine since lunchtime I feel surprisingly cold after cycling into a wind that has been steadfastly against me for much of the afternoon. The wind convinces me that I have turned the pedals quite enough for one day so I take the opportunity to finish earlier than planned at Ciry-Salsogne, a small village a few miles east of the city of Soissons in the direction of Reims. The geographical position of Ciry-Salsogne makes it a well-placed springboard for my start tomorrow morning. By setting off from here the heavy commuting traffic in the city of Soissons will be behind me so I won't have to start the day jostling for space on busy city roads. Ciry-Salsogne is also where I take my leave of the east-to-west axis of the Aisne valley and head off south towards the River Marne. The latitude here is forty-nine degrees, which puts me level with the northern suburbs of Paris, or put another way about a quarter of the way from the English Channel to the Mediterranean.

When drawing up my plans for the trip I decided against factoring in specific 'non-cycle' days, although assuming that my estimates for my total Channel-Mediterranean distance, and my mileage-per-day calculations are correct, I should have two spare days I can use as the fancy takes me. This built-in flexibility allows me a bit of wriggle room to deal with unforeseen circumstances should any arise; a complicated mechanic problem perhaps, a bout of very bad weather or illness, or any injuries to more than my pride should I take a tumble along the way. Today seems to be a good candidate for an early finish for no other reason than I feel like one. Stopping mid-afternoon does nibble into my notional spare day 'allowance' but only by a couple of hours. I can't make a habit of stopping early as the terrain will be more challenging further south and I may well need time in the bag to compensate for the slower progress the larger hills south of Burgundy will demand from me.

I am the sole inhabitant of Ciry-Salsogne campsite, in fact there is no sign of anyone here barring the lady in the rather basic shed-type reception to whom I have just paid eight euros. Surely this must raise the question of how a place such as this covers wages, never mind the other running costs. Camping is allowed anywhere on a very large and roughly square field, which has hedging on two sides with dense woodland beyond. A pretty lake forms much of the southern edge of the site. There are no defined pitches as such so I am spoilt for choice as to where to put the tent. A few unoccupied caravans are positioned near the lake; some are covered with tarpaulins for over-wintering, others have the paraphernalia of last summer left outside: tables, barbeques and the like. Most of the caravans have that weathered and somewhat forgotten appearance that comes with not having had visitors over the winter. It is from near one of these forlorn-looking caravans that I borrow a white plastic chair, which I find upended and resting against some hedging.

After a day of my own company, it is very pleasant to enjoy the presence of other people during the evenings; it is one of the experiences I look forward to whenever I arrive at a new campsite.

Unfortunately this will not be possible at Ciry-Salsogne as the campsite is totally deserted and a bit out of the way, so I set about making my evening a pleasant if solitary experience.

I pitch the tent in the furthest corner of the campsite and well away from the road. Here my little home can sit on a raised grassy platform ten feet from the edge of the lake with an unrestricted view over the water. In front of me the rim of the lake is edged with reed and clumps of bullrushes. To my left eight white-barked trees overhang the water in a short row; aspen or birch, I think, but I'm not sure. The lakeside is surrounded by attractive bushes that sparkle as the light breeze flutters their iridescent lime-green leaves. The late afternoon sun is catching the movement of the foliage and creating a beautiful kaleidoscopic effect. There is nothing particular that I have to do this afternoon so I spend the time enjoying the tranquil view over the lake from the comfort of the borrowed plastic chair. A pair of moorhens swim side by side a few yards from me. The sun feels warm, and hints of spring are all around me, who could ask for more?

Great crested grebes live here, resplendent with their smart neck ruffs and spiky head plumage. Further into the lake they dive repeatedly for food, each time re-emerging many yards from where they submerged. The hidden presence of frogs and toads is given away by their raucous croaking but unfortunately, they are too well hidden for me to see. Watching this display of nature for the rest of the afternoon with my feet up would suit me very nicely but I have remembered that there are clothes to be washed and it would be foolish not to take advantage of the sun to dry them, especially as the white-barked trees provide such convenient posts for my impromptu washing line.

Thirty-one miles since breakfast makes today one of the shortest days for a while. It may be a modest distance that I have covered, but today marks the end of my first week as a would-be cycle-tourist and to be honest it feels to me like I have ticked off a bit of a milestone. A – week ago I was very much the novice cycle-tourer and just seven days later I have pedalled getting on for two hundred and fifty miles, which is the same as cycling from London to Amsterdam. It has been camping every night and self-sufficiency all the way; my plan seems to be working out. How very fortunate to have enjoyed a full week without rain. Admittedly some of the days have been cooler than expected and a couple of overnight frosts have been far harsher than I bargained for, but now I have the experience of those nights under my belt I feel confident that my tent and sleeping bag, indeed all of my equipment, is up to the job. Thinking back, even when my water bottles froze solid on the coldest of nights the temperature was just about manageable, although if I'm honest it would concern me quite a bit if I thought such temperatures were coming my way again.

Rain is sure to arrive sooner or later and when it does, I don't expect my Gore-Tex jacket to let me down as it has proved itself impermeable during torrential downpours on the uplands of Dartmoor. The weak link in my equipment, if indeed there is one, is my tent. Will it withstand heavy rain? Could its thin fabric resist strong winds if it were tested? My little shelter has not yet endured heavy rain or stormy winds so it will very be interesting to see how it copes. Ever the big spender, I bought my tent, brand new I should point out, on eBay for just twenty-nine pounds and ninety-five pence – bargain! I know at that price that I'm pushing my luck a bit but what is the worst that can happen? Oh yes, the tent can be blown to tatters and leak like a sieve!

# Week Two

*Day 8 – Friday 23rd April*

*Departments of Aisne and Seine-et-Marne: From Ciry-Salsogne to la ville-sans-nom!*

It is only ten minutes after eight and I'm ready to load up the two-wheeler and set off. What is going on? Only an hour ago I unzipped the tent and gazed out at a beautiful clear blue sky; not only that but when I opened up the tent porch the arms of the sun reached in through the open door and gave me a warm hug. I doubt there is a better way to start any day.

    I have to say that I slept pretty well even though I was woken up several times during the night because the nocturnal wildlife that calls this place home was less than considerate. Owls hooted throughout the hours of darkness and at about five o'clock an angry snarl sliced the night air just as dawn crept over the land. When I first heard the sound in the half-light of the tent, I was quite alarmed, but after a few rather disturbing minutes the snarl moderated to a series of grunts and snorts, which sounded altogether less threatening. Before falling back to sleep I was undecided whether the sound was just a hedgehog rummaging outside the tent, or a larger animal, further away, a wild boar perhaps. I know boars are widespread in some parts of France so why not here?

Hungry or amorous hedgehogs, wild boar, or some other creature. I shall never know, unfortunately.

Not only has this morning started warm but there is no dew and I know after recent mornings that this is a real bonus; my pleasure on realising that I don't have to pack up a soaking wet tent is quite disproportionate. Little things matter a great deal when you are camping, I am learning. The absence of dew puts me on the cusp of being cock-a-hoop, which some will doubtless consider a rather tragic overreaction, others may think I need to get a life, but let me tell you that in my new world as a would-be cycle-traveller a dry tent when you get up is mighty significant and a thing of wonder. No grass is stuck to the groundsheet, no cold water runs down the fabric walls, I don't have to clean wet mud off the tent pegs, and the whole process of packing my accommodation away for the day's journey is so much better. In fact the process of decamping is easier all round and far quicker. Not only that but later this afternoon, when I set up the tent again, I will not get wet and I will not be covered with bits of mud and grass clippings. Joy of joys, or am I sounding like a bit of a wimp?

Three texts to my Nokia 3310 before I set off provide an additional lift for the day ahead: the family are all well, they wish me good luck, and they tell me that the weather is set fair across central France. The text is reassuring on all fronts and provides a very welcome reconnection with home.

Today begins with the measured euphoria brought about by being ready to set off in unusually good time, but the opportunity is scuppered because the lake has mesmerised me and I have been glued to 'my' plastic chair for some time. Twenty minutes ago, I saw what I believe to be a coypu swimming lazily across the lake twenty-five yards in front of me and I have been transfixed ever since. The creature swam for ten to twelve feet before gracefully diving under the surface in what was an unexpected and magical start to my day. About fifteen years ago the family and I had our first sighting of a coypu (*ragondin* to the locals) in the Vendée area of western France. At the time the main impression the animal made on me was that it was very much bigger than I expected and had disproportionately large and very orange teeth. The creature I have just seen seemed smaller than the Vendée animal but far too large to be an otter so I cannot think of anything else it could be. Hoping for a return of the coypu (which I know sounds like a low-budget film) I sit on the chair watching a pair of grebes. A couple of coots arrive a little later resplendent with their distinctive white forehead and red eyes; they continually '*tut-tut-tut*' to each other as they swim side by side along the edge of the reed bed. Close to where they are swimming an untidy nest has been built into the reeds just a few inches clear of the water and I can see that at least one of the six eggs it contains is broken. Unfortunately the nest has received no attention that I have seen. Abandoned, it appears, with all six eggs lost.

It would be very pleasant indeed just to sit here all day overlooking my private nature reserve, but the need to make some kind of a start to the day is becoming pressing, so the plastic chair is taken back to its caravan and I conduct a few rudimentary checks on the bike. The tyre pressures feel fine, the forks are lifted so I can spin the front wheel just to confirm that the brake blocks aren't rubbing against the rim. As everything seems to be in good order mechanically it's time for me to attach the panniers and fasten the bungee cords to the remainder of the load to make sure it stays in place. It is time to depart Ciry-Salsogne campsite, which for all its lack of human contact I have grown rather fond of. A manageable thirty-one-mile trip lies ahead, and as far as I know there is just one summit that exceeds a thousand feet. Such a hill would have alarmed me a week ago but no more because even if I am reduced to a bit of huffing and puffing, I am confident that I will be able to take it in my stride.

I wheel out of Ciry-Salsogne campsite just after nine o'clock. In the village I cycle past a group of young mothers chatting together. I guess they have just said *au revoir* to their children at the village primary school. One lady sees me and calls, '*Bon courage!*' loudly in my direction, causing other mums to look around and join in the chorus. I am surprised by this seemingly well-practised chant until I learn later that *'bon courage'* is a long-established call of encouragement in France for someone undertaking an arduous task or a test. The literal translation is quite simply *'good luck'* although in the context of what I was doing it means something along the lines of: *'keep going, you CAN do it.'*

At this stage I am blissfully unaware of the large hill hidden from view by a bend in the road ahead; the incline doesn't feature on the map in front of me. A hill is one thing but hiding a hill from a man on a bike is simply not playing cricket. *Bon courage* is indeed required as I end up pushing the bike for the next two miles. Pushing is harder on the legs than pedalling, and slower too, and this particular hill robs me of a full hour until it is kind enough to flatten out and allow me to get back on the bike so I can get back to the job in hand.

The D6 country road meanders beside fields of vivid yellow mustard, which, added to the parasol of deep blue sky above makes the few miles to the town of Fère-en-Tardenois particularly picturesque. In the town I pause for a drink under the shade of the ancient covered market. The building is open on all sides and has a particularly grand vaulted-timber roof. Its huge, ancient roof trusses are supported by a central row of sturdy wooden columns, clearly many centuries old. It is a beautiful old building and one that would have fascinated Nicolaus Pevsner, the great British-German architectural historian who wrote the mammoth and highly acclaimed forty-six volumes of *The Buildings of England*.

Between Fère-en-Tardenois and my intended destination at the town of Trelou I come across the antithesis of the National Front sign I passed earlier in the week in Picardy. Here a single sentence is scrawled in bold black paint on an otherwise clean concrete wall; the harsh block letters read *'Le Fuck Le Pen'*, a reference no doubt to Marine Le Pen or her father, Jean-Marie Le Pen, both leaders of the French National Front party. Whatever your politics you have to agree the point is deftly made in just four words.

Leaving the graffiti behind to make its impression on others no doubt, I continue along the narrow rural road as it twists and turns through a pleasant landscape that is textured with clumps of trees, old hedging, and a patchwork of small fields. A few miles short of Trelou I come across a red granite plinth that has been erected at a fork in the road; the polished stone forms the centrepiece of the small and well-tended garden that is the poignant memorial to Lieutenant Henri Despots, Sergent-Chef Rene Assailly, and Sapeur Michel Julien, all three local firemen who lost their lives here in June 1977 when their fire engine crashed as they were responding to an emergency. It is a sobering and sad sight but I am pleased to observe that although over thirty years have passed since the tragedy occurred the little memorial garden is still highly valued and so well cared for.

The views are dramatic from my elevated position on the bike and the plateau in front of me offers far-reaching views of the picturesque road ahead as it passes through a contoured landscape made up of shadowy valleys, small hills, and a patchwork of bright flower-filled fields. It is an enticing view, but what draws the eye more than all else is the bright blue sky streaked with cirrus clouds high in the atmosphere. The Latin word *'cirrus'* means wisp of hair, which is a very apt description of the clouds above me. Rounding a bend, I come to the unexpected and rather strange sight of a building with a massive wine bottle emerging from the middle of its flat roof. The bottle is at least twenty feet high. A vineyard! Glancing down at the cyclometer I realise with some astonishment that it has taken me a full week and two hundred and fifty-four miles to come across my first vineyard. How is this even possible in France? A quick look at my map confirms that I am now cycling between the Rivers Aisne and Marne and heading directly south towards the departments of Ile-de-France and Champagne. I really am about to enter the land of the noble plant, it seems.

I arrive at the town of Trelou-sur-Marne in the Hauts-de-France region with exactly thirty miles under my belt. It has been an enjoyable day, although the hills have been quite taxing at times. As I enter Trelou-sur-Marne I strike up conversation with two passers-by who tell me the local campsite is closed until after Easter but there is an alternative site at Dormans, which is a small town a couple of miles from here, albeit in the wrong direction. They then explain directions to another campsite at Chateau-Thierry; this second site is ten miles further on but much more in the general direction that I need to travel in, so after weighing up both options I am persuaded that as ten miles more today is ten miles less tomorrow, Chateau-Thierry is the way to go.

The road from Trelou to Chateau-Thierry follows the *Route Touristique-du-Champagne*. I make good speed for just over an hour when I come upon a small but well-stocked cycle shop on the outskirts of Chateau-Thierry. I pop into the shop for interest more than anything else and end up buying an absolutely minute bottle of cycle oil; by minute I mean not much bigger than the size of a pen top. My front wheel has been squeaking for the last couple of days, so hopefully I now have the cure in my pocket.

The campsite at Chateau-Thierry, like the one at Trelou, is also closed; this is unwelcome news, of course, but what can I do? Nothing but refrain from salty language, exert pressure on the pedals, adopt the chin-up attitude, and crack on. Charly-sur-Marne, here I come. But here's the thing, I am no longer flagging, my second wind has come from somewhere and I am bolstered by glorious weather and a splendid route. And what is this I see ahead of me if it is not a McDonald's restaurant at the roundabout? I may not be their greatest fan but there is a time and place for everything and this is exactly the time and precisely the place for me to buy a double cheeseburger, frites, and a large Coke (milkshake is never available from French McDonald's, I am aghast to learn). Outdoor seating allows me to bask in the sun and enjoy a massively calorific boost. I take half an hour to refuel, ponder over my map, and enjoy being amid the bustle of people: this is all very pleasant indeed and makes a most welcome break.

More than two hundred and fifty miles have passed since I left England and I have just realised that there are no photographs of me on the journey, not one. Some empirical evidence will be needed when I return home just to prove that I haven't cheated. Let's be honest, I could have stayed in Dover for a month, or pedalled into Belgium where the land is billiard-table flat and wandered between pubs in a country renowned for the variety and quality of its craft beers. True to my word, I am indeed in France, and heading for the Mediterranean as planned, so to prove the point I ask a lady at the outdoor table next to me if she would oblige. Photograph duly taken and my refuelling complete, I continue into the city of Chateau-Thierry.

Having crossed a road bridge that spans the River Marne in the middle of the city, I come to a major intersection where all roads and footpaths are subject to extensive alteration. As part of the work every road sign has been removed, and all lane markings have been stripped away along with the tarmac. Excavation is widespread. An alternative road layout, clearly and repeatedly signed *'Deviation'* has been constructed using hundreds, and I mean hundreds, of enormous red and white plastic blocks placed in long rows to separate the various lanes of traffic. Each of these rectangular blocks is like super-Lego in design with each interlocking piece being a good two feet square and four feet long. The whole area covers several hundred yards and in all truth resembles a very large go-kart track. The situation is creating near-terminal confusion for all drivers and if the entertainment value of the scene could be measured by the number of onlookers then Chateau-Thierry has created a very successful pop-up visitor attraction right here in the middle of the city. As exciting entertainment goes this is absolutely top drawer, full of visual thrills and regular near misses and I really cannot recommend it highly enough. As for me? Well, I opt for the only sensible option and push my bike until I am well clear of the spectacle.

All signage has been uprooted along with the road surface and of course I need to find my way out of the city. Fortunately for me the flow of the river matches my intended direction of travel so by keeping La Marne to my left I have a navigational aid *par excellence* until I am clear of the entertaining chaos and once again happily cycling between the rows of vines that grow on both sides of the river.

Vines, thousands of acres of them I would say, stretch as far as the eye can see in every direction. This early in the season the plants have yet to develop so all that is visible are leafless stems, lots of buds, and some initial shoots. The lines of plants are supported by thousands and thousands of stakes, evenly placed and five feet high. The stakes are positioned in long rows eight to ten feet apart for maximum crop yield; after encouraging the vines to climb and ultimately to fruit, the stakes support the weight of the bunches of grapes until the harvest begins in mid-September. The lines of stakes are linked horizontally by four thick wires stacked one above the other in the form of a fence. Scores of identical fields stretch far into the distance where they blur into a single mass as the sun glints off tens of thousands of yards of metal wire. The whole scene looks like a massive gossamer-threaded spider's web; it is quite surreal to see and actually rather beautiful in an odd sort of way.

Colourful and often artistic signs advertising the individual Champagne houses are dotted along the roadside as I cycle along. Most of these enterprises look to be small concerns, family businesses making use of a small parcel of land, which in some cases totals just a few acres. The global prestige of Champagne conjures up thoughts of considerable wealth, but I see no outward signs of a moneyed population living in these wine-dependant hamlets, for the most part the vineyards are small and the houses look modest. A few miles on and an Aston Martin glides past me, but barring this single exception there is nothing visible to distinguish the earnings per capita of the vintners in this part of Champagne from those of the farmers growing mustard further north. After a long but very pleasurable afternoon of cycling through wine country I arrive at my overnight campsite dead on six-thirty.

The location of today's campsite must remain under wraps. Let me explain: I arrive at an anonymous and well-maintained campsite and after a pleasant exchange of greetings Madame at reception starts booking me in. This involves the now familiar process of examining my passport and recording my details in a ledger. At first Madame seems agitated, vexed even; I assume it is because I have turned up rather late, perhaps I have unwittingly delayed the end of her working day, but not so, thankfully. Apparently, the minimum overnight campsite charge is eight euros and twenty cents. Madame looks deep in thought for a moment before decreeing that for a 'true' traveller such as myself the amount is both excessive and unreasonable, so with an elegant yet decisive flourish of her pen over the records book she announces that I should pay just three euros and twenty cents. At this point she leans slowly forward over the counter towards me to reinforce her insistence that this one-off act of kindness is granted on the explicit condition that the location of her rebellious act of generosity must remain a secret. Naturally I take this to mean *in perpetuum* in its full legal sense.

As if to underline the potential gravity to her, and perhaps to me for all I know, should this clandestine act of generosity ever become known, several gallic hand gestures are accompanied by a flurry of words that are spoken far too rapidly for me to comprehend. Nevertheless, it is crystal clear that Madame considers the issuing of a receipt in such unique circumstances an unnecessary risk somewhat akin to leaving a trail of evidence that would reveal her *modus operandi*. It is a most unusual encounter but Madame has been very thoughtful and I am most grateful for her kindness.

It is a good two to three hours later than usual by the time I start sorting out my camping arrangements for the night, so the tent is pitched at speed and its interior organised in quick order. This flurry of effort allows me to shower and eat by eight, which is as good a time as any to cycle into the town that must remain secret and find a suitable venue to write up my journal, over a beer or perhaps two, naturally.

In *'la ville sans nom'* (the town with no name) I find a pub that would be called a sports bar in England, although the only connection with sport seems to be a large wall-mounted television showing horse and trap racing. The event in question looks rather like modern-day chariot racing without quite so much violence, a French passion I assume as I have never seen it anywhere else. A cheerful bunch of around twelve men are glued to the screen; they are all jolly and highly animated and give the pub a very lively atmosphere. I carry my beer and valuables bag to a large corner table where I lay my map out next to my notebook and beer and set about writing my recollections of the last twenty-four hours.

Fifty-one miles of pedalling since breakfast is by a fraction my furthest daily mileage to date. Today's journey has seen me track a wide arc in order to bypass the northern suburbs of Paris before arriving here, which I feel I can safely reveal without compromising Madame's anonymity, is one of the dozens of satellite communities that lie just south of the capital. Today's extra mileage will put me in good stead for the journey ahead especially if my progress is hampered by unforeseen rain or winds, both of which are overdue.

Ninety minutes and three pages of writing later the chariot racing ends and the attention of a dozen happy and, by the look of it, 'well-oiled' Frenchmen turn towards me. They look my way, talk amongst themselves, then turn back to look at me again. I am quite obviously the sole topic of discussion; their interest in what I am doing is being expressed in a rather excited but clearly good-humoured fashion. For me, the feeling is rather like sitting in the front row at a pantomime and being slightly apprehensive that I am about to receive the uninvited but well-meaning attentions of the star act. I cannot hide amongst the audience here so I smile and raise my glass to acknowledge them.

Raising your glass must be a secret sign in the-town-with-no-name because the men suddenly bound over *en masse*, huddle round my table and home in first on my map and then my notebook. These two possessions seem to have increased their curiosity, which quickly develops into a light-hearted and enthusiastic interrogation. A crescendo is reached when two of the men take my map, one at each end, and unroll the whole thing: eleven feet long, remember. *'Zut Alors! Mon Dieu!'* and all that. A flurry of questions follows: Where are you from? Where were you last night? Are you staying in hotels? Where are you going next? Where will you go after Montpellier? Each question is answered and understood as best as we all can using my limited vocabulary and their smattering of English. Still, questions come my way: Are you really alone? What do you do for food? What work do you do? Does your wife not mind? Each of my answers is excitedly discussed amongst the men and then conveyed at some volume to all of other customers and staff in the pub. The whole bar then erupts in what I can only describe as a crescendo of alcohol-fuelled gallic encouragement. Naturally enough this includes many, many, shouts of, *'Bon courage!'* This peaks at a chant that continues for several over-enthusiastic minutes.

The peak of this excitement occurs when, quite unexpectedly, a man runs over from the bar towards where I am sitting. He joins the group of men leaning over my table and shakes my hand vigorously, then in an unanticipated and sudden action (which I have to say, surprises me more than you will ever imagine) Jean-Marcelle, or whatever he is called, bends down and squeezes my calf muscles before announcing his approval with considerable gusto! It appears that I have just passed his impromptu cycling credibility test as he immediately offers to buy me a beer. The muscle-testing Frenchman then declares that I should aim for Montpellier by the end of tomorrow and not in three weeks' time as planned. I have to decline his kind offer of beer as two have already been plonked on my table by the other men. After three hours in the sports bar I depart to a flurry of back slapping and a shouted chorus of, *'Bon courage!'* I am greatly buoyed by the confidence and good cheer these strangers have expressed in me.

Pushing the bike back to the tent, albeit slightly unsteady on my feet, I cannot help but smile broadly at the reception I received in the pub. Once back at the campsite I am unable to find my torch so I cannot see what is making the inside of my canvas home go round and round. *Bon courage*, time for sleep.

*Day 9 – Saturday 24th April*

*Department of Seine-et-Marne:*

*From La-Ville-Sans-Nom to Bray-sur-Seine*

The start of the weekend greets me with glorious weather and a surprisingly clear head so I decamp in an uncharacteristically snappy fashion and set off from the town-with-no-name to continue my travels into the exquisite Marne valley.

This part of France owes its appearance almost entirely to the hand of man. Here the landscape has been sculpted over many centuries for wine production and little else. Most local wine is made from the Pinot Meunier grape variety. The River Marne was developing as a major trading route by the 1830s when access to markets further afield allowed the vintners to expand their businesses rapidly. Consequently the number of acres devoted to cultivating grapes in the valley expanded considerably about this time. The visual result is laid out before me as a continuous tapestry of rolling vineyards. What a place this sunlit valley is to pedal through on a morning such as this.

It has become something of a daily habit for me to scrutinise the map just before setting off each morning. This is not so much to familiarise myself with the places I will pass through, as that is clearly visible to me as a bright line drawn across the map as I cycle along; checking the map is much more about giving me an idea of the terrain to expect for the day ahead. It is a few miles into today's journey when I remember I've not yet looked at the route, so I pull over to examine the map and see to my dismay that eight of the next fourteen or so miles are hilly. Within an hour of setting off the sun is beating down and it becomes surprisingly warm for April. I am particularly glad to have my full quota of four litres of water on board, even though at one kilogram per litre the liquid adds four kilos or nearly nine pounds to my already excessively heavy load.

Listening to the faint whisper of the tyres gripping the tarmac and the occasional birdsong I am absorbed in a world of my own thoughts as I potter along the rural lane at eight miles an hour. Surrounding me is a beautiful sunlit landscape that lends itself to allowing the mind to wander, so I wonder what my family are doing at home, then my mind moves on to the days and places ahead, the chances of rain, and the need to restock with food. My thoughts then unexpectedly return to yesterday and it is impossible for me to stifle a smile when I recall the bond of secrecy between myself and the campsite receptionist, and of course how the pub customers asked question after question, tested my legs, bought me beer, and chanted *'bon courage'* – what a unique experience the pub was. It was an evening that I'll remember with great fondness long after the trip ends.

Signs on the verge confirm that I am still following the *'Route Touristique de Champagne'* – it is a very picturesque road that requires little navigation on my part. This leaves me free to consider the two options yesterday's extra distance now offers me: 1) I can make an easy day of it today and stop at my pre-planned destination, but I shall probably be there by lunchtime, or 2) I can steal a march and make good use of yesterday's additional twenty miles by pressing on further south. In all truth I am reluctant to cast aside the hard-won benefits now that I have them in the bag, and as I cycle along, I warm to the idea of pressing on to the ancient city of Provins, which will be within reach at the end of the afternoon with a bit of extra effort.

Our family stayed at Provins about fifteen years ago so I know that the town is a pleasing and historic place and the campsite is full of useful facilities such as washing machines and hot showers. It also sports its own restaurant. So, having convinced myself that a night at

Provins is a worthy goal I step up the pace a little and daydream the morning away by pedalling on autopilot with the warm sun on my face.

I may not have brilliant ideas too often but although I say so myself, one comes to me as I am pedalling along: After just over a week of cycle touring it is glaringly obvious to me that I have overpacked the bike with many items I simply don't need. For example, I am carrying duplicate items of clothing, which I now realise are completely unnecessary, I am carrying books I have yet to open and probably never will, and I have considerable duplication of maps. As a case in point I am carrying sixteen maps of the *Local France* series by Michelin. It seemed a good idea at the time to bring these larger-scale maps but they haven't been looked at once, so why do I need to haul their weight for the rest of the trip when my roll-out map is proving to be perfectly adequate? Taken together, these bits and pieces add very considerably to the weight I have to transport every mile. Extra weight means more effort on my behalf, to say nothing of the additional strain it must be putting on the bike components.

My brilliant idea relies on the fact that twelve days after I return home to Devon, my wife and I are driving *Piers* (our open-top Morgan sports car) from Devon to Alsace. We have pre-booked a couple of nights at a hotel in the city of Troyes, which is less than an hour's drive from Provins. My idea is to appeal to the benevolent nature of the campsite staff in the hope that they will agree to store my excess belongings on the understanding that I will collect them when I pass this way again in early June. Assuming this would be acceptable to them the only flaw in the idea is the design of *Piers*. Morgan car design is firmly rooted in the 1930s; each car is hand-made with a metal body supported on a wooden chassis made of ash. Morgans have no boot of any kind so all luggage must be carried on a small rack on the back of the car or wedged in the even smaller space behind the two seats. I should be able to find room for my extra cycling bits. Where there's a will and all that!

My rate of pedalling increases exponentially due to a burst of optimism created by the prospect of enjoying the rest of my little adventure on a semi-lightweight bike. I whizz along the flat road ahead in a state of mild euphoria as I run through a mental checklist of exactly what I can offload: a pair of trousers, one spare jumper at least, a pair of shorts, maybe two inner tubes (after all, I am carrying three with me), surely my Nikon D90 camera handbook is ridiculous cargo if not quite as ridiculous as *One Thousand Helpful Cycling Tips*, a book I bought on eBay just before leaving. What was I thinking of?

I am not a cyclist and I need all the help I can get – that's what I was thinking.

Anyway, now that I have a few hundred miles and nine days of cycling behind me my confidence has grown. I don't need the helpful cycling tips book or its weight!

The region of *Île-de-France* is centred around Paris and is made up of several departments. Not surprisingly it is the most highly populated of the eighteen French regions; not only that, it generates roughly a fifth of the country's total wealth. Ile-de-France is home to a diverse spread of world-class cultural experiences ranging from the Louvre to Disneyland, from Montmartre to the Rive Gauche, and from Chantilly to the Palace of Versailles. In the great scheme of all things French, this region is unquestionably very grand and important, but for a bloke on a bike there is no tangible difference now that I am in Ile-de-France, I am still cycling through the splendour of rural France and overnighting in little villages along the way. This is a cultural highlight in its own way.

Once clear of the market town of La Ferte Gaucher the landscape becomes somewhat featureless. Large open fields stripped clear of hedges lie to both sides of the road; there are few trees here and not a building in sight. As I look ahead the road trudges its way over the vast expanse of a high-level plain and for mile after mile the road is perfectly straight, so I wonder if it has Roman origins. After an hour or so the road starts to develop a gentle roll. A series of false horizons meet me as I 'summit' each shallow hill; a small hill replaces another small hill like waves arriving on a beach. The undulations are nowhere near steep enough to require me to push the bike but after a while their unforgiving repetition becomes energy sapping.

Exactly twenty miles after leaving Le Ferte Gaucher I arrive in Provins. My breathing is deep now and to be honest I am starting to flag a bit. The heat of today has made cycling strenuous and it comes as a considerable relief that the town's campsite will signal journey's end. As a benchmark of today's effort, I have drained three water bottles in the last two hours and my supply is now at zero for the first time since leaving Devon.

I arrive at the city of Provins from the north by cycling down a road that drops a couple of hundred feet from the plateau down a series of steep bends. There are no complaints from me as this is the largest hill of the day by a healthy margin and I'm going down it. After a few minutes of blissful freewheeling, I emerge invigorated into the busy town centre where the sun reflects brightly off the pale stone buildings. The city feels airless and notably hotter than it did on the plateau above.

I pedal around the main streets in the middle of town until I come upon a tourist information board with a map. The location of the campsite is marked, which is good news until I notice exactly where the site is. Disheartened? I should say so. No, let's be honest, I am crestfallen when I realise that the site is at the top of the big hill I've just freewheeled down. The location puzzles me because the plateau above Provins is completely flat, and yet I recognised absolutely nothing from my visit here some years ago. Certainly I saw no campsite. At the edge of the plateau, on top of the hill, there is a roundabout where four roads converge; it makes sense that this is where the campsite sign would be so I must simply have missed it.

The oppressive afternoon heat makes me reluctant to tackle the hill without being sure that the campsite is indeed on the plateau so I ask two different people, both of whom confirm its location and give me roughly the same directions. Unfortunately neither of their directions is particularly clear, although to be fair that's down to my limited French more than anything.

I retrace my route from the centre of town to the bottom of the zigzag hill. Before starting the climb I notice a pedestrian, who I assume to be a local, on the footpath walking away from me up the hill. The slim lady is wearing a pale blue skirt with matching handbag and a white blouse, she has fair hair in an immaculate bob style, how very French she looks. '*Excuse moi, madame,*' I say, gliding to a halt next to her. '*Je voudrais directions pour le camping, s'il vous plaît?*'

Madame turns towards me and directs me up the hill. '*Après la première gauche.*' I can't help but notice she has a great deal of make-up on and large hands. I thank her for her helpful assistance and bid her good day. She calls out, '*Bon courage!*' in a rather deep voice as I pedal away and whilst it is she who has wished me courage, it strikes me that it is Madame who is taking the brave step.

One bend further on I have no option but to get off the bike and push it, panniers and all, up the steepest section of road. Once back on the plateau I pause, steady myself on the handlebars, and wheeze for a bit. My hope is that some stability will return to my respiratory system and my face, which must have changed in colour to heart-attack red, will return to its usual shade. Next, I circumnavigate the roundabout paying particular attention to each sign as I do so. The four roads that meet at the roundabout lead to Paris, Nogent-sur-Seine, Sens, and Montereau, but there is absolutely no road sign pointing to the elusive campsite. As you can imagine I am annoyed and deflated in equal measure by now, but I am also stubbornly determined not to be outwitted by any gallic sloppiness in the provision of road signs.

I counter this apparent incompetence by the French highways department by cycling a mile along each of the four roads, which converge 'spoke like' on the roundabout. Sixty minutes and eight miles later I am back at the roundabout and I am hot and I am irritated, in fact I was hot and irritated an hour ago, but I am even more so now as all roads have been checked with absolutely no evidence of any campsite. It is now late afternoon and my options are running out at about the same speed as my patience. I reckon I have three hours of daylight left to find a campsite, which if I'm honest and think with my sensible head on should be plenty of time.

The next tactic in my seemingly endless quest to find a pitch for the night is to position myself where the busiest road joins the roundabout for one last throw of the dice. My logic is that by standing right next to the roundabout I have a captive audience of drivers who are obligated to halt at the junction thereby giving me the perfect chance to attract their attention and ask them for directions. I decide to apply a quasi-scientific approach and select for conversation only those drivers who look up to the job; by the law of averages one of them will surely be familiar with Provins campsite. Over the next ten minutes I ignore a surprising number of cars that pause at the give-way sign next to me as none of the occupants appear to offer much promise. A few more minutes and I am blessed with the arrival of a driver who looks the part, and to prove the efficacy of my process of natural selection (Darwin would have been proud) the driver speaks near-perfect English. The driver is enthusiastically confident that if I cycle back down the hill (yes, that hill again) I will see a small sign part-way down the incline on the left. I thank him and express my appreciation as he drives off towards Sens. My faith in the human race has been restored along with my happy disposition. I take a few photos of the roundabout for future reference, to remind me of the joyless and torrid time I have had here, and as a useful prompt when I write up my journal.

Just before cycling away, I glance over my shoulder to make sure it is safe to set off when I spot a bizarre convoy of cars heading towards the roundabout. The vehicles are barely three or four feet apart and are being driven very, very, slowly. A few sound their horns loudly as they pass me at no more than walking speed. This impromptu horn blasting is clearly contagious as it escalates very quickly until all vehicles are blasting away; it is a deafening cacophony by the time all thirty or forty cars in the convoy join in.

Without warning all cars halt midway around the roundabout. They stop in concert as if ordered to do so by some secret command, so close to each other that every entrance and exit is simultaneously obstructed. Nobody seems even slightly concerned, indeed they clearly think this is great fun. Now that all the cars are stationary some of the occupants clamber out accompanied by much laughter from the other drivers and passengers. Loud and excitable conversation follows coupled with vigorous arm gestures seemingly directed at me. Eventually, I grasp that they have spotted my camera and want me to take photographs of them; naturally, I oblige. Some who are standing next to their vehicles bow in my direction, most others applaud, several sound car horns. I seem to have met with their approval.

Button-hole flowers and smart clothes for all suggests they are driving to or from a wedding. I am unconvinced of their sobriety and it seems to me they are between venues and that alcohol has already played its part, judging by the level of merriment on display. Near the middle of this cavalcade of madness are two cars that attract my attention more than most. The first is one of those very small microcars that only the French and Italians seem to favour. The outside of the little car is festooned with balloons, dozens of them. Someone, and I sincerely hope it was the owner, has 'enhanced' the paintwork of the whole car with enthusiastic and random splodges of fluorescent paint. The interior is crammed with so many people that I am amazed they are not suffocating, perhaps some already have. As if that were not enough a second small car is painted white but has splodges of black in the sort of pattern you would much rather expect to see on a Frisian cow. Anyway this second car is gloriously adorned with an oversized plastic tractor strapped onto its roof. The tractor is accompanied – why wouldn't it be? – by a large, partly inflated killer whale. Finally an over-large 'besom' type broom, which must be a good eight feet long, is strapped to the rear bumper. I suspect this whole cavalcade is the French equivalent of the Young Farmers having a wedding. Photos done, vigorous arm waving exchanged, multiple calls of *'bon courage'* taken care of, and I can get back to the tricky business of locating somewhere to spend tonight, although by now I am convinced the holy grail would be easier to find. Now where is this campsite?

If my last shot doesn't locate Provins campsite, I will have no choice but to press on to the next town or even the one after that, or perhaps I will just have to try my hand at wild camping after all. The most pressing task right now though is to top up my water bottles. To give myself the very best chance of finding the site I decide to stop at every corner on my way down the hill. At the first corner a most helpful elderly lady comes over to me and before I even ask, she explains that the sign no longer exists because the campsite closed two or three years ago. In some ways this is absolutely not what I want to hear but I am very grateful to her for resolving the conundrum once and for all. I resign myself not only to having to find somewhere else to camp tonight, but to hauling all of my luggage to the end of my journey, even the items I hoped to offload to my car a few weeks from now. Anyway, it's only another seven hundred or so miles. *C'est la vie.* You've got to laugh!

First things first – water. The search for Provins campsite has taken me two hours, a wasted two hours at the end of what has turned into a rather long, hot day.

I am probably incapable of cycling another ten, fifteen, or possibly twenty miles unless I get hold of several litres of water. Fortunately I can see that some men renovating a building across the road are mixing concrete, so they must have water. After a brief chat the best part of half a gallon fills my three bottles from their hosepipe. It may or may not be the cleanest water but as one of the builders glugged several mouthfuls before he filled my bottles I'm guessing it will be fine.

Throughout the journey I have done my best to avoid main roads wherever possible. This strategy has been partly for personal safety as cycling near lorries has always struck me as inherently perilous whenever I have seen it, and partly because the *raison d'être* underpinning my trip is that the journey will allow me to experience the very best of rural France, under my own steam, and at a leisurely pace. But sometimes rules have to be broken, and now is just such an occasion if I am to reach Bray-sur-Seine with sufficient daylight to give me a fighting chance of finding somewhere to pitch the tent, campsite or not. Two large water bottles are secured in their cradles and I gulp down the complete contents of the third bottle before refilling it and setting off to cover the fifteen miles to Bray-sur-Seine. It will be a relief to be pedalling with purpose once more after all the time I have lost this afternoon.

Any ideas I may have about leaving Provins are thwarted before they even start when I glance down and see a completely flat front tyre. Today is turning into quite a day, or more probably a day to forget, although for reasons I cannot quite fathom I am surprisingly philosophical and sanguine about the unwelcome discovery of a flat tyre. A puncture was bound to happen sooner or later, and yes, it would have been better had it not happened right now, but on the other hand it could well have occurred at a more inconvenient time. At least here the sun is out, the road ahead is downhill, and best of all it is a front-wheel puncture so I don't have to unload the bike as I would have done in order to get at the back wheel. To save precious time I simply replace the inner tube with a new one, leaving the repair for later. Voila!

Can you believe it? My pleasure at the prospect of getting back on the bike is very short lived when I hear an unmistakable '*hhhssssss*' from the front wheel? 'Not ideal' is the most acceptable translation of the brief Anglo-Saxon phraseology that accompanies the sound of a brand-new inner tube failing and releasing air. Once my blood pressure and pulse rate are restored, I am genuinely puzzled by this unwelcome development because the new inner tube was checked before being fitted. Naturally I scrutinised the tyre to identify the cause of the original puncture because quite obviously any sharp object that remained would puncture the new tube as soon as it was inflated.

I conduct another check and much to my dismay a minute hole is revealed half an inch from the valve. I decide not to risk a second new inner tube and opt for repairing the puncture. I know this will sound woefully unprepared, but prior to this very moment the last puncture I mended was on one of our children's bikes two decades ago, but then you can't make punctures happen, can you!

Job done, tools away, and the bike and I are freewheeling back into Provins in no time at all. Fifty-three miles of pedalling is quite enough for a day but thankfully there is still life in the old legs and I am up for a few more miles. This is just as well as I have no other choice. It has taken six hours and twenty-three minutes of pedalling to reach this point. Any proficient cyclist would consider this an embarrassingly long time for fifty-odd miles, but not me, no embarrassment whatsoever, because up to this moment I have covered one hundred and two miles in the last two days and I am feeling rather buoyed by this new personal record.

Have I bleated on about mustard fields before? Yes, yes, I know I have, but I have to again because the scene laid out before me really has the wow factor. The evening sun is very low in the sky and the little flowers have turned to gold, pure gold, even though King Midas is nowhere to be seen. The sight of tens of thousands of the smallest flowerheads gently waving as I cycle past, well, it gladdens the heart, and then just when I think there can be no better moment to be alive, I cross the River Seine and another milestone is ticked off.

What is this if it's not the campsite at Bray-sur-Seine? Booking in is accompanied by me asking my usual questions in bumbling French: Are the showers included in the fee? Are they hot or cold? The owner answers as I was hoping on both points and after settling myself in, I find that everything at the site proves to be spot on except for a very noisy party that went on (and on) until well after midnight, thirty yards or so from my tent. Plenty of alcohol was involved, I would guess, but there was no trouble to be fair, just exuberant fun.

53.35 miles in a day; now that's something to send a bloke to sleep, party or not.

## Day 10 – Sunday 25th April

## Departments of Seine-et-Marne and Yonne: From Bray-sur-Seine to Villeneuve-sur-Yonne

A Carrefour supermarket is conveniently situated in Bray-sur-Seine so I make it my first port of call after pedalling away from the campsite. Pre-packed sandwiches are in danger of becoming established as my lunch of choice for the simple reason that they are quick and easy. Today is Sunday so I buy some Breton shortbread by way of a modest treat, and because I know how to live it up. Luckily for me the French no longer close shops and supermarkets on Sundays, as was the case nationwide until not so many years ago. Once provisioned up I look forward to a day on the bike, which should involve around thirty miles of pedalling and no hills of note. That sounds about right for a Sunday, which traditionally at least is meant to be a day off. I cycle alongside the mighty River Yonne and into the town of Villeneuve-sur-Yonne by mid-afternoon after an uneventful but pleasant few hours of pedalling. I passed lots of mustard fields on the way here but I will assume you've heard enough of them so I'm missing them out, glorious though they were.

Camping Savail is very pleasing indeed. The proprietor interrupts her Sunday afternoon not only to book me in but to walk me around the whole campsite showing me the facilities. The site is very quiet and the only other occupants are three generations of the same family in a nearby caravan. By four o'clock my tent is all sorted out and I am ready to explore the town that lies on the opposite side of the river from the campsite. The sun is warm and bright, and civilisation beckons.

Villeneuve-sur-Yonne is set within the region of Bourgogne-Franche-Comte. The town dates to the twelfth century and nowadays its five thousand residents enjoy living in a small and pleasingly picturesque town that has expanded beyond the few remaining sections of the city's ancient walls.

Before the year 1504, when the city burned down, Villeneuve was one of eight locations across the country where residences were maintained by and for the French kings. After the French Revolution Villeneuve's name was changed from '*le-Roi*' (the king) to '*sur-Yonne*' (on the Yonne). After the town was rebadged, a few hundred years of largely uneventful existence followed until 1946 when the then-mayor, one Marcel Petiot, was guillotined having been found guilty of the deaths of forty-six townspeople during the war. Today Villeneuve-sur-Yonne is a beautiful and peaceful place, which I set off to explore, camera in hand, by walking over a substantial stone bridge that crosses the river. From the bridge, an impressive church (*Église Notre-Dame de l'Assomption*) dominates my view ahead. Pope Alexandre III blessed the first stone of the church in 1163, a date that coincides with the building of Notre-Dame Cathedral in Paris. To the left of the church the original fortified entrance to the town and some sections of the medieval walls still remain.

Porte-de-Joigne is one of the original fortified entrances into Villeneuve and once I have passed under its stone arch a path leads me into a small park before continuing as an attractive riverside walk. Once in the park, a wide gravel footpath runs from the entrance gently downhill until it reaches the banks of the River Yonne. Either side of the footpath is lined with trees, and as I walk along the bright afternoon sun creates an ever-moving pattern of dappled light as it shines through the foliage onto the crowds of people gathered in the park to visit the outdoor antique market.

So, this is why the middle of town looks so deserted. A few of the more upmarket stallholders have turned their pitches into elaborate scaled-down versions of complete rooms. Several of these grander displays have pseudo walls and ceilings made from cream canvas sheeting suspended from metal frames. Each 'room' is created in the style of some grand chateau and is beautifully fitted out with carpets, fine furniture, and ceramics; antique paintings even hang on the faux walls. These vendors really have gone the extra mile and they deserve all the trade they are attracting. I take a few photographs but I am not especially at ease with street photography; it always strikes me as a bit of an imposition to take photographs that include complete strangers even if they are not the intended feature of the image. I enjoy wandering around the market and I find several small items that I could easily be tempted to buy to take home as gifts, but more luggage really isn't an option for me, so after a most interesting time at the *brocante* I return to Camping Savail.

Today the bike and I are ten days into our little adventure and remarkably I am under budget, so having completed the little jobs that need doing at the tent I make my way back over the bridge into Villeneuve to treat myself to an evening meal. First I check out a couple of likely places spotted this afternoon. Staff are closing the shutters just as I turn up. Trading finishes at seven o'clock on Sundays, which strikes me as odd. Fortunately, an *Amstel Bière* sign is hanging from a building further down the road. This looks a good bet until I realise that this pub has already closed for the day.

I have crossed the stone bridge from the campsite three times today, each time passing a small restaurant just off the end of the bridge called Fruits du Dragon. I didn't expect to come across Vietnamese food in the Yonne valley but this seems to be the only restaurant open and it looks worth a go. The restaurant is run by a lady called Fouet Oanh, who explains that her first name is French and her surname is Vietnamese. Fruits de Dragon is a modest family business where Fouet runs front of house and her husband works behind the scenes cooking. The restaurant has few customers this evening which may well be the usual state of affairs on a Sunday. In my humble opinion they deserve to be busier; they are pleasant and hard-working people who have provided me with a very tasty three-course meal at a most reasonable price, and if I lived here, I would be a regular customer. My time in Villeneuve-sur-Yonne has ended on a very positive note thanks to Fouet and Mr Oanh.

My unusually brief notes are written up in the restaurant after my meal. I have pedalled a rather meagre twenty-seven and a half miles since this morning, a modest amount it may be but it has added to my total, which now weighs in at 363 miles in about a week and a half.

# Day 11 – Monday 26th April

## Department of Yonne:

## From Villeneuve-sur-Yonne to St. Florentin

After pausing briefly to buy a few items for lunch I am clear of Villeneuve by nine-thirty and heading south across open farmland. The morning is cooler than yesterday but it is another sunny start and I am grateful for that. A modest distance lies ahead over untaxing countryside, well, that's my expectation for today and if this proves to be the case it seems as good a way as any to start a new week. I am uncertain as to the exact distance from Villeneuve-sur-Yonne to Florentin as this is the only section of the whole trip that I have no map to refer to, not that I expect this to be a problem as I shall simply use the River Yonne as my guiding star for the second time in a few days.

A few miles after setting off I spot a sign that reads *'Chemin-du-Haulage'*. The words are deeply etched into a weathered wooden fingerboard at the side of the road. I take the sign as my personal invitation to exchange the road for a more interesting route. After carefully pushing the bike down a steep (think one-in-two steep) and rather slippery grass embankment I come to a riverside path. It is a bit disappointing to discover that this path is no more than a 'sheep-track' right-of-way that is overgrown and has no sign of recent use. My spontaneous act of going *'off piste'* immediately feels somewhat short of my smartest move. That said, I am keen to have a break from the tarmac for a while so I follow the riverbank even though the track ahead is not the well-defined towpath I had in mind. A leap of faith, perhaps, but what's the worst that can happen? Let's give it a go.

The track heads off in exactly the direction needed although I have no idea if it will peter out before the next town or become impassable in some way. I guess I just have to accept that in the end I may be forced to retrace my way back here to resume cycling on the road. On the other hand, the path could improve and provide me with a beautiful riverside journey. Nothing ventured, nothing gained, and all that. Pedalling along the track brings with it a greater sense of freedom than cycling on the road; the change of scenery is refreshing and although my progress is slow and uneven, the little track makes the journey feel quite adventurous. That said, I need to stay alert and keep an eye out for stones, hollows, and ruts if I am to avoid the risk of toppling into the water flowing just a couple of feet to my left.

The river looks for all the world like a wide ribbon of glimmering silk as it flows silently by my side. Sunlight flashes between the poplar trees that line the far bank as I pedal along and after barely thirty minutes of carefully avoiding pitfalls in the track, the narrow surface becomes smoother and hazard free. What a joy this waterside route is proving to be now that the track is less demanding and I am freed up to look around me rather than just ahead of the front wheel. Balls of foliage hang high in the branches, dozens of them on some of the bigger trees. The largest of these leaf-globes must be four feet in diameter; it is only mistletoe, of course, but what an interesting feature this parasitic plant makes as it silently extracts water and nutrients from the host trees. It is easier to make headway here now the track is wider, and earlier concerns that it may dwindle to nothing or become obstructed in some way are put aside and replaced with the simple joy of being alone in the great outdoors: no buildings, no traffic, no rain, no wind, absolutely nothing to improve upon really.

Stopping for a drink coincides with the sight of several butterflies skipping in happy flight along the hedge tops. There are several species here including the peacock, which is easy to identify, as is the orange tip, but I also see some type of fritillary, then a little further on what looks like a ringlet, but I cannot be sure. The long grass and untended hedgerows next to the river are alive with the chorus of nature and bird song, the buzz of insects abound, and just occasionally I hear a frog or toad croak. Could anything be better? The simple splendour of this place entices me to halt periodically just to savour the view, relish the tranquillity, or enjoy the small details of the natural world that surrounds me. Quite often these breaks coincide with the sighting of herons, there must be dozens of these silent statuesque creatures that call this beautiful river their home.

After a couple of hours of pleasantly bumping along the narrow waterside track I return to the real world as the river, the bike and I arrive at the little town of Joigny together. Joigny looks to be a pretty place but instead of stopping I decide to press on for another six miles to the town of Migennes in order to pick up a proper cycle path. From Migennes the path in question stays with the River Yonne for the fifteen miles to the town of Auxerre, at which point it switches its allegiance from the Yonne to the Armançon River, which it then follows for the one hundred and fifty miles to Burgundy and the beautiful city of Dijon.

Migennes marks a significant point in any north-to-south journey across France because the Burgundy canal, which is one of the great manmade French waterways, starts here in the town. The canal, which was over fifty years in the making, links the English Channel with the Mediterranean Sea by connecting the Rivers Seine and Yonne in the north of France, to the Saône and Rhône in the south. The canal is an incredible feat of engineering with nearly two hundred locks in its 150-mile (242-kilometre) length. The locks raise the waterway to a maximum elevation of 1,240 feet (378 metres), which the canal reaches at Pouilly-en-Auxois.

The *Comité National pour le Fleurissement de la France* (The National Committee for the Flowering of France). Can anyone think up a more appealing title for a committee? I very much doubt it. The members of this august group have erected a yellow sign informing me and others that the town of Migennes has been awarded two stars in the *Ville Fleurie* category. Of course summer is still ten to twelve weeks away so evidence of the town's floral splendour is scant, which is a shame. Nevertheless, upon arriving in the centre of town I discover that Migennes boasts a fine and picturesque marina, which, whilst not in the least bit floral, is very pleasing to the eye.

After a few minutes spent admiring the pleasure craft berthed at a pontoon I walk to the tourist information office where I hope to confirm locations of the various campsites along the route of the canal. This will be particularly helpful as the canal is going to be my companion for the next few days. Dismounting from the bike brings disappointment because a notice informs me that on Mondays the tourist office only provides information between two and five. Of course it does! Why would any tourist possibly require information before mid-afternoon? And how foolish of me to forget the glaringly obvious point that if you don't start your French lunchbreak until eleven, how can you possibly be ready to return to work until 2pm at the very earliest? Don't be fooled by this venting; I am not annoyed in any way.

The exquisitely slender steeple that is set aloft on Migennes Church is my first sighting of an architectural feature that I hope and expect will become prominent in the coming days. Burgundy is famed for the patterned, multi-coloured tiling seen on many of its buildings. Polychrome glazed tiles have been used for roofing here since the thirteenth century. Originally such expensive adornments were limited to cathedrals, but realising that a colourful roof signalled opulence the style gained popularity with the wealthy and soon the coloured tiles were adopted by the great landowners, and by the fifteenth century the fashion had spread in popularity to the urban bourgeoisie. The tall thin steeple in front of me is improbably elegant and visually very striking, with its lozenge-shaped tiles laid to form a repeating vertical pattern using different colours.

Leaving the colourful rooves behind for now, I cycle out of Migennes on a purpose-built towpath. The path is six to eight feet wide here, separated from the canal by a narrow grass embankment and surfaced with loose gravel, which I discover within minutes is not a great surface to cycle on. I'll just have to see how it goes.

Sixty miles due west of this point lies the Loire. There is a long-held belief that the weather in France improves immeasurably south of the Loire valley. I have no idea whatsoever if this claim is supported by empirical meteorological evidence but this lack of factual backup matters not to me, as it is far better to travel in hope than in expectation. Naturally, the prospect of a few warm or even hot sunny days spurs me on no end.

Gravel crunches beneath the bike as the tyres push surface stones aside and against one another. Pedalling is the most constant feature of my journey and however much it may be repetitive, I have discovered, somewhat to my surprise I should add, that pedalling is not in the slightest bit tedious. Not only that but I have come to the conclusion that I am actually rather well suited to cycling, which I have come to realise is a most civilised way of getting from A to B, especially so if traffic can be avoided most of the time, as it is here, by the river.

Very infrequently I come across long and low-slung vessels that are putt-putt-putting along the canal. Most of these barges do not appear to be connected with commercial trade in any way although many would have started life having to pay their way by hauling goods. Most of the boats that slowly pass me are used for pleasure. Doubtless some will have been hired to holidaymakers so there is a commercial element to their use, but the majority of boats I see are floating homes, used by retirees who are comfortably off or people striving for a better work-life balance, as they would probably put it. Good luck to them in their search for tranquillity, I say. As for me, I am looking forward to spending the remainder of today enjoying a slow journey along the gravel towpath in the splendid company of the Burgundy canal. It should be an especially relaxing prospect as navigation and map reading are both redundant here on the towpath. The scenery is pretty this afternoon, the weather benign, nature surrounds me, and the world is a mellow and unchallenging place. What a pleasant place this is to glide along at a rather lazy six and a bit miles per hour.

The Burgundy canal is far wider than the others I have come across since leaving Calais and the waterway is arrow straight, literally, for as far as I can see. Vessels are an infrequent sight here and fellow humans have been non-existent since leaving Migennes, so it is quite a surprise to see a fellow cyclist heading towards me. As practised by solo travellers who bump into each other the world over we stop to exchange a few words. Michel lives in the Alpine region of France near Montreux and is cycling with a very loose timetable from his home in the mountains to the north coast of France, then he intends to follow the North Sea cycle route towards Denmark before returning through northern Germany and possibly Poland to his alpine home. He wishes to be home in time for the winter skiing season, otherwise he is quite unhindered by any time limit or exact route. Michel is a retired postal worker whose cycling adventures have become an annual event since he finished work. He tells me that south of here I will find campsites at St Florentin, at Alesia, and near Vandenois-en-Auxois. Each of the sites lie near the canal, which is very convenient.

Apparently, the cycle path south of here is not tarmacked. This is useful if disappointing information as forcing the wheels through loose and sometimes deep gravel becomes more tiring as each mile ticks by. In all truth, I had been looking forward to a few days of easy pedalling along a smooth bitumen surface. Fortunately for me my *'velo'* has a suspension seat pillar and the front forks can be adjusted to activate suspension on the front wheel. I have yet to meddle with the forks but I assume doing so will dampen the effect of the uneven path. I don't know if that's going to be necessary but it's an option if needed. Michel adds that the gravel surface continues for at least the next hundred miles, after which cycling changes to a smooth asphalt surface. I describe the route north of here to Michel, pointing out some campsites along the way and recommending the Fruit-de-dragon restaurant. Twenty minutes or so later we bid each other a safe journey and set off in opposite directions to mutual calls of, *'Bon courage!'*

I am gently bumping my way south towards Brienon-Armançon on the loosely packed gravel towpath without a care in the world, when I glance down at the handlebars and notice that my cyclometer is missing. The black plastic cradle into which the device clips is still in position next to the right handlebar grip but my trusty mileage recorder has gone. *'Quelle horreur'* may sound over-the-top but this little piece of equipment would be near the pinnacle of any list of items that are important to me on the trip. Not much bigger than a small box of matches, its primary use is to record distance but it also measures current and average speed. Its small LCD display helps me judge where I am, and occasionally, if I am cycling along a monotonous stretch of road, it provides a point of focus, which adds interest. Admittedly the loss of the cyclometer is not like having my tent fall apart or my bike stolen, but right now it feels quite a blow so I set off to retrace my route in the hope that the device fell off when I laid my bike on the grass to speak to Michel. If I'm lucky I'll be able to locate where we chatted as the grass will be downtrodden. I hope it will, because on this section of cycle path one mile of canal is pretty well identical to the next.

Fifteen minutes later I spot a patch of embankment where the grass looks disturbed if not exactly flattened, and right there, where the gravel meets the grass, is my cyclometer. It's quite a relief to have it securely gripped in its holder again.

A few miles further and I arrive at St. Florentin just as thirty-three miles are notched up since this morning. The distance has taken me around four and a half hours, so I've been doing around seven miles per hour or thereabouts, an average sort of day for me in terms of distance and time. I have now pedalled a total of 397 miles, the same as cycling from London to Edinburgh.

After booking in for the night and getting on with my campsite routine I ponder the pleasing prospect of finding some food and hopefully a beer, if St. Florentin has a pub.

First on my list of priorities after the tent is sorted out is a shower, and me rabbiting on about shower design is probably not what you expect at this juncture. Neither do I, to be frank, but please bear with me. The pros and cons of the experience of this afternoon's shower make such an impression that it would be remiss of me not to share the details with you:

The disabled persons' shower is the only one open out of season and the proprietor has told me that this is the one I must use. Opening the door, I discover that the shower block is nothing short of a visual wonder. There is opulence wherever I look and the title 'shower facility' does it a great injustice. Consequently, and very deservedly I rebrand it *The Ablutions Hub*, which is a far more fitting title. The washroom facilities are clearly brand new; the cobalt-blue tiles and lavish stainless-steel fittings shout *expensive!* The facility really is more in keeping with a five-star hotel than any campsite. Aesthetically the *Ablutions Hub* would be difficult to improve upon.

My first impressions of the shower are very good. Water is dispensed in a generous, hot flow, which is always welcome after a day on the bike. Unfortunately, the duration of this watery pleasure is limited because hot water is dispensed in short powerful bursts, which after precisely nine seconds stops abruptly. This is an unfaltering sequence for the duration of my shower so I can be accurate with timings – and if anyone is in the least bit interested this equates to exactly sixty-seven bursts of water during a ten-minute shower. Moving on!

No, I can't, another nine seconds pass and the water flow stops suddenly. This requires me to press a large wall-mounted plunge button to generate the next hot deluge. I don't wish to sound petty but there is no soap tray, or a shower seat, or handrails, so the shower would be a challenge for some less able people, I would have thought. Yes, you're right – the whole facility is brand new and perhaps these adornments are still to be fitted.

But here's the thing! All this short-water-blast kerfuffle is simply the warm-up act as the real irritation has yet to be unleashed on me. Forty or so aqua jets into my shower – I say forty, but who knows, who cares! – and without warning, my sense of sight is removed instantaneously and – I am plunged into total darkness – The lights are on a timer!

So, I am now deprived of light, deprived of sight, and deprived of water, as all things halt conterminously! You would be correct to assume that I am not pleased, and to make matters worse this cacophony of sensory deprivation coincides with me dropping the soap into the pitch-black void of the shower tray. I dare not move! Who would? Naturally, I stand rigid because I know the soap bar is sliding stealthily and silently across the shower tray in a sinister attempt to upend me; it now poses a potentially lethal slip hazard. In a desperate act of self-preservation, I lunge for the hand rail, forgetting that it has yet to be installed. The frustration causes me to emit a flurry of salty language into the steamy dark space around me. I fumble and slide around in the pitch-black death-trap trying to recover my bearings when after about nine seconds (clearly the time it takes to get things done around here), I remember that the main light switch for the shower block is situated on the wall next to the entrance door. This is a good twenty feet away, of course it is, so I stand still for a while to take stock of my whereabouts and try to visualise a mental map of my surroundings and the route to the entrance.

I am now standing in the shower and the water has stopped (naturally). I am pretty sure that the shower door is to my left and behind me but try as I might, I can't remember if the shower tray has a lip. That said I have no difficulty whatsoever in visualising tripping over the said lip and ramming my foot into the edge of the ceramic tray. Doubtless this will involve excruciating pain and an injury that will render me unable to pedal for days if not weeks, maybe a lifetime. Being (of necessity, it appears) a cautious chap, I pause a little longer to take stock but concentrate as I might, I don't recall any other impediments to a safe exit from the shower cubicle. So that being the case I must have at least an even chance of navigating my way to the brighter and lighter world that would come with reaching the light switch near the entrance door, without mishap or injury.

As you will doubtless understand, I need to take several deep breaths to steady my nerve and help muster the courage needed to set off on the hazardous twenty-foot quest for the light switch. So, once I have allowed myself to reoxygenate and for my pulse to return to two figures, I gingerly grope my way around the slippery wet walls of the inky black shower cubical. Then, having successfully felt my way to the waist-high door handle, I manage to operate the lever without opening the door into my face and disintegrating my nose and cheekbones in the process. There is a God.

Before I make my next step, I hover, chameleon-like, to consider my next move, then, after a suitable delay needed to compose myself and prepare for whatever misfortune and searing pain is about to come my way, I lift my right foot an unnecessary height above the floor in the style of one of those ornamental Greek soldiers with pompoms on their shoes. Perhaps I should explain: If I could see anything, such an exaggerated foot action would look ridiculous, but I can't see, so necessity prevails just in case the shower tray has a ceramic lip.

Once beyond the shower door my feet make contact with the stone floor. It is stone cold (obviously). As quickly as you could say, *'Oh, I've just gone tits up – that hurt!'* I transform the floor into a deathly slip-hazard by dripping water copiously all over. Now, why I hadn't thought to bring a Zimmer frame fitted with non-slip rubber feet, is quite beyond me. Without such a frame I take two dozen or so short nervous steps to cross the floor in the style of a novice at an ice-rink after one too many stiff drinks. As you will imagine, seeing a thin horizontal sliver of light penetrating the darkness from under the main entrance door of the *Ablutions Hub* is a great relief to me. Thankfully the light, however dim, will make my final few yards less perilous than I expect. Part-way across the vast expanse of tiled floor that is no-man's land, as it were, it suddenly hits me that any moment, and without warning, a stranger may enter, at which point my naked form will suffer near terminal embarrassment. Thankfully, I am spared this ultimate indignity and a few seconds later I reach the switch whereupon I am instantly bathed in light.

Thank you for listening to my rant. It has been exceptionally cathartic for me and I feel very much better now that I have vented.

Outside the warm steamy interior of the *Ablutions Hub* I set off to walk back to the tent. The temperature has tumbled considerably in the last half hour and I am reminded that it is still early in the year. Glad to be back inside my flexible little home I rummage through the contents of a pannier bag until my fingers close around the neck of a bottle of wine – *Vielle Cave* to be precise. It has *Vin de Table de France* printed on the label; let's just say the wine was dirt cheap and snatched from the less prestigious end of the alcohol display on a whim. I expect plonk rather than vintage.

Having discovered the *Vielle Cave* you may be disappointed to learn that I can no longer be bothered going out on some potentially futile trek into town to seek out a pub to buy beer and write up my journal. It seems far better, especially now I have wine at hand, that I write my notes here in the tent. Anyway, if further justification is needed let me add that after my near-death experience in the shower wine is needed to steady my nerves, which are still frayed.

Making use of the remaining daylight to write up today's events, whilst lying prone due to lack of space, I should add, is most uncomfortable, but with no alternative I just have to get on with it by balancing my weight on my left elbow in order to free up the other hand to write. Writing is far less comfortable scrunched up in a peapod tent than it would have been at a table in some bar, but it works out all right providing I move every few sentences to keep the blood circulating. The wine, I should say, unlike my blood circulates rather well, and although it's hard to believe, the plonk actually ends up tasting quite acceptable. More to the point, it helps me no end in my quest for words. Once the journal is written up and darkness encroaches my thoughts switch to the journey ahead, and a choice I must make, two days from now, about the route ahead: In simple terms the choice is between an easier way or a more challenging way.

The easy route, let's call it route one, follows the Canal de Bourgogne south to Pont d'Ouche where it turns in a fish-hook shape before going back on itself in a northeasterly direction. Route one is the longer of the two routes, in fact its extra distance will probably add a full day of cycling to reach the point where both routes next converge, which is at Beaune, a pretty Burgundian town between Dijon and Chalon-sur-Saone. On the other hand, distance is the only disadvantage of route one, which on the plus side is flat throughout and would allow me to visit the city of Dijon. The canalside cycle path and little city of

Dijon are both very beautiful; not only that, there is a well-placed campsite just outside the city at Lac du Dijon. In essence, route one ticks all the boxes provided that I am happy with the extra time and distance involved.

Route two, like route one, heads due south from here and sticks with the Canal de Bourgogne until it reaches Pont d'Ouche where the routes part company. From this point route one stays with the canal and trundles northeast; route two, on the other hand, leaves the canal and continues south. It then pretty well keeps going in that direction on a rural road, climbing quite quickly as the route sets off over the Morvens. The Morven hills are a thickly forested mountain massif that reaches three thousand feet in elevation. In short, route two is more direct but far hillier. I fall asleep wondering if flat and longer, or short and more hilly (bigger hills than I have had to take on so far) will be my route of choice. It's a bit tricky, really, but I don't have to decide now or even tomorrow for that matter, and in reality, the weather on the day will have some bearing on my decision.

# Day 12 – Tuesday 27th April

## Department of Yonne:

## From St. Florentin to Lézinnes

Yesterday afternoon I failed to notice that a main train line runs alongside the perimeter of the campsite. Had I spotted it before I pitched the tent, I would have set up on the far side of the site rather than directly under to the railway embankment. (How can anyone miss a railway line? Schoolboy error, methinks!) Anyway, that is exactly what happened and as a result, I have woken up early after a night made restless by passing traffic and intermittent trains. What I could really do with is a few more hours' sleep, but today has started as one of those very annoying *'I can't sleep so I may as well get up'* days. On the plus side the day greets me with a cloudless sky and a beautiful low sun, which casts its long orange fingers across the campsite, and for the first time in several days it is chilly, very chilly, but fortunately for campers like me there is some warmth from the sun, just a hint. I seem to be the first person on the site to welcome the day and I am ravenous so I set about cooking three eggs and a packet of bacon lardons.

In true outdoor style all the ingredients are tossed into the shallow pan balanced atop the storm cooker. Breakfast bubbles very close to the rim and for a moment I fear I may have overdone the quantity; fortunately for me it looks more perilous than it really is and nothing is lost. Wisps of steam rise slowly from the pan and drift over the tent on this windless morning. The aroma is wonderful, and I am reminded that an outdoor breakfast really is one of life's great moments. I monitor the progress of the cooking while cupping a mug of tea. This deals with thirst and cold hands simultaneously. It is black tea, unfortunately, as I have no milk, but tea is tea, is it not? As this is my first tea in many days even *sans lait* it is especially delicious. My piping hot breakfast is forked straight from the pan while I stand up and survey the campsite. Absolutely nothing stirs – no people, no trains, no traffic, nothing in fact to detract from the wonderful taste of a 'Full English'. I had three eggs for breakfast this morning! This is because I am English; a local person could never eat three eggs because for a Frenchman *un oeuf* is always enough! Pitiful, I know, but there's nobody here to share that little gem with me, except you, and you are a captive audience.

What a breakfast, now for lunch! The half baguette left over from yesterday is still perfect so I fill it to overflowing with some locally produced three-pepper pâté topped with chunky slabs of beef tomato. It is a feast to behold, let me assure you. Next, the cooker is cleaned and packed away and I make final checks of the pitch for missed equipment before silently wheeling out of the campsite, leaving the other residents deep in slumber. Lucky them, I think to myself. Perhaps they didn't hear the trains or maybe they are all geriatric and stone deaf, who knows?

Five minutes after leaving the village of St. Florentin I am delighted to wake up to the fact that the tow path has lost the loose gravel of the last couple of days. Here the track has been compressed into a hard, smooth surface by the thousands of feet, paws, hooves, and bicycles that have passed this way for decades, and pedalling is going to be all the better for it.

This stretch of the Armançon River doubles as the Canal de Bourgogne and this morning the waterway looks particularly serene in the post-dawn sunlight. Wide slivers of translucent mist hang motionless over the still water while the tree shadows from the far side of the canal stretch out to touch the bank next to me. I'm pretty sure that if the shadows could touch the riverbank, they would give it a gentle shake just to wake it up, but stretch as they might the shadows fall just short and so the canal slumbers on in silence. As I pedal along those bits of path that remain dark and shadowy under the trees the air retains its overnight chill. These cool sensations on my skin are only fleeting and each time I emerge from below the overhanging branches the light hits me with its sudden intensity and warmth. The brilliant light illuminates otherwise invisible clusters of the tiniest flies, which pogo-stick up and down in the haze above the sunlit track. All of this wonderment exists under a cobalt sky – what a sight! It makes me glad to have set off before the sky gets lighter as the sun climbs higher into the sky.

Humans may seem to be an endangered species along this part of the waterway but herons are a regular sight, sharing the canal with several varieties of duck that I can't identify and a large water vole, which I unwittingly disturb. The vole leaves an expanding V-shaped wake as it swims from the exposed water in the centre of the canal towards the protection of the grassy bank. How magical is it to be surrounded by nature? And however much there is for me to see here I know that so much more is hidden from view. If I focus, the clues of wildlife are all around me, be it the plop of a frog entering the water, an occasional croak, or sometimes the sound of a small flock of passerine birds tweeting excitedly in the bushes and then falling silent as I near. Such delights continue for several miles; there is nothing to distract from the appeal of this place, no people, no roads, no buildings. The only sign of human activity is the wood yard that I can just about make out through the mist on the far bank of the canal, but it is still too early in the day for activity and no-one has arrived to deal yet with the piles of roughly hewn tree trunks stacked for transportation. Nothing, it seems, breaks the magic of the canal at this early hour and I am fortunate enough to enjoy a few more miles of canalside tranquillity before I arrive at the little town of Flogny-la-Chapelle. The sight of a supermarket conveniently situated just yards from the canal thrusts me back into the modern world. Everything has to be somewhere, I guess, and the shop is ideally positioned for me to restock.

Whenever I leave my bike unattended and outside a place such as a supermarket, I leave the rear panniers attached simply because they are too cumbersome and heavy to carry around. Also both my bulging panniers wouldn't fit into a shopping trolley together, not even a large one. Unfortunately, I feel that I should be guarded against the opportunist thief, however unlikely this may be in rural France. It really would be a monumental problem were my possessions to be stolen. Accordingly, I always secure the bike to some sturdy structure using a steel cable and combination lock. I back this up with a bike alarm – it really doesn't look like it packs a punch but take it from me, it is fearsome!

To most passers-by I'm sure my electronic bike alarm must look insignificant and harmless. Visually it is rather like a mini remote control for a television. The alarm is permanently attached to the handlebars as a visual deterrent for any passing thieves who would be alert to such things if they were worth their salt.

When activated the alarm emits a high-pitched antisocial noise. Setting the alarm requires a three-digit code then pressing the 'ARM' button. Once primed the movement-activated alarm emits three short but piercing beeps just to confirm it is working. Even the 'armed' sound is guaranteed to turn heads. The noise is not so bad in a large open supermarket car park such as here, but I have to admit that it was rather more startling to the customers using the outdoor seating area at the McDonald's I stopped at some days ago, although to be fair, as far as I know nobody choked on their McMonsterBurger or whatever they were gorging on when I tested it, and, rather more to the point, nobody nicked my bike. Of course, the thing about crime prevention, and alarms are no exception, is that you never really know if people are deterred or just irritated.

Ten minutes later my shopping has been done, the alarm is deactivated, and I'm back on the bike setting off towards to Tonnerre.

The ride from Flogny-le-Chappelle to Tonnerre is uneventful and not in the least bit energy sapping. My arrival at the canalside town of Tonnerre coincides with sandwich o'clock, which is absolutely ideal because I am starving. My lunch is a pleasant affair, which I enjoy seated at a wooden canalside picnic table kindly provided by the local *Maire*. I divide my time between pondering over my map for points of interest between here and the hamlet of Lézinnes, and devouring the quite humungous pâté and tomato baguette that I constructed after breakfast.

At the adjacent picnic table, a group of people are engaged in lively conversation over lunch and a bottle of wine. We start chatting and they inform me that they are renovating a house in the town, then very enthusiastically they persuade me that whatever my plans are, I really must cycle into Tonnerre. Unfortunately, other than picking up a word that sounds like 'fuss' I cannot make out exactly what it is they want me to see. I am unaware that the town is particularly worth exploring but as locals usually know best, when lunch is over I set off into Tonnerre, which I discover to be especially quaint and a very pleasing place indeed, so much so that I take to pushing the bike through the quiet streets to give me more time to admire the detail of the place.

Many of the old houses here in Tonnerre have un-rendered natural stone walls which are tinted a pleasing hue of warm ochre by the early afternoon sun. Several houses have colourful highlights on some feature or another, aquamarine window frames here, a door painted in beautiful Alizarin crimson over there. By way of an impromptu experiment, by squinting and half closing my eyes the view of the narrow street before me, with its ancient little houses, is transformed into quite the prettiest watercolour painting, then, on nothing more than a whim I follow a dark and rather nondescript side-alley just off the middle of town. The alley is very narrow and looks extremely old and after a hundred yards or so it opens into a sunlit natural ampitheatre where by some good fortune, I find that I have stumbled across what must be the 'fuss' I misheard over lunch.

Before me is the *'Tonnerre Fosse'*, a quite remarkable natural feature that starts life deep under the town. The fosse is a water source that gently erupts from the hidden depths of some underground chamber at the considerable rate of three hundred litres per second. In times of spate the flow increases tenfold, which must be an astonishing sight. The crystal-clear waters of this karst spring rise to the surface in the centre of a circular stone structure over forty feet in diameter. Although now disused, the open-sided building that encircles the fosse enabled full use of this constant flow of pure water as the town's wash-house.

Coming upon an old *lavoir* is a common enough sight in France, although I have never seen one in this league before. Three hundred years ago, the semi-circular building before me was constructed in a half-rotunda shape with a shallow sloping roof. It was built to protect the washer women who toiled beneath it from very hot or inclement weather. The whole place has stood the test of time well and is remarkably well preserved. Immediately behind the *lavoir* and set high above its bubbling waters is a small crescent of higgledy-piggledy homes that peer down onto the fosse. These charming little houses cling to the edge of an escarpment that towers vertically above. The whole place is exceptionally charming, but for me the real surprise of the Tonnerre Fosse, and what makes it a special place indeed, is that nobody has defaced the place with any form of commercialisation, not even a small café or gift shop. The Tonnerre Fosse really is a hidden gem, which I hope stays as unique and alluring as it is today.

Leaving the enchanting fosse behind me I follow the course of the waters as they are channelled away from the wash-house and through the town along a wide stone leet. Eventually the watercourse arrives at a little bridge where the water from the fosse joins a small river, and it is here, at this junction of waterways that I find the setting for yet another of Tonnerre's architectural charms.

The river view in front of me is quite simply idyllic. As I stand on the bridge, a stone wall replaces what would have been a natural riverbank to my right. The wall is softened by overhanging bushes and trees and at its base the River Armançon caresses the ivory-coloured stone blocks as it flows gently by on its way out of Tonnerre. The riverbank to my left is made up of a row of very old houses that are built right up to the water's edge; each little house has been constructed of off-white stone and has a pretty first-floor balcony overhanging the river. The metal railings that edge the adjoining balconies run the full length of the four houses and are painted in a mixture of Windsor blue and cadmium yellow; the result is a very warm and very French green.

Continuing this beautifully co-ordinated colour theme, the inhabitants have hung French green curtains at their cottage windows and as a final touch an outdoor table and two chairs have been placed on the balcony of the last house; the table has a large umbrella in matching French green, naturally – this ties the scene together perfectly and offers a photo opportunity *par excellence*. This is one of those rarely stumbled upon and never forgotten scenes that are so simple, so pleasing, and so evocative of rural France.

Later I learn that the town of Tonnerre dates to Roman times when it was known as Tornodorum. Apparently, it is claimed that the name is derived from the Roman word for fortress (*castrum*), which puzzles me because, as I discover some weeks later when I get my dictionary off the shelf at home, the literal translation of *tonnerre* in French is thunder or fracas. Tonnerre seems to be no place for disorder but surely its name must be connected to the mighty and thunderous upswell of water in times of flood. This seems entirely logical to me, but then I am no historian.

My afternoon in Tonnerre has been fascinating and a great joy. The hours have flown since my picnic table lunch, where let's be honest, were it not for the good fortune of a chance conversation I would never have visited Tonnerre. The place has turned out to be one of the highlights of my trip so far.

After pulling myself away from the tranquil beauty of the riverside cottages I resume my travels south along the D905 until, at Lézinnes, I am reunited once more with the River Armançon. The time has simply flown by this afternoon and I am astounded that it is a quarter to six when I arrive at my overnight campsite. The Lézinnes site is rather small but it is beautifully manicured, and its thirty-two level pitches are just a five-minute walk from the river; perfect, if you ask me.

After twelve consecutive days of living in a tent I have developed a bit of a routine for setting up camp. It is twenty-two degrees centigrade here in the hamlet of Lézinnes. Sunshine and a light breeze are always welcome, and my sequence of jobs on such a lovely evening must revolve around taking advantage of the weather. This evening my routine is:

1. Partially erect the tent by putting up the inner tent to expose it to the air; an hour in the sun should rid the fabric of any hint of damp.
2. Next, my large microfibre bath towel is hung over the bike to dry it and freshen it up after my morning wash.
3. I turn the outer tent inside out then lay it flat on the grass for the breeze and sun to do their work. The two opposite corners are secured with heavy pannier bags in case of wind.
4. Leave the tent disassembled as above and go for a shower.
5. Having located the wash room, wash my clothing by hand (today this is done without soap as I am running low).
6. When my clothes have been washed, I return to the tent and drape the wet items over the bike to dry. Sometimes I use a short line tethered between trees, but not today.
7. Once the outer tent is dry, which occurs surprisingly quickly on an evening such as this, it is placed over the inner tent and attached to the poles. Finally, the guy ropes are secured and adjusted, and tent pegs finish the job.
8. I start writing up my notebook (bullet points only) so I don't forget any minor yet interesting events.
9. Flash up the storm cooker using meths and a match, then prepare, cook, and enjoy my meal.
10. Wash dishes and clean the cooker components, which are then packed into themselves, Russian doll style.
11. Visit the town for a beer, write up my journal in detail.

Today, like many of the last twelve days, or at least since I got myself a bit of a system going, I've followed the above routine more or less as soon as I select my pitch, although to be fair I have yet to pitch the tent when it is raining. Rain would inevitably force me to cancel many of the steps above as I would want to erect my shelter as soon as I could.

Tonight's evening meal comes in the shape of two cans. First: *cannelloni (100% pur boeuf)*, which is self-explanatory, and secondly a can of six *quenelles de veau sauce Lyonnaise aux champignons*. The title sounded good, I thought, although I have absolutely no idea what *quenelles* are. Let's just say that I will not be trying them again. My rather disappointing meal is a snappy affair because it is still a pleasantly warm evening and I wish to see what lies beyond the campsite, hopefully an alehouse.

Like so many of the small communities scattered across rural France Lézinnes is a sleepy little place; the hamlet has no obvious centre that I can find although I do come across a pub that is busy with customers. An ultra-large TV is mounted high on a wall. Generally I am not a supporter of televisions in pubs as they are usually intrusive and often replace conversation by being too loud. Here in Lézinnes the television is set on 'Meteo', a channel solely dedicated to broadcasting the weather, so in a blatant change of attitude to pub TVs I divide my time between completing today's journal and absorbing meteorological information for the days and places ahead.

Two young Frenchmen at the table next to me are drinking dark red beer. I am reasonably well travelled but I have never seen red beer anywhere on the planet! Light brown beer, yes; dark brown beer, of course; beer that is almost black; and white beer in Belgium, but never red. They tell me they are drinking *bière fraise*, which is simply draught beer with strawberry syrup added. It's a new one for me so I conclude the evening by giving it a go; it is not unpleasant but not really to my taste as it is neither beer nor fruit juice, but I am glad to have had the chance to taste it. I conclude the evening by noting in my journal that I have travelled just over thirty miles in four hours today and that my running total now stands at four hundred and twenty-seven miles.

## Day 13 – Wednesday 28th April

### Departments of Yonne and Cote-d'Or:

### From Lézinnes to Venaray-les-Laumes

I have been looking back over the distances I have cycled since leaving Calais. Twenty or so miles on day one caused cramp, let's just say that my prospects for the journey ahead didn't seem at all favourable at the time. A few days on and twenty miles had risen to thirty and within a week almost forty, then when forced to do so by campsites that were unexpectedly closed, I discovered that I could actually pedal over fifty miles in one day. 'Fifty miles in a day!' I hear you call. Yes, and I did it without seizing up. Who'd have thought?

But now, as my second week on a bike draws to a close, I realise the increase in distance has halted and I am now very comfortable pedalling thirty miles a day or thereabouts. Yesterday, while I was browsing over my map stretched out over the large pub table, it crossed my mind that I really should check to see if I will actually be on schedule to catch the bus from Montpellier back to the UK if I continue my somewhat pitiful thirty miles per day. A quick calculation of the distance to the south of France divided by the days available shows I am not actually running late, but neither do I have any time spare, so it would be very useful for me to put in a big mileage day or even two, just to give me a bit of a buffer, as it were.

Well, that was my line of thinking last night, but waking up this morning at twenty-five past nine is not the ideal start to any day pencilled in as one for more effort. All is not lost, I convince myself, providing I get my skates on, so after a rather uncharacteristic flurry of high-energy pre-departure activity I pedal out of the site less than forty minutes after opening my eyes. Half an hour of purposeful activity revolving those pedals gets the blood circulating and the joints moving freely. It's amazing what can be achieved by turbo packing the equipment and speed-fuelling myself with water and chocolate. Lézinnes and its campsite are soon behind me and my meteorological good fortune holds as today is yet again a sunny one. Surely this fine weather cannot last.

Like most mornings of late I head straight for the canal where a sign on the gated towpath informs me that it is a dedicated cycle route, the first since leaving the Tarka Trail. The Canal de Bourgogne cycle way is flat and level and makes for easy cycling, so much so that I am encouraged to pedal quicker than usual, ten to twelve miles per hour, in fact. Now this may not be fast to most cyclists but for me, it is little short of whizzing along. The village of Ancy-le-Franc comes along five miles after Lézinnes, then the hamlets of Nuits and Aisy-sur-Armançon follow in quick succession before I wheel into the village of Rougemont. Like so many of the settlements that straddle the canal the place is little more than a church and a few dozen houses. I exit Rougemont just a couple of minutes later.

Three miles along the cycle path and I come to Buffon, a small place with less than two hundred residents and the home of the *Grande Forge du Buffon*. Whilst I may not have heard of it before, the Grande Forge is a place of significant historical interest for it is an integrated ironworks established around 1770 by George-Louis Leclerc de Buffon. Monsieur Buffon used the most advanced thinking of the time to create, on a single site, a blast furnace, a forge, and a slitting mill, all of which were powered by water. Well Ahead of its time his business functioned successfully for a century before it became dormant; the forge lay derelict for the next hundred years before being resurrected as a museum in 1979.

Next I come to Montbard, an inviting huddle spanning the River Brenne. It lies thirty minutes on the bike beyond Buffon and although no more than a big village, it is the largest inhabited place I have come upon since leaving Tonnerre. Montbard is also where I talk to the first cycle travellers I have seen since I chatted to Michel, the retired Swiss postman, a few days ago. The three Australian cyclists I bump into in the centre of Montbard are retracing a trip made on a bicycle in 1934 by one of their mothers. The trio of men started their travels in Gloucester, then crossed over to France and have since made their way south via Paris and the Dijon canal. We swap experiences in the warm sunshine and depart with a cheery, *'Bon courage!'*

Before leaving Montbard I make a visit to the town's tourist information office, which I find is staffed by a most helpful lady who phones ahead to confirm that the next campsite on my list is indeed open. She also provides me with four pints of icy cold water from the office drinks dispenser. This is exactly what I need because although it is very pleasant cycling in the sun, I have found today's temperature of 27-28 degrees to be very hot on the bike, especially as very little shade is available on the cycle path. I may well have said this before but I really have been incredibly lucky with the weather. When I left Devon my hope was for a day or two of dry weather; all I wanted was for it to be fine enough for me to become familiar with pitching my tent. I just needed sufficient practice that I could set camp without fumbling should the weather turn against me. And with the exception of some strong headwinds, a few cool nights, and one night that was freezing I have been blessed with sixteen days of the most splendid weather.

Rotating the pedals now comes automatically to me; sometimes it really does feel as if I have known nothing else. Not only that but when I'm on the bike, unlike when I'm driving the car, there is no need to concentrate on where I'm going, especially on towpaths such as here where my mind can wander and I am free to absorb the scenery and wildlife that surrounds me, or just ponder over the route and days ahead.

Once clear of Montbard I ease into my go-to cycling speed of three times walking pace. This is an especially tranquil and beautiful part of France and to rush in such a place would be little short of a sin. Over the next couple of hours, I am rewarded by seeing the best part of two dozen grey herons.

Venarey-les-Laumes is the home of Camping Municipal Alesia, which is a well-established and attractive campsite with many large trees and well-tended grass. The site looks especially welcoming on a warm and sunny afternoon such as this. Soon after arriving I am indebted to the young owners of the site who kindly give me some *alcool à brûler* (meths) and a few cans of beer. Unbeknown to me they had watched me taking photographs of their campsite and asked if I would email the images to them when I get back to the UK so they can be used as website illustrations. As it happens, the light is particularly sharp this afternoon and the new spring foliage looks stunning silhouetted as it is by shafts of sunlight. It is an exchange I am delighted to agree to.

## Day 14 – Thursday 29th April

## Department of Côte-d' Or:

## Venaray-les-Laumes to Pouilly-en-Auxois

This morning's breakfast is best described as dishevelled! The meal really is a visual disgrace, but using up all of the perishable or fragile ingredients I have at hand is both pragmatic and saves waste. One monster field mushroom, several misshapen beef tomatoes, and a box of six eggs (well, you can't really transport eggs on a bicycle, can you?). Everything is thrown into a single deep pan and placed on the Trangia, where it is blasted to hell and back. Presentation may be appalling but it tastes great and after demolishing the panful I am fully fuelled for a morning on the bike. Unfortunately I cannot set off before paying the price for my gluttony, which is to clean the virtually indestructible layer that has been case-hardened onto my aluminium pan-cum-plate. Where is a non-stick surface when you need one?

My pre-departure preparations follow a simple routine: The outer tent is unclipped from the pole ends and shaken vigorously to remove the excess dew and rain; it is then draped over the low hedge that surrounds my pitch to drip whilst I battle with the sleeping bag. Unlike my tent the sleeping bag is dry but being rain-free doesn't make its stowage an easy task and it always requires great effort just to force it into its far-too-small outer bag. It must be rolled up then squeezed as hard as humanly possible to expel the last vestiges of air. To have any chance of squashing it inside its bag I have to kneel on it. Once I manage to squeeze it in, I pull the compression straps taut to squeeze out any air that remains after the beating it has just had.

Next is my very thin but highly effective self-inflating mattress; it is the easiest of the items to pack as it deflates very quickly. Then I pack the items I use daily: my wind-up torch, the Trangia, a few cooking utensils, my washing gear, are all packed into the pannier bags. Once the panniers are full the drawstrings are pulled tight to keep any rain at bay, and finally the pannier tops are folded over and sealed with clips. Then, if I expect to cycle in traffic or if rain is likely, the bright yellow waterproof covers are pulled out of the velcroed bottom pocket of each pannier and the elasticated sides of the covers are stretched up and over the bags. The bright pull-over covers increase my visibility to other road users and hopefully they will create another barrier between my possessions and rain and spray.

I am ready to leave at a respectable enough nine-thirty but getting into any sort of cycling rhythm seems beyond me this morning; I have no idea why this should be as usually I climb onto the bike and within twenty minutes of setting off momentum builds steadily commensurate with the terrain and surface. Not so today, unfortunately, and as a result it takes me a full two hours to cover the first ten miles. There is absolutely no good reason for this as the surface is fine, there is no headwind, and the bike has no faults, nevertheless my legs are decidedly reluctant. That mega-breakfast, perhaps.

As I dawdle along on two wheels, I remind myself that the speed and progress needed, beyond that required to reach Montpellier on time, really doesn't matter a bit. Every now and again I need to remember that this trip is a simply delightful opportunity to embrace retirement, it is no more and no less, and it really shouldn't morph into an endurance test. I put my thirty-year career behind me eighteen months ago and life is very different without the routine of work. Like most people I miss colleagues but not the desk, not the targets, nor the meetings, especially not some of the meetings. It has taken a while to adjust but I feel that this trip has already washed the last bits of work out of my system, if that makes sense. I don't mean in any purging sort of way, it's just that life moves on, new priorities emerge. Maybe this trip is my new target, although I don't think I'm comfortable with the thought when I put it like that, and I hope that in retrospect ending the bike trip won't simply be like completing another job from the in-tray. I don't think it will, I must make sure it doesn't.

Information boards tell me that I am now cycling along *'La Veloroute du Canal de Bourgogne en Pays D'Auxois Morvan'*. It is an hour since I left the campsite, and encouraged by a bright and sunny day I am now getting into my cycling rhythm at long last. The *veloroute* is level, more or less straight, and picturesque enough. To my right a field of lush grass is made colourful and fragrant by an abundant scattering of wildflowers; the blooms share the field with a small herd of white Charolais cattle. The cows are engrossed with eating but still find time to lift their heads and watch me pass. I stop to peer at them and we share a few moments of mutual inquisitiveness until we become bored with each other's company and resume our respective tasks of ruminating and pedalling.

Every now and again the unhindered progress of the canal is punctuated by lock gates, which more often than not are accompanied by a single-storey lock-keeper's cottage. The cottage before me looks rather forlorn but nevertheless its red pan-tiled roof and rustic wooden door make for a pretty sight. Some blue paint remains on the door, matched on the window frames but only fragments of colour remain as most of the original coating has succumbed to time and weather. Above the door a chunky cast-iron plaque displays a large number 8, the name *'Écluse des Carrons'* (Carrons Lock) is embossed into the metal below the number. The old-fashioned script informs me that here at Carrons Lock I am 14.7 kilometres beyond Pont Royal and 4.3 kilometres north of Pouilly. Having said that, there are several villages called Pouilly in this area, so exactly which Pouilly it is that lies three miles ahead I am not at all not clear.

As morning turns to afternoon, I keep my eyes open for somewhere to stop for lunch. A picnic table like yesterday or a village bench would be my choice but such stops have proved few and far between and today a pile of logs at the side of the towpath has to do. Each log is four or five feet long and several thousand are stacked to waist height in a row that must be a hundred yards long. After propping the bike against the logs a full bottle of water disappears at speed. Although the wood pile appears heavy and well anchored it proves unstable when I try to sit on it so after a couple of shortbread biscuits and a few minutes' rest I set off to find a more suitable place. A little further on a sign for the delightfully named village of *'Saucy'* makes me smile.

Another mile passes when I come upon a traditional English narrowboat proudly flying a red ensign on the stern. As a former Royal Navy man I am naturally drawn to any ensign, red or white, neither of which I expect to see hoisted in the middle of France and certainly not on the stern of an English narrowboat. Emblazoned in brightly painted 3D lettering on the port side of its long, thin cabin are the words: 'Dragonfly – No: 367. – C and S Hargreaves. Aylesbury.' The vessel is tied alongside the opposite bank to me but the English owners notice me and we enjoy the opportunity to converse across the water. The owners of this splendid boat are Charles and Julie Hargreaves, who kindly enquire about my plans for lunch and ask if I would like to join them on the boat. They tell me that I can cross over to their side of the canal if I continue along the towpath to a bridge less than a mile ahead. Twenty minutes, two miles, and one bridge later and I am laying the bike down on the grassy canal verge next to *Dragonfly*.

The narrowboat *Dragonfly* is quite lovely to look at, rather beautiful in fact. Her glistening hull and cabin are painted oxford blue, a smart pair of black chimney stacks are positioned one for'ard and one midships, both chimneys are short and squat and have wide bands of highly polished brass that glints in the sun like pure gold – set against the glossy black paint the brass banding looks striking. The long, thin vessel is tied alongside by a hefty pleated rope, which runs from a cleat on the bows to a metal stake driven into the grassy bank. On board we talk about France, travel in general, our respective journeys, and of course about narrowboats, of which I know little. Charles and Julie explain that they have owned the boat for twenty years and now they have retired they divide each month into three weeks on the canal and a week at home in the UK.

Sitting in their snug galley we enjoy lunch together, the *piece de resistance* of which is a cup of Yorkshire tea and a generous slice of Julie's homemade flapjack. Tea with fresh milk, my first since leaving England fourteen days ago – could life get any better! Our meal together is unhurried and a delightful way to break the day. I may still have 20-25 miles of cycling to put in today but on this delightful boat with such good company the distance is easily put to the back of my mind. The Hargreaves tell me that when they bought the narrowboat it already had 'C & S Hargreaves' painted on the sides. By pure coincidence they are 'C & J Hargreaves' but for authenticity they decided to retain the boat's original name.

After lunch they give me a tour of their boat and being guided round by this knowledgeable and friendly couple was quite fascinating. Starting at the bows I was shown the modern cooking and seating areas, next the midships engine compartment, then most interestingly of all the stern of the boat, which houses the aft or rear cabin. The aft cabin was originally the living quarters for the bargee and his family and is known as the boatman's cabin. It is a very small space indeed even for a couple and it stretches the imagination that a whole family could have lived in such a minute cabin. I learned that all traditional English narrowboats are built to a width of six feet ten inches. Somehow the little cabin, which is no more than six and a half feet by eight feet, contains an array of storage cupboards, a double bunk, and a small coal burner that acts as both a heater and a stove for cooking. When I stand up in the boatman's cabin there are several very hefty black metal rods suspended horizontally from the deckhead (ceiling); the rods facilitate steerage from inside the cabin.

Towards the bows, in the space once used to carry commercial goods, Charles and Julie have installed a few modern appliances: a full-size fridge, a second cooker, and a combined washer dryer. They have also fitted a second log burner in a for'ard compartment, which they can use as a more spacious lounge as they require. It was especially interesting to learn that they have preserved the tiny boatman's cabin just as it would have been a century ago, and for all its minute dimensions and its clunky overhead steerage ironmongery, the boatman's cabin is their accommodation of choice, even though they have created a roomier and more modern alternative towards the bows.

After an extremely pleasant couple of hours, it is cheerio rather than *bon courage* as I leave the kindness and good company of the Hargreaves and set off again.

Threatening clouds have been gathering while I was on the narrowboat. At the start of this morning the barometer read 1,022 and it has now fallen to 996; this significant fall in pressure has taken just six hours and I fear it's a rather ominous sign of what's to come. Charles and Julie warned me that tomorrow's forecast is grim and as if to reinforce the point a warm wind steadily picks up pace all afternoon. Time will tell but I feel that my meteorological good fortune is about to run out.

The wind direction fluctuates as I cycle along; sometimes it blows directly into my face but more often than not it blows across me from right to left, from west to east. Cycling with a falling barometer, a rising wind, and the rather lazy disposition that is the byproduct of a long and relaxing lunch does not make for good progress, so I try boosting my pedalling speed by listening to music. For the fourth time since leaving England I try to auto-scan my MP3 player for a local radio station but as with all my earlier attempts this proves unsuccessful. The MP3 was bought a few weeks before I set off and I am not in the least bit familiar with how to operate the tiny contraption. In short, I can't be at all sure if the problem lies with me or the device; perhaps I am simply in an area of poor reception but who knows? Eventually I give up trying to tune the radio and listen instead to 'Tapestry', the acclaimed album by Carol King that I preloaded before I left home.

By astute use of gaffer tape I stick the MP3 player to the handlebar bag in front of me. This enables me to alter tracks and volume one-handed as I cycle along without the need to stop. The ability to adjust the volume whilst cycling is surprisingly necessary as the sound generated by cycling over gravel varies from a quiet background sound to a loud irritating rumble that obliterates the music.

It will come as no surprise to hear that never has my cycle journey across France been boring, although there have been occasions, albeit short and infrequent, when my concentration has been tested by uninspiring or repetitious scenery. Such times have been few and far between but right now, mid-afternoon on Thursday the 29th of April – repetitive landscape surrounds me and such times call for inventiveness: I have no empirical evidence to support my claim but it strikes me that listening to music, especially a jaunty and uplifting melody, increases mean pedalling speed by a good two miles per hour. This may sound miniscule but in my case, in the world of the painfully slow cyclist, this equates to an increase of about twenty per cent.

It is whilst keeping tabs on the speedometer that I notice the somewhat inane fact that the thin wire that stretches from the MP3 taped to the handlebar bag up to the earpiece in my left ear, functions rather excellently as a wind gauge, a mini *'Gustometer'* if you will. A strong wind blows the earpiece wire level with my left elbow, like the hand on a clock moving swiftly from six to eight. This is an entirely futile fact, I appreciate, but this is how I have taken to entertain myself this afternoon. I shall monitor the *'Gustometer'* (patent pending just as soon as I get home, let me tell you) as I progress, and I promise to report back to you as required. If you hear nothing from me, assume the experiment is inconclusive so writing more about it is simply a pointless waste of my time and yours.

As I approach the village of St. Thibault a large chateau comes into view. The basic structure looks sound from a distance but as I get closer it is clear that nearly all of the windows have gone along with much of the building's charm. Boarded-up windows strip even the most elegant building of so much appeal and I can't help but wonder if the *Autoroute du Soleil*, which thunders barely two hundred yards away, has contributed to the demise of this once splendid residence. Of course, over the years large numbers of grand houses the length and breadth of France have fallen into disrepair. In part this is because under French inheritance law an estate does not automatically pass to the surviving spouse intact; children are the first in line to inherit, and French law prohibits any child from being disinherited. The inevitable outcome of this system is that once proud family estates are subdivided and broken up.

The *'Conseil Municipal'* or town council of Pouilly-en-Auxois ensure that visitors to their town are well informed about the local area by the generous use of display boards that contain historical photographs, together with interesting facts about the town's heritage and its relationship with the canal, the information boards overlook the canal in the middle of Pouilly-en-Auxois. They are also next to a large glass canopy, which I discover offers protection from the weather to a very odd-looking mechanical contraption called *'Le Tourer Électrique'*.

*Le Tourer* looks for all the world like a massive floating dodgem car. It is around twenty feet long and painted a sandy beige tone rather like the colour used to camouflage tanks for desert operations. It has overhead rods (surprisingly dodgem-car-esque, if I may say so) from which the vessel once received power. In its heyday this floating oddity was used to maintain the canal by scooping up surplus weeds, thereby reducing the problem of boat propellers becoming snagged. *Le Tourer Électrique* is unquestionably quaint and exceedingly bizarre, yet however improbable the design appears at first sight, it was clearly very effective as it operated as a weed scoop here on the canal from 1893 right up to 1987.

Not far from this improbable de-weeding relic is a steep and rather high embankment, at the base of which is a comparatively small black hole marking the rather sinister-looking entrance to a canal tunnel. Constructed during the 1820s this marvellous example of civil engineering is still in use today. Unfortunately the tunnel was built for barges and not bicycles, and as no tow path exists through the tunnel I am unable to explore it beyond peeping into its dark, damp, and somewhat intimidating entrance.

On arriving at the campsite my details are noted, I pay for my stay, and listen as the campsite facilities are explained to me. The proprietor then informs me that tomorrow's weather should not cause me any problems but I should expect it to deteriorate markedly the day after that. Either way I am welcome to stay for one or two nights and the proprietor suggests that I pay for one night and decide in the morning if I wish to stay longer. This seems an eminently sensible option, the outcome of which will depend on whether or not I wake up feeling up to the strenuous pedalling that will be required to carry me over the hills to Beaune. Naturally the weather on the day will influence what I decide to do. I will also need to bear in mind that the French take national holidays very seriously and two days from now is May Day. Most food shops will be closed and campsites may well be fully booked for the holiday weekend. Fortunately no decision is needed until the morning; right now it's time to find a pitch and set up camp.

It's now eight o'clock and I am sat in a local restaurant. I ordered a pizza, as much as anything because I am intrigued at the prospect of whatever a 'Greek' pizza is, and although it sounds like a bit of a culinary experiment, in the event it turns out to be very tasty, although eating in any restaurant 'solo' is a not the best way to enjoy an evening out.

Don't get me wrong, there is nothing gloomy about my time in this evening's choice of eatery because quite unwittingly the restaurant entertains me royally. Unlikely as it may sound entertainment is provided by two intriguing pieces of kitchen paraphernalia. The first of these is a standalone cold-service counter, which is fitted with little wheels for mobility. Visualise a narrow pool-table-sized structure, or bar-billiards if you are of a certain age, and you about have it. The cold-service counter is very sturdy; a squat hip roof made of coloured glass squares set within a metal frame provides a cover, the frame has gable ends just like a roof on a doll's house, and visually the whole design looks very 1970s. Having been wheeled into full view by a member of the kitchen staff, the cold-service counter is initially left unattended, but after a few minutes of dormancy (this may be well practiced and done purely for dramatic effect for all I know), a different member of staff wanders over to the contraption. She adjusts the position of the mobile service counter slightly, then pauses briefly before pressing a button.

This causes a high-pitched bell to ring out. That's got everyone's attention, I think. Then to my astonishment the gable-ended glass roof starts to elevate. The upward movement is slow motion, a bit juddery, and totally silent, a bit like what I imagine watching levitation would be, until the movement suddenly stops. At this point the little bell rings again and the glass roof comes to a somewhat shaky halt three feet above the service area, which, it is now revealed, contains little bowls of food and the like. The device is then wheeled around the corner, I assume for the use of other customers who are out of my sight. I feel some disappointment for them as no doubt they have paid to consume the contents of this antiquated-musical-food-dispenser and no matter how splendid their eating experience may be, watching the roof elevate is worth a few franks of anyone's money.

That little episode may not strike you as massively entertaining but take it from me that after another day of watching alternate knees rising rhythmically towards my elbows for thirty miles, a 1970s rolling buffet with a bell-ringing elevating roof is a wondrous thing to behold!

As I near the end of my meal a different staff member walks over to what looks to be a butcher's block. This is not just any butcher's block but one of extreme substance and weight; its aged and rolling wooden surface is a good twelve inches thick, or as we are in France a good thirty centimetres. The block is desk height, mounted on sturdy wooden legs, and I guess five feet long. At one end a pile of dainty oval wicker baskets are stacked one inside the other; there are around twenty baskets in all. At the opposite end of the block – the business end, as it were – a long, thin, metal trough is suspended just below the thick wooden surface. Between these two points rests a most fearsome cleaver, its heavy-duty blade more than capable of instantly dispatching man or beast. I am somewhat nervous as to the purpose of the device as this is the land of the despatching instrument, after all. The cleaver is fitted with a long wooden handle, and end to end, from the tip of its well-used handle to the far end of the metal blade the cleaver must be four feet long if it's an inch. The far end of the blade has a circular hole through which a substantial metal rod passes; the metal rod anchors the blade to the thick wooden base while allowing it to pivot in a chopping action as required.

I am aghast that in these modern risk-averse times the operator is not dressed in full protective clothing. In England chainmail gloves, a suitably visored helmet, and probably a dayglow smock would be the order of the day. On second thoughts this is France after all, so maybe not. The operator leaves the machine unattended, *(Mon dieu, quelle riske!)* and disappears into the kitchen via swinging saloon doors. Then I realise they are probably going to return with some unfortunate small victim. Naturally, I'm very glad that I've finished eating. Feathered or furry and cute would be my guess. A few minutes later the waitress returns cradling something rather larger than I was expecting in her arms. The motionless victim is concealed, quivering I would think, under a sheet of red and white gingham material. I imagine I am not alone in being on tenterhooks that some unfortunate *lapin* has just been separated from its cosy warren and its furry mates. I cannot be sure that it is a rabbit, of course, and it's entirely possible that some other unpleasant spectacle is about to unfold. Naturally, I take a substantial glug of wine so that I am suitably fortified for whatever is about to follow.

I wish I was sitting further away. I've almost got a front-row seat, for goodness' sake. So I take another glug of wine, top up my glass, and I'm about as braced as I can be for the horror story about to unfold. I'm expecting the speedy if unfortunate demise of some helpless local fauna, and I know that without question I will feel very squeamish whenever the *coup de grâce* is finally delivered. Frogs, perhaps, fresh from the canal. Oh no, I do hope not. I like frogs.

A few minutes later, somewhat to my surprise and very much to my relief, the device is put to use and I observe nothing more menacing than a baguette being portioned, albeit by a slicer of industrial proportions.

Meal and entertainment concluded, I finish writing my notes by recording that I have pedalled for three hours and fifty-one minutes and I am now thirty miles further south from last night's campsite. Surprisingly, I think, not a single vineyard has been seen along the whole of the one hundred and twenty miles I have cycled with the Canal de Bourgogne by my side.

The final sentence of the day in my spiral notebook records for posterity that my time in the restaurant, and for the enjoyment of two beers, a Greek pizza, and some good old-fashioned music-hall-type entertainment cost me just over fifteen euros.

It is dark by the time I return to the campsite where I crank up the wind-up torch so I can sort out my sleeping bag. Minutes later I crawl inside and fall asleep wondering if tomorrow's weather forecast will indeed bring the long overdue rain.

# Week Three

*Day 15 – Friday 30ᵗʰ April*

*Departments of Côte-d' Or and Saône-et-Loire: From Pouilly-en-Auxois to Chalon-sur-Saône*

I am startled by the sound of wind-driven rain as it batters my flimsy home. This is not the gentle wake-up call I would have found acceptable. Outside, Friday 30ᵗʰ has heralded its arrival in no uncertain fashion. Inside, my tent is notably cooler than it's been on recent mornings. I listen to the unwelcome noises that surround me while trying to estimate the ferocity of the rain without actually seeing it. It won't surprise you that I can't muster any enthusiasm for disturbing my snug sleeping bag just so I can move forward enough to unzip the door and stick my head outside into what sounds like a maelstrom. Instead, from the warmth and comfort of my sleeping bag, I look up at the tent roof while contemplating the slim hope that the rain has actually stopped and the noise is simply water being blown down from the overhead trees against the tent fabric. Unfortunately, having only half the facts will never sort out this quandary so I bow to the inevitable, crawl halfway out of the sleeping bag and unzip the tent door.

Teeming rain is the mesmerising sight before me. Proverbial stair-rods home in on the large areas of surface water that have appeared over my grassy surroundings overnight. I'm transfixed by the sight of dome-shaped bubbles drifting across the surface of a large puddle that now forms a large wind-rippled doormat at the entrance to the tent. I can't work out if the cloud is very low or if it's just foggy outside, either way I can't see very far. Some of the outside air sneaks into the tent down the side of my face. It may feel much colder than yesterday but that it doesn't alter the fact that it's now decision time. This morning the weather may be uninviting but what's the point in spending the whole day in the tent just to keep dry, I would find that excruciatingly tedious even if there was enough room to swing a cat, which there is not. It's more likely that if I decide to stay here, I will end up walking into town just to alleviate the boredom. So, if I am going to get wet, I might as well be properly wet and the best way to do that is to man up (can we still say that?) I need to get on that bike, and head for Pouilly-en-Auxois, anyway, who knows, the rain may stop, or is that just being ridiculous?

Languishing in my sleeping bag for a few extra minutes gives me a bit of time to enjoy the last of its warmth. I use the time to work out the best sequence to pack my possessions as I need to keep everything that really matters as dry as possible. Once I have a plan, I get dressed at pace to retain body heat. Kneeling down on the ground sheet is the best way to roll up the still-warm sleeping bag, but it is very dull in the tent and my haste backfires in the half-light when the material becomes stuck in the zip. Even with help from my torch I cannot release the jammed zip so I give up on it for now and stow the bag in its compression sack. I can deal with it later. Once both panniers are packed, I double check the waterproof inserts are folded over tightly. Next I pull over the yellow rain covers, making sure they are a snug fit. Then, the panniers are clipped onto the bike and the tent is stacked in its usual position on top of the bike rack along with the other small bags.

I have a quick 'stand-up' breakfast of water and Breton shortbread sheltering against the trunk of a large tree. I have yet to try cycling in the rain wearing all my extra layers of clothing but today is a day that demands it, so I put on my Gore-Tex jacket, Gore-Tex shoes, and finally the waterproof overtrousers. Fortunately all my wet-weather clothing is very loose fitting so I should be able to pedal unhindered by clothes that cling. That's the hope, anyway.

The world is a still and silent place as I cycle away from last night's pitch and into a rural landscape largely hidden from view under a shroud of fog and low cloud. The rain continues to fall steadily and I shiver involuntarily. Not surprisingly I am the only person out and about on this opaque and dreary morning. It takes me a while to wake up to the fact that sometime in the last hour the wind has stopped completely, that's a bonus!

The small lizard that scurries between the wet rocks at the side of the road is unaware that it is the highlight of the first few miles. Initially I am surprised by the sight of the reptile but on reflection, had today been sunny and warm the little creature would not have seemed at all out of place. A mile further on, a lone donkey stands motionless at the edge of its field; its head is down as the stair-rods of rain give us both a good soaking. The animal has a forlorn expression on its face and I expect that I look exactly the same.

Beyond the town of Pouilly I join the towpath again and resume my encounters with herons and a lone jay that flies towards me from the densely wooded embankment on the far side of the canal. A couple of miles on and I spot a V-shaped wake of something swimming; it is an animal rather than a duck and far larger than a water vole, so on the off chance that the creature may not have spotted me I get off and push the bike stealthily.

A coypu! What a privilege, but only a brief one because as soon as the animal senses me it glides silently under the water and disappears out of sight. I'm in no rush so after laying the bike down on the grass embankment, I stand back from the canal and use the hedge for shelter from the rain. I wait a good fifteen minutes for the mammal to reappear but unfortunately it doesn't oblige. Here the banks of the canal are edged with thick undergrowth; there are endless places for creatures to hide. I'd like to think the coypu has found such as place and is now watching me, watching it, watching me!

Pedalling in heavy rain isn't so bad, really; 'once you are wet, you are wet' about sums it up, although to be fair the waterproofs are doing a pretty good job. After ten miles of towpath cycling on this wet and foggy morning my reward is the sight of a very pretty cottage next to the canal. Like most lock-keepers' dwellings, this one is a single-storey building of very modest proportions. The little house has walls painted cream and burgundy paint for the porch, front door, and shutters. On the loose gravel under the two front windows of the cottage rests a large selection of cast-iron pans and stoves; the ironmongery all looks freshy painted in gloss black and is being used to display plants. Everything is orderly and smart and looks very splendid indeed, even on a morning as overcast and gloomy as today. But this little building stands out from the many other lock-keepers' cottages I've passed because its outer walls are smothered, quite literally, with old tools. A vast quantity of bygone implements, all restored and painted black, are attached to the walls to create a fascinating vertical display of museum quality and interest. There are sickles and bowsaws, tongs and hammers from a forge, I can see hand tools such as augers and chisels, a few pliers, some tinsnips, various stonemasons' hammers, a large jack plane, several horseshoes, the list could go on for there must be well over a hundred items on display.

Above the burgundy front door a large cast-iron name plate reads '*Ese-du-Grand-Pre*'. Above the name is a number four, and between the number and the eaves of the cottage is a sundial; wall mounted, naturally.

Fifty or so yards beyond the cottage the canal is serviced by a lock gate where the same industrious effort and imaginative skill has been used to brighten up the place. Trios of barrels, all smartly painted and stacked on the verge, two for the base and a third on top. Painted metal urns and stoneware pots sit next to the lock gates, indeed everywhere I turn artistic flair and hard work are on show, a labour of love and dedication if ever I saw one. I hope that whoever created this special place receives the praise deserved, they have improved my day immeasurably and added much interest to an otherwise run-of-the-mill place. I leave with a smile on my face, like most others who pass this way I expect.

As I cycle away from the heavy wooden lock gates the canal immediately opens into a wide basin, which is home to several motor cruisers. A few restored barges are moored to the bank and two other barges are waiting mid-canal to enter the lock. One of these vessels, the *Tigre d'Or*, is very striking with its immaculate and shiny black hull, spotless white wheelhouse, and polished chrome fittings. Clearly once used to transport goods the barge is now a much-cared-for home that shouts Art Deco with its black and silver paint, its geometric wheel house, and its clean-cut lines. *(I learn later that the* Tigre d'Or *series of boats was built in the Netherlands by Amels to a highly acclaimed design by one Terrence Disdale.)*

Leaving the midstream vessels to continue their travels I cycle clear of the canal basin and beyond the row of trees that flank the canal for the next half mile. A combination of low cloud, thick fog, and trees hide the view to my left for some miles until the vista opens out suddenly and I am surprised to discover that the canal is actually following a contour around the hillside and running high above the valley floor. It looks somewhat out of place at this elevation and to be honest it feels rather strange to be pedalling on a towpath hundreds of feet higher than the valley below. Eventually the cloud fragments and lifts in places, and as it does so a pleasing patchwork of fields is revealed in the countryside below, while on the higher ground a distant chateau commands the far side of the valley. Whisps of feathery white cloud contrast with the dark sky behind the chateau, making the grand building look very atmospheric. Ahead of me I can just about make out the shape of a range of hills a few miles to the south. The lower slopes are swathed in haze and hints of woodland but the hilltops are completely hidden by low cloud. I assume it is the Morvan mountains that I'm looking at. The range once formed a northerly extension to the much higher and once-volcanic *Massif Central*.

The Morvan Hills are composed of granite and basalt and I expect them to test me more than anything so far. Cycling beside the

Burgundy canal has been a wonderful experience that has provided me with a great deal of interest, but the end of our journey together has now been reached, as I have finally decided against staying with the towpath to Dijon (route one, you may recall), in preference to setting off over the hills. Coincidentally, a quick glance at the cyclometer shows that to this exact point I have pedalled precisely five hundred miles since I left Devon – time for an understated self-gratulatory *'bon courage'* perhaps? The heavier rain has eased, at least for now, which is a relief as the waterproof overtrousers I have worn since breakfast are simply too hot to wear now. Uncomfortable waterproofs, the sudden improvement in the weather, and the approach of hills convince me that it is time to change into shorts for the uphill stretch ahead.

With the canal behind me and winding its way gently to Dijon I swap the towpath for a quiet country road that is delightful to cycle along as it meanders through the forested lower slopes of the Morvan Hills. There is no wind here amongst the trees and the rain has stopped. Every now and then I am showered by a windblown cascade of water droplets from the ceiling of overhanging trees – an occasional light dousing down just to keep me on my toes, I fancy. It is surprisingly dark here in the woodland where low cloud and fog hang in the air; tall trees close in on me from all sides, silence envelops the forest, and although I know it will sound silly, if I stop and think about it this forest is an eerie and foreboding place to be.

Having rounded a foggy corner, bold white chevrons painted onto the road surface give me fair warning of the steep gradient ahead, while to my left sturdy, galvanised crash barriers edge the road. Dense forest obscures most of the view beyond the barriers but occasionally a gap appears that allows me to peer into the valley far below. It surprises me just how much altitude I have gained in only a few miles. To the south, the summits of larger mountains are hidden by angry pewter-coloured clouds; beyond these higher summits ominous dark vertical slashes streak the sky, warning me of heavy rain ahead.

My progress up the hill is steady and slow and manageable for a while but then the gradient of the narrow road becomes even steeper and I am forced to stand up on the pedals and lean into the hill. Shifting my centre of gravity forward certainly helps me power the bike, but only until the road becomes steeper, forcing me to go even slower. Eventually momentum is lost and I am reduced to crawling, at which point I can no longer stop the front wheel from zig-zagging or prevent the instability that comes with it. As I expected it would, the ascent beats my stubbornness to pedal to the top and I have no choice but to get off the bike and admit defeat. This inevitable outcome is probably just as well as my heart rate and breathing have increased exponentially.

Yet more chevrons on the wet tarmac, painted closer together now. A challenging road ahead, it seems.

A paltry twelve miles is all I have managed so far today. Two hours is the time it takes me to push the bike the next three miles; shoving the bike uphill is hard going and by the time I get back on the saddle the torrential rain has returned. Maybe it doesn't matter anymore as I am completely soaked, bare legs and all, but oh how the rain is coming down. The cloud is much thicker now, a real pea-souper as they used to say and I feel forced to put on reflective clothing even though traffic is non-existent. Now that I think about it, I have seen absolutely no cars today. I know this is a back-of-beyond sort of place but not one human, that's a bit odd. Has something happened? Front and rear LED lights are set to flashing mode to make me more visible should a car appear out of the gloom. I reckon I've done all I can to make myself safe: Red Gore-Tex jacket, yellow fluorescent tabard, yellow pannier covers, red cycle helmet, and flashing lights – I am lit up like a Christmas tree, and nobody would want to drive into a Christmas tree, would they?

I don't want to bleat on but right now I am drenched, I am truly drenched! The rain has seeped inside my jacket and from there it has leeched into every part of my clothing. My torso is wet and below my waist absolutely everything is soaked – socks, underwear, legs, inside my shoes, the lot. Still, if I can't take a joke and all that! An unexpected highlight occurs when a pair of dim yellow headlights emerge from the heavy rain and the small car behind them drives cautiously down the hill. Its wheels leave a minor wake as they drive towards me through the rainwater that flows down the tarmac.

Another thirty minutes and I come to the summit, indicated by a noticeboard, which is just as well because without the wooden sign I would have absolutely no idea if the summit was yards or miles away thanks to the low cloud that's swirling between the trees and all around me. Right now, I am pleased, in fact I am extraordinarily pleased to have made it to the top and a mild euphoria starts to creep upon me until it crosses my mind that this 'summit' may turn out to be just the first of many. The weather deprives me of the panoramic view promised on the map but I don't really care about the view, in fact I don't care a jot, and I don't care because I am hungry and I am exceedingly wet. Not only that, but when I think about it, it is an affront to common decency that the rain should dare to pervade my whole body. It is exactly at moments such as this that I really wish my luggage contained that elixir of all ills: a hipflask of Islay malt whisky, 'Laphroaig Select' ideally, which, had a glug been available, would have given me an instant blast of inner warmth with its glorious taste, all smoky and peaty and aromatic, but this hilltop is no place for fantasy.

Given my sodden and uncomfortable bodily state it would be entirely reasonable for me to be downbeat here at the summit. Yes, I am jaded because I am soaked through, but I am not downbeat, not a bit of if it even if I sound a bit that way. In fact I am cheered by the heady anticipation that comes with knowing I am about to reap the reward that all hills eventually gift the cyclist: From this summit I can freewheel downhill in whichever direction I choose, and if my map is anything to go by a run of five or six miles of effortless pleasure lies ahead. But here's the rub: after being rained on from above for most of today, I know that going faster will not necessarily be the best idea; any increase in downhill speed will be matched by a comparable increase in the volume of water thrown up at me from the front tyre from the road surface. Do I care? Absolutely not.

Setting off to freewheel from the top of the Morvan is not quite like pushing off down the Cresta run, I'll grant you, but the start of my downhill ride is not without its excitement as the heavy rain that runs from my helmet travels down my forehead and into my eyes. My visibility is hampered so much that I am forced to use the brakes to restrict the bike to no more than fifteen miles an hour on the straight and very much less going around bends.

It may sound a bit far-fetched but the truth is that this extraordinary deluge of rain has transformed my downhill journey through the woods into something quite magical. On my right pulpits of rock emerge from the misty treescape like buttresses holding back the forest. In places the rocks reach right down to the edge of the road. Water tumbles out of every crevice and the little cascades gather together and form mini waterfalls; in turn these congregate to create streams that cross the road before tumbling joyfully under the crash barrier on their frantic way to the valley below. But water is world-class when it comes to finding options and while some of it takes the direct route to the valley floor another stream bubbles and foams along a deep natural gulley at the side of the road just to keep me company for a while.

This misty, soaking wet, and atmospheric forest is a truly exhilarating sight right now and as much as sunny weather would be pleasant, I wouldn't swap the opportunity to experience the forest as it is now for anything. Mysterious, raw, sinister, and dramatic, yet beautiful and enchanting at the same time. This is a place to enjoy, not a place to rush through; surely this is one of the best shows that nature can put on. And if all this were not enough, just for good measure, the impetuous gurgling stream to my right appears to be challenging me to a race as we match each other pace for pace down the hill. Suddenly a small clearing in the forest to my left permits me a glimpse of the meadowland far below and at this exact moment a single shaft of sunlight hits the valley floor and illuminates the farmsteads hundreds of feet below. What a location this is on a day such as today.

In benign weather this is probably just another very pretty place, but today, with the roadside rock buttresses flowing with cascades of water, and the battalions of trees peering at me through the mist, it really is quite fantastic, and just when I thought the scene could get no better, a brilliant sunbeam appears like a theatre spotlight. Who would have thought that a bright patch of grass with its miniature farmstead on the valley floor would be the act that steals the show?

Slowly but surely the rain eases, water no longer runs into my eyes, my speed picks up because I can see properly, and soon mile after mile just whizzes along. Pedalling feels effortless, even in wet clothing, so I press on through lunchtime to make up lost time until I reach the beautiful town of Beaune. Beaune, the wine capital of Burgundy, is a delightful small city that our family came upon some years ago. We spent an interesting day here and visited the *Hospices de Beaune*, also known as Hotel Dieu, which is a wonderfully preserved hospital dating to 1443, originally built to treat the many casualties of the Hundred Years War between England and France. The Hotel Dieu is a stunning example of Northern Renaissance architecture with its half-timbered galleries and an astonishingly artistic roof covered in tiles laid in the ornate, colourful, and patterned style so typical of this part of eastern France. Nowadays the Hotel Dieu functions day to day as a museum, but once a year, every year since the mid-1800s, in fact, the building hosts a prestigious three-day wine auction.

I take lunch sat in the drizzle, enjoying the damp comfort offered by a wooden bench with a view of the Hotel Dieu Museum. Once refuelled I set off with thirty miles already under my belt. I'm not entirely sure how so many miles were clocked up after such a slow start but I'll take it anyway. Thirty miles in the bag is a great way to start the afternoon and the distance done encourages me to have a go at putting in a bit of a shift this afternoon.

I depart Beaune at its southwest corner through the town park where smart tourist signs point me towards Pommard. Pommard is a village three miles from Beaune along the *Voie-des-Vignes*. The 'Way of the Wines' is a dedicated cycle route that makes use of a network of tracks that weave their narrow way between the vineyards. Today these ancient rustic lanes are still used by vintners and grape pickers, as they have been for centuries.

The *Voie-des-Vignes* runs from Beaune to the village of Santeney and along the way it offers wine buffs the opportunity to stop at some of the great vineyards that are centred on the highly acclaimed wine-producing villages of Meursault and Puligny-Montrachet.

The interconnected lanes of the *Voie-des-Vignes* undulate and meander, but for me at least they create a haphazard and confusing route. My progress is indirect and disappointingly slow because I have to stop at every intersection to decide which of several lanes I need to follow. Before I've even got into my swing vigorous rain returns and blurs what, until a few minutes ago, was a clear view of the vineyards surrounding me. I press on for another thirty minutes in the downpour, but with navigation nearly impossible and getting wetter by the minute my heart is no longer in it. It won't surprise you that I decide to cut my losses and leave the narrow lanes, so I can backtrack to the main road. The town of Chalon-sur-Saône is firmly in my sights for tonight. Arriving there will make today another fifty-miler, the first one for some time. It will be pleasing to have another big day in the bag at the end of today.

The main road from Beaune to Chalon-sur-Saône is by some margin the least cycle-friendly road I have travelled on since leaving Calais. The D19 is a four-lane dual carriageway; put simply it is a horror story waiting to happen. It's raining hard (of course it is) and there is a high volume of traffic. Great stretches of surface water lie everywhere and I am not in the least bit comfortable with what faces me for the next couple of hours. I check my lights and set them to flashing for maximum visibility but that's about it by way of self-preservation. The trunk road runs parallel to, and three miles to the east of the *Autoroute du Soleil* motorway. Rather foolishly it's slipped my mind that not only is today Friday, the end of the working week, but it is also the start of a long holiday weekend across France. The D19 road is toll-free and it is the obvious alternative for anyone driving to the same tourist destinations that the nearby *'motorway to the sun'* funnels cars towards. Unsurprisingly the road I am on is the highway of choice for motorists not wishing to pay a hefty *péage* (toll).

The road has no hard shoulder so the bike and I hug the edge of the carriageway out of necessity, well, out of necessity and fear to be totally honest. In places the lip of the tarmac has crumbled away, which causes me to give more than a passing thought to the probable outcome should my front wheel catch some invisible rain-filled pothole and fling me and the bike in front of some passing lorry. Doubtless such an event would involve much inconvenience to other road users and several local authorities, to say nothing of the large pile of paperwork it would generate for the local gendarmerie. To be fair, most drivers are considerate and give me a wide berth, but occasionally a vehicle, and it is usually a lorry, drives far too close for comfort. Good fortune stays with me and although passing lorries cause the bike and me to tremble in unison, the only harm done to us is when we are engulfed in a billowing vortex of dirty spray, which is followed, a second or two later, by a buffeting wind that destabilises the bike as the slipstream hits us. It is most unnerving. On reflection exchanging the confusion of the deserted grape-pickers' tracks for this multi-lane highway may not be my finest decision, but I have made my choice and there is no alternative but to put my head down, press on for a couple of hours, and pretend the lorries are elsewhere.

I wouldn't have bet money on it whatsoever, but somehow I have avoided the hidden water-filled potholes and entered Chalon in one piece via the city's busy industrial and commercial sector. I am now in the department of Saône-et-Loire, and with a population of forty-five thousand Chalon-sur-Saône is the department's largest city. Because of its location on the river, Chalon-sur-Saône has been an important centre of population since Roman times. Two thousand years ago Chalon was situated on the Via Agrippa, that vast network of Roman roads built right across Gaul under the direction of Emperor Marcus Agrippa. Far be it for me to do Chalon or its proud residents a disservice, but as far as I can tell not very much has happened here for many centuries, although more recently Chalon-sur-Saône did become famous as the home of Nicephore Niepce who invented photography in the nineteenth century, or heliography as it was called back in the day.

By another stroke of absolute genius (one of several that I've had today, in case it's slipped your mind) I arrive in the city at rush hour. My primary task is to look out for campsite signs whilst at the same time remaining alert enough to avoid the traffic that is weaving all around me. My task of self-preservation is made far more challenging because the road funnels into a bottleneck the same shape and just as effective as any Victorian wicker fish trap. Here, high metal safety barriers have been erected on both sides of the carriageway, a lower one down the middle eliminates any chance of escape, and within minutes I find myself being carried along as part of a conveyor of slow-moving traffic. Somehow, I have ended up on a flyover where the four-lane road and all of its traffic have simply been squeezed together and elevated above the city. Surprisingly this proves a blessing in disguise because the traffic is now wedged together so firmly that it has been forced to a standstill. The result is that I am lost rather than vulnerable and lost; this is a good thing indeed because once again it is raining heavily and what little visibility is left at the end of the afternoon is reducing by the minute.

Vehicles crawl along within two feet of my left pannier while others are a similar distance ahead of me and behind. The nearside safety barrier is to my immediate right; in short, they have me surrounded. Late afternoon becomes evening prematurely with the arrival of a sinister black sky, which has rolled in above the city. My watch tells me it should still be daylight yet I am surrounded by car lights, bright red in front of me and white behind. The lights reflect on the wet road surface and catch the brief flashes of individual raindrops as they fall in their thousands from the ever-darkening sky looming above me. From my elevated position on the busy flyover, I can see shop displays and streetlights glowing in the busy city below and little cars scurrying through the town centre. It's a surreal sight when the time of day is taken into account as there could so easily be bright sunshine now.

Looking around me, I reckon that as long as traffic is nose to tail and creeping slowly to its destination I am pretty safe, nevertheless I know that I'm very insignificant and the drivers surrounding me are peering through swishing windscreen wipers at the smudged world beyond the glass. Let's just say that my situation is not an entirely comforting prospect.

At the back of my mind, but creeping to the front pretty speedily, let me say, is the thought that sooner or later this log jam of traffic will burst, and the hundreds of drivers stuck on the flyover with me are late and probably impatient. So I reckon I'm probably an even bet for coming out of this unscathed once the traffic starts to move again. In the meantime, from the comparative safety of the stationary Chalon log jam I settle back in the saddle and watch the illuminated raindrops falling all around me. Fortunately for me my good fortune holds fast and after another twenty minutes on the flyover (it seems longer) the road dips down and regains its position at ground level whereupon we cross the mighty River Saône, where it is no exaggeration to say that the bike and I both sigh in relief that we remain uncrumpled. Finding the campsite proves easy as it's located on the western bank of the river; not only that, the site is conveniently placed for a walk into the city should I feel up to it later.

Checking in is a speedy process and within minutes I set about seeking out a suitable pitch. Generally, this is a simple enough task but here it takes far longer than usual as most pitches have a compact gravel base. Unforgiving solid surfaces may be ideal for motorhomes and caravans but like anyone else in a tent I don't want stones protruding through the groundsheet. Eventually I find a pitch with less gravel than most and some threadbare grass. The almost impenetrable ground forces me to get angry with the tent pegs, which end up slightly bent. Giving the pegs a healthy thump was foolish of me because they are now barely secure enough to withstand the guy rope tension. I'll just have to trust to luck and hope it's not windy overnight.

After unloading the bike, I unroll the tent only to discover water inside; a good couple of pints are sloshing around on top of the sewn-in groundsheet that forms my combined living room and bedroom floor. Let's just say it is not really what I want to see but it is hardly a disaster and I can sort it out later. I know there has been a great deal of rain today but it still surprises me just how much has managed to find its way into my little home. The sight reinforces my lifelong belief that rain is sneaky stuff that should never be trusted. Yes, the rolled-up tent has been exposed to all weathers on top of the bike rack since this morning but it's been completely encased in its nylon bag, which I thought was fully waterproof until now. Anyway, apparently it is not and the rain has won the day. Fortunately, when cycling high on the flyover I noticed a Carrefour supermarket below; it cannot be too far from here so it's back on the bike with a plan in mind.

Carrefour does me proud and I find all I am seeking and more besides, and soon I am cycling back to the tent armed with four packets of tomato soup, a large baguette, some black-bean sauce, a packet of fruit pastries that are peach, I think, and another that may prove to be raspberry. The pastries have reached the last day of their 'best-before' date and are on an offer that simply cannot be refused, so I have come away with twenty pastries in total for just a few euros. It would have been rude not to scoop them up, don't you think? Oh! And I also bought the item I actually went for – a large, and I mean 'wash your very large car' large, sponge!

I am back by seven. The rain has stopped, and the sponge works a treat when I put it to use emptying the bilges of my tent. I knew that a few years' service in Her Majesty's Royal Navy would come in handy one day. Before eating I carry my sleeping bag and a few bike tools to the campsite laundry room where I utilise the counter as a makeshift bench: the sleeping bag is laid out for repair but unfortunately try as I might I am unable to dislodge the material I jammed in the zip this morning. I end up having to cut the fabric free before patching up the cut section with gaffer tape. Finally I give the zip a bit of poke with a small screwdriver to release the bits of chewed-up sleeping bag. It is all highly skilled stuff, as you can tell, but however 'Heath Robinson' my efforts may sound to you, after some attention the zip functions perfectly smoothly for three-quarters of its length. Unfortunately, after this point further movement is halted by the taped repair. I reckon the sleeping bag will zip up to a point just above my elbows from now on. Ideal! Well, almost.

While strolling back to the tent from my makeshift shed, I meet a Dutch couple staying in a nearby caravan. They walk over to me and enquire if I was the person they had seen crossing the flyover on a bicycle during the storm. I confirmed that I am indeed that very cyclist (while hoping I hadn't nearly caused them to have a collision, of course), they then surprised me by handing me a few cold beers. As far as I can tell this kind gesture is because although they don't know me from Adam, they are relieved and surprised that I survived the flyover experience. That's three of us, then. The alcohol is Alfa Edal Pils which is brewed in their home town of Arnhem; they hand me a plastic cup and even offer me food in their caravan. What thoughtful and kind people. I am very tempted at the prospect of company for the evening but feel that I should make my excuses as I am very wet and I can't risk my clothes making their caravan seats damp. They understand my predicament and invite me to knock on their door at any time should I need anything.

While I am wandering back to my tent carrying the bodged sleeping bag, the bike tools and the beer, the memory of reading Kate Adie's book *The Kindness of Strangers* comes to mind. The thought makes me reflect on the sensationalised gloom we are fed every day in news reports, and yet when you think about it, whatever else may be going on, there is so much to be cheerful about in the world, and my new acquaintances from the Netherlands prove the point wonderfully.

My evening meal is the antithesis of fine dining and should any passing Frenchman observe, I will have gone a long way to confirming the widely held French belief that *Les Rosbifs* (the British) are philistines when it comes to feeding themselves. What is it they say? *'The British eat to live and the French live to eat'*. Anyway, it's probably better that you judge for yourself. My main course is the family can of black-bean sauce, heated up I should point out, and used as a dip for my baguette. That's it. I told you it wasn't fancy. Dessert on the other hand is no less than a dozen little French pastries. It is a speedy meal, it is tasty, and it is filling, not only that but it hits the spot and creates very little washing up. How can anyone possibly need more?

After my meal is finished I reflect back over today's route, and I would like to share with you that I am actually quite happy with the distance I have covered since this morning, and I am pleased with overcoming the largest hills so far. Not only that, but I have endured some pretty appalling weather on the way, to say nothing of perilous encounters with traffic, firstly on the trunk road and then on the flyover. And given all this, the bike has carried me and the luggage for fifty-one miles today; in return I've pushed it for at least three miles since we left Pouilly this morning. Another day on the bike has ended, my fourteenth in France, thirteen dry days and one very wet. I would certainly have settled for that when I left England.

*1 – Leaving our house in North Devon.*

THE ADVENTURER WITHIN

*2 – Leaving the white cliffs of Dover & England behind.*

*3 – When in Rome! The viewpoint near Campagne-des-Guines.*

4 – *Traditional boulangerie in the village of Licques.*

5 – *Language mix-up with the motorcyclist near Devres.*

*6 – 6-egg omelette breakfast at Montreuil.*

*7 – British War Grave cemetery at Wavans, near the Somme.*

*8 – Major Byford-McCudden VC, DSO & Bar, MC & Bar, MM.*

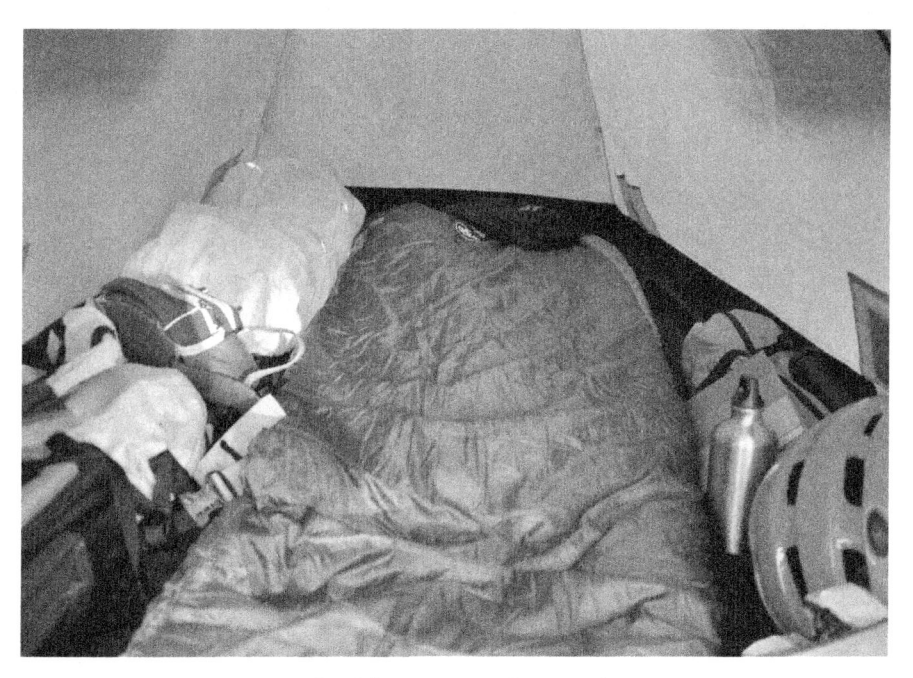

*9 – No room to swing a cat!*

*10 – Tent with a view at Ciry-Salsogne.*

DAVID PAUL ELLIOTT

*11 – Traffic chaos at Chateau-Thierry.*

*12 – The hilarious roundabout parade near Provins.*

*13 - Track along the banks of the Armançon.*

DAVID PAUL ELLIOTT

*14 – Refreshments on the Canal de Bourgogne towpath.*

*15 – Lunch at Tonnerre, Yonne.*

THE ADVENTURER WITHIN

*16 – The Tonnerre Fosse.*

*17 – Pretty cottages, Armançon River, Tonnerre.*

*18 – Lock-keeper's cottage near Pouilly-en-Auxois. Côte-d'Or.*

*19 – I've cracked 500 miles, now that's a surprise!*

THE ADVENTURER WITHIN

*20 – Deluge on the Voie-des-Vignes, Burgundy.*

*21 – The first of several punctures at Chalon-sur-Saône.*

*22 – A new tyre at last.*

THE ADVENTURER WITHIN

*23 – The happy postman at Villars-les-Dombes.*

*24 – Using my fire-hazard porch at Meyrieu-les-Étangs.*

*25 – Dry, Damp, Wet or Soaking, let's sort it out.*

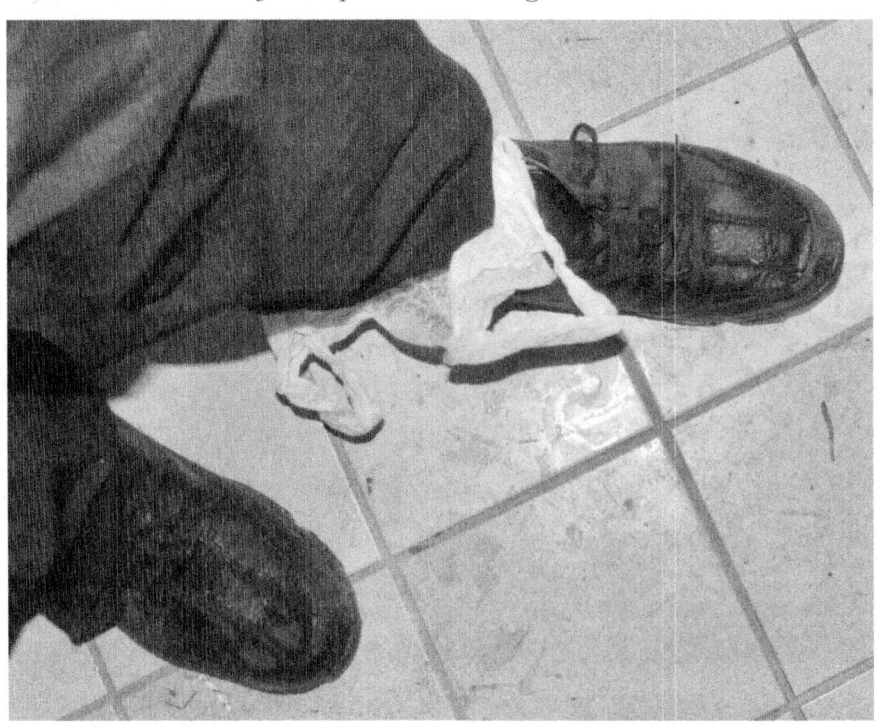

*26 - Waterproof feet – but not for the fashion conscious.*

*27 – Unseasonally cold for May, near Hauterives, Provence.*

*28 – Colourful abstract house.*

29 – *The whip snake in Auvergne-Rhône-Alps.*

30 – *Prancing horse outside the city of Romans, Isère.*

*31 – The café in Grignan after the festivities.*

*32 – Arc de Triomphe d'Orange, Vaucluse.*

*33 – Le Pont des Armenières en route to Barthelasse Island, Avignon.*

THE ADVENTURER WITHIN

*34 – The Papal Palais in Avignon.*

*35 – The drawbridge near Arles as painted by Van Gogh.*

*36 – Daudet's Windmill of 'Master Cornille's Secret' fame.*

THE ADVENTURER WITHIN

*37 – A well-earned beer at Fontvieille.*

*38 – Shortly after my beer in Fontvieille I was caught out in a surprise delute as I returned to Arles.*

*39 – The N113 expressway – not a place for bicycles or the feint hearted.*

*40 – A formation of flamingos in the Camargue.*

THE ADVENTURER WITHIN

*41 – St Maries-de-la-Mer – I've actually arrived.*

*42 – The sweet taste of success – My coast-to-coast reward.*

DAVID PAUL ELLIOTT

*43 – Broken spokes – the least of my disintegrating bike's problems.*

THE ADVENTURER WITHIN

*44 – The energetic band outside the church in St Maries-de-la-Mer.*

DAVID PAUL ELLIOTT

*45 – Time to write up my notes before a celebratory meal.*

THE ADVENTURER WITHIN

*46 – My transport to England – The European Bike Express.*

*47 – The return ferry to Dover and the last leg.*

*48 – Buckingham Palace – don't camp outside my place.*

# Day 16 – Saturday 1st May

## Department of Saône-et-Loire:

## From Chalon-sur-Saône to absolutely nowhere!

Forget the hard gravel camping surfaces, Chalon-sur-Saône campsite leaves me with very favourable impressions as it has provided me with the best shower facilities so far, and the site has a small but very pleasant restaurant with seating for around forty and a view over the River Saône. A sizeable shipping facility on the opposite side of the river with large gantry cranes for loading and unloading vessels is a surprise to see so far inland, and although it's clearly industrial it's an interesting rather than unsightly outlook. Upstream from the campsite and the shipyard is the impressive Pont de Bourgogne bridge, which spans the Saône. Perhaps it would have been interesting to explore the city today but on balance it seems prudent to press on. After all, an overcast day is better used for cycling than exploring.

I set off in good time, very probably spurred on by yesterday's fifty-four-mile effort. That said, I fancy a more leisurely time of it today. The weather may be overcast but it's also dry and cool and that sort of weather will do me very nicely indeed for a day on the bike. I've decided to take the proprietor's advice and follow the green tourist route through the vineyards just to the south of here rather than return to the busy trunk road that I used yesterday.

The city is almost deserted as I leave, which seems a bit odd as the holiday weekend has started and this is a tourist destination. Having said that, I am quite happy that I can just get on with finding my way out of the city without having to jostle with traffic and people.

The day starts like any other for the first fifteen minutes as I allow myself a bit of time to get into the rhythm of pedalling. Unexpectedly, my steady and relaxing start is interrupted by a disturbingly loud crack from the bike. On inspection I discover not some mechanical failure to the metal, which is what it sounded like, but simply a puncture. Not a great way to start the day, but the puncture's occurred close to a bus shelter, which, as there's nobody around, I utilise as a temporary workshop. Its wooden lath seat makes the perfect bench for me to set about sorting the bike out. Unfortunately, it is the rear tyre that has punctured so I have to unload the tent, the panniers, and the canoe bags in order to disengage the chain from the derailleur gears just so that I can remove the back wheel. The tyre has covered over five hundred miles of travel, heavily laden travel at that, so I can't complain about a puncture and twenty-five minutes later the repair is completed, the bike is reloaded, the bus shelter is reinstated to its original purpose, and I can set off once more to find the green route out of town.

Three-quarters of a mile further into today's journey and the bike suffers a relapse when it has another puncture; the same wheel again, which necessitates unloading the bike for a second time. Irritating? More than a bit irritating, if I am honest. I know it's only a bit of time that I've lost and it's not a big problem as such, but one puncture a day should be more than enough for anyone, don't you think? The second puncture occurs near the main railway station and conveniently close to a seat, which I utilise as a bench once I have unloaded the luggage and flipped the bike upside-down for repair. Chain and gears are disengaged, tyre removed, innertube out, hole located and fixed, test, re-test, and reassemble. Another repair, another reload, and I'm once again ready to head south, out of the city.

A hundred yards on I notice a signpost that points me towards the green cycle route – excellent! Well, it would have been except I have just had my third puncture of the morning and I am still less than three miles from the campsite. Checking the rear tyre reveals a rupture in its wall. The clearly visible split is about half an inch long; this is a new and far more challenging turn of events. Perhaps the rubber wall has been weakened by whatever caused the first two punctures. A puncture to the innertube can be easily fixed but a split tyre will be far trickier. I ponder for some time about just how to tackle it but in the end, I can think of nothing durable enough to prevent the innertube from protruding through the split under pressure and being pinched by the tyre wall into yet another puncture. Although it seems completely futile, I have a half-hearted attempt at mending the inside of the tyre wall by using a rubber innertube patch to reinforce the tyre lining. Once the glue holding the patch has set, I line the inside of the tyre with several layers of gaffer tape to provide extra strength and to spread the air pressure over a wider area of tyre wall surrounding the split. I put no money whatsoever on this working and once my bodge is done I replace the wheel and reload the bike. Instead of getting on the bike and pedalling it seems sensible to push the bike back towards the campsite, a test flight of my unconventional repair, as it were.

Fifteen minutes into my hike the tyre is again flat. This comes as no surprise but it gives me fair warning that I must push the bike slowly and carefully, making sure that I avoid uneven surfaces, kerbs, potholes and the like. Without the inflated tyre to cushion it the wheel rim now bears the full weight of the bike and its load and a replacement wheel may be difficult to find, and costly.

It is entirely possible that I am not wearing my happy face when I arrive back at the campsite. I secure the bike to some railings before walking into town looking for a bike shop that has a 700mm x 420mm tyre and a couple of new inner tubes. Ideally the tyre needs to be puncture resistant but not all are I was astounded to discover. Unfortunately I draw a blank at the various locations that the good-natured and helpful people of Chalon direct me to; it is a bank holiday weekend, after all, and France has literally shut up shop – every one of them, it seems.

While walking back to the site I remember seeing a massive indoor shopping centre as I was cycling over the flyover yesterday evening. It's about a mile from here, I would guess, and certainly worth the effort of a stroll in the absence of anything more pressing to do. On reaching the complex I find several promising outlets but in keeping with everywhere else in the city they are all closed; rather unhelpfully not a single shop displays any indication of when they will reopen. All bike repair options are now exhausted so I wander back to the site, pay for a second night and put the tent up on exactly the same pitch as yesterday. I use the time to text home and write up my notes for the day so far.

In the great scheme of things an enforced day of rest is not a big deal, although I could do to sort the tyre out on Monday morning. If I can do that, I'll be in a position to set off by midday at the latest. Two spare days are factored into my plan for circumstances such as this so if I lose today, tomorrow, and then Monday morning I will still be only half a day behind schedule. I cannot risk another tyre failing so erring on the side of caution I decide it'll be prudent to buy two new tyres; one I will fit to the wheel, the other can be attached on top of my luggage with a bungee cord as an emergency spare.

Sunday the 16th of May must see me in Montpellier, no ifs, no buts, so I don't see that I have much choice but to eliminate the risk of losing another day on a tyre hunt.

I stroll towards Chalon just to pass some time when I come across an outdoor market. Unlike the rest of the city the market is filled with people. A very large pizza makes a tasty and impromptu lunch; it is large to the point of being unseemly but for six and a half euros it would have been wrong not to buy one. Perhaps it is a family size. Who cares? I was very hungry and it's disappeared now!

All told, I reckon I've walked eight to ten miles today since I wheeled the bike back to the campsite. I have been on my feet all day and the change of muscle use from cycling to walking is not appreciated by my body. I take the hint that my tender feet are giving me and return to the tent where I have a simply wonderful time repairing two inner tubes and sorting the rest out. The third is too far gone and has to be thrown away. Anyway, I now have two serviceable if repaired tubes as my safety net against future punctures. Today the bike and I have covered the not-so-grand total of four point six miles. *'Bon courage,'* as they say!

## Day 17 – Sunday 2nd May

### Department of Saône-et-Loire

### Chalon-sur-Saône

I walk out of the site by nine-thirty. Why? You may well ask; it is a Sunday, after all, and as you know I have a completely blank itinerary for today. Well, I have heard of a large out-of-town shopping area with several hypermarkets, so even though it is Sunday and a holiday weekend to boot surely it is worth a go. A long shot, perhaps, but maybe some mega supermarket will buck the trend and open up; maybe they will even sell bike tyres. This is the land of the Tour de France, for goodness' sake. Surely they can't all throw the towel in for a holiday weekend, what's the matter with them?

My walk to the shopping complex is a drab experience by any measure that fails to enthuse any part of me. This is because I am cold, it is a thoroughly miserable day, and ahead of me lies the inescapable prospect of another day and a half in a city I would rather move on from. I have places to go, don't they know?

As expected, the shopping complex is sterile and functional, like big shopping centres everywhere. The first thing that strikes me is the immense size of the car park; it looks absolutely vast. Nearly all of several thousand parking spaces are empty. This is not a good sign for someone hoping to make a purchase, but I have arrived early, and it is Sunday after all, so perhaps the stores have yet to open, and who knows, maybe the staff have parked out of sight and everything is about to open. A nice thought but I'm not convinced this place will be a hive of commercial activity anytime soon.

McDonald's, on the other hand, is putting on an admirable display of fortitude and capitalism. Good for them, I say. Staff are visible inside but the door is locked so I sit outside probably looking a tad forlorn, waiting for them to open, which they do at ten-thirty prompt. Whatever you think of McDonald's, they really do turn out a splendid cup of *café au lait* – tasty, large, and modestly priced at just one euro. Being the first out of the blocks, as it were, I have my choice of all the inside tables so I grab a first-class position with a picture window and a radiator: free warmth and a front-row seat for when the shopping mall erupts into a frenzy of purchasing. I doubt anyone could wish for more on a Sunday morning.

The *Chalon Journal* is kindly provided free for McDonald's customers so I have a crack at reading it. Sadly, too many large French words prevent me from gleaning much information. Nevertheless, an hour soon passes and at eleven-thirty, having been beaten into submission by the sight of the still-empty car park, I give up all hope of finding bike spares today.

Thankfully, Chalon remains dry under a dull overcast sky as I trudge my way back across the city via an island in the middle of the River Saône. Initially at least, the island doesn't meet my expectations, which were along the lines of *Île de la Cité* in Paris. Chalon's River Island fails to ooze the historical interest I'd hoped for until quite by chance, I come across the old quarter where a lively open market is in full swing. The streets are thronged with shoppers, displays of fruit and vegetables are piled high on the covered barrows used by the market traders. It's a vibrant and interesting place, which I depart from with some tomatoes, a few mushrooms, and a small onion. My somewhat desperate quest for a bike shop had been put to the back of my mind until a stallholder rekindles my hopes by suggesting that if I head toward Chalon's main railway station I will pass a specialist bike shop that opens every Sunday. Naturally, off I trot through the quiet streets of the city until half an hour later, eureka! A bike shop.

*Europe Velos* looks extensive and promising until I get closer and read the notice on the door, which explains that the shop is in fact closed every *Dimanche et Lundi*. My heart sinks because until this precise moment I had completely forgotten that many shops in France close on Mondays, bank holiday or not, by long-standing tradition. Tomorrow is Monday and a holiday Monday at that. Suddenly it seems to me that there is a very real probability that I will lose a third day's cycling, in which case I will have a day and a half to catch up on. After my initial concerns have subsided and I've made a few quick mental calculations, I'm reassured that if I cycle an extra five to ten miles each day between here and Montpellier, I can make up all the lost time and distance. Where there's a will, and all that. The quest for an elusive bicycle shop may have proved futile but I've given it my best shot and more besides, so I decide to spend the remainder of today at leisure. It's not really much of a decision, to be fair. What else can I do?

The main railway station is near here somewhere; it's bound to be open (or is it?) and a large bar of chocolate is entirely appropriate at any time of need and obviously this is such a time. The station and its shop are indeed open for business and an uncharacteristic rush of blood to the head causes me to forget the daily budget and spend three and a half euros on a *Sunday Times*, and, as it is now lunchtime, I lighten my wallet by a further six and a half euros for a toasted ham and cheese sandwich, a chocolate biscuit, and a coffee. Not bad, a decent lunch and a large wedge of reading matter for just ten euros. I'll take that. Not only that but I enjoy the luxury of a comfy seat in the café for the best part of two hours while I very much enjoy catching up on current affairs from Britain and around the planet.

Back at the site I set about separating the rear wheel from the forks, and then the chain from the derailleur system. Next, the tyre is removed from the wheel ready to take to the shop for repair first thing in the morning. While removing the wheel I discover a single broken spoke, which I remove to make sure the snapped metal doesn't cause me or the bike another problem. It's while kneeling on the grass beavering away at the bike that I notice the front of the tent, which should be a symmetrical dome shape, is bent at a distinctly jaunty angle. The front of the tent looks lopsided. How have I not noticed that until now?

The dome shape of the tent is created by two long fibreglass support rods that thread diagonally, corner to corner, through loops in the tent fabric. Once in position the fibreglass rods form the shape of an 'X', which, when viewed from above, is raised at the intersection of the two rods. This stretches the tent fabric into shape while leaving each of the four corners resting on the ground like feet. Each of the two rods is around ten feet long and constructed of six separate interlocking fibreglass sections. After a quick examination I discover that one of the fibreglass sections has snapped. Aside from strengthening the break with my trusty gaffer tape there is little to be done other than considering a splint of some sort if the tape isn't up to the job. Even lopsided, the tent is still igloo shaped, more or less, and the distortion shouldn't affect its waterproof integrity.

The entrance to my tent has a sort of micro porch, which remains distorted even after my tent pole repair, and although the porch only provides a few square feet of extra floor space I have found it to be the ideal place for cooking when it is raining. Now it's lopsided it's a bit smaller but it should still provide me with a place to cook as long as I'm extra cautious to ensure the cooker doesn't ignite the tent. To be fair this has always been a bit of a risk because even without the distortion less than a foot separates the nylon wall of the porch from the hot cooker. This modest 'safety' margin is a little less now.

Sunday the second of May ends in a glorious fashion with me using the offset little porch to cook a veggie omelette from six eggs (is that still veggie?) along with the tomatoes, mushrooms, and onion that I bought from the outdoor market. My pudding was going to be the chocolate from the railway station shop, and such extravagance would have been a fine end to the day, but I have just realised that forgot to buy some, which is a disappointment, to put it mildly. I blame being distracted by the cheese and ham toastie. Anyway, let's end an odd sort of a weekend on a positive note: Against the odds my porch cooking went off very well – *'sans incident'* as the locals would put it, and as nothing ignited there has been absolutely no need for the *Service d'Incendie* to be summonsed, which is a relief to everyone, especially me!

## Day 18 – Monday 3rd May

## Departments of Saône-et-Loire and Ain: From Chalon-sur-Saône to Pont-de-Vaux

I hoof it out of the campsite at a determined pace on what is a pleasant enough morning. I am carrying the damaged tyre, the rear wheel, and as always, the handlebar bag of my can't-afford-to-lose items. At the last minute I decided to take the wheel with me as it will save time if I can get the shop staff to fit the new tyre, if they do that, I will be absolutely certain that the replacement tyre is the correct size and that air doesn't escape before I leave the shop. The retail park is reached in quick order and I make the large Carrefour hypermarket my first port of call. *(Mon dieu, c'est ouvert!!)* Carrefour has an admirable array of bicycle parts and *'accessories'*. The tyre display is surprisingly large and very well stocked, but virtually all the tyres available are of the twenty-six-inch imperial size favoured in the UK. This strikes me as astonishing because as far as I know the 700mm tyre is favoured on the continent, as one would expect in the land of metric measurements.

So, having drawn a blank at Carrefour it is one down, three to go. Next, I visit *'Feuvent'*, a specialist tyre fitter. To be fair I know this place is a bit of a long shot as it is obvious from what's going on that they cater for cars and vans, and, as I soon discover, not tyres for push bikes, but it was worth a try. Two down, two to go. Decathlon and Intersport remain my potential saviours. Decathlon staff are very helpful indeed; they have a Michelin version of my tyre in stock so I buy two and an innertube *(chambre à air)*. I then pay an extra five euros to have the tyre fitted by them. Altogether I spend forty-seven euros and eighty cents, which by any measure punches a massive hole in my twenty euros a day budget. Anyway, needs must and I am very relieved that after marking time for over sixty hours here in Chalon everything is once again in order and I will be able to set off later this morning. *Magnifique!* The wheel is fixed and as I'm now in full-blown *'lets-crack-on-I've-got-places-to-go'* mode, I hot-step it back to the campsite to deconstruct the tent and pack up all my worldly possessions.

Two-and-a-bit days later than planned I bid my farewell to Chalon-sur-Saone along the D987 road, which exits the city in a southeasterly direction. I am relieved to say that the triple torment caused by the E15 motorway, the E608 dual carriageway, and the city ring road are all avoided this morning, as is the elevated flyover on which I made my precarious way into the city on Friday. Cycling clear of the city is still a bit of a challenge simply due to the volume of traffic. I guess the city is sparking back to life after the holiday break so it shouldn't be a surprise. The road out of town is well maintained and straight. This is not always a good thing as roads with a good surface and no bends can attract more than their fair share of speeding traffic. Today many of the vehicles, just as they did when I arrived here three days ago, pass much too close for comfort. Although pedalling on this busy road may not qualify as relaxing cycling it is far better than marking time waiting for repair shops to open. Six miles on and the bike and I are well clear of the built-up area; the speeding cars seem to be miles ahead now and I can breathe a sigh of relief that the bike and I can once again set a slow pace through the picturesque French countryside.

An umbrella of brooding low cloud hangs above me, dark grey and sullen; the clouds are at odds with a morning that has remained dry so far. Looking up, the realistic question seems not to be if it will rain, but when and how much.

The landscape south of the city is agrarian in all directions as far as the eye can see. In the far distance the horizon is hinted at by a thin horizontal line of olive green that sits between the beige farmland and the charcoal clouds. The line indicates a range of low mountains, I would guess. Next to the road barley grows; the stems are already over a foot tall, making the crops here notably more advanced than those I saw further north only last week. Two weeks ago, in Picardy and the Somme, the crops had yet to break the surface of the soil. Stalks of barley sway in waves as I cycle past, pushed and pulled by the breeze. The whiskered heads move in formation like a well-practised Mexican wave rippling from one side of the field to the other. It is a beautiful and mesmerising sight.

The first village I come to this morning is Ouroux-sur-Saône. Here the road I have followed for the last hour turns east leaving me to continue south on the D933 as it runs parallel to the Saône River for the next twelve miles to the village of Cuisery, which is reached and exited almost simultaneously because of its diminutive size.

As I leave Cuisery village I pass an ancient split-level farmhouse on my left. In such homes the ground floor accommodates animals and the family lives on the first floor above their livestock. Farmhouses of this design have been used for centuries but they are an increasingly rare sight in modern-day France. I like very much that some of the old traditional ways still cling on in out-of-the-way hamlets such as Cuisery. *'Grange maison'* or house-barn buildings such as this are still seen in the mountains of Basque northern Spain but this is the first such building that I have come across in France. It is early afternoon as I exchange the department of Saône-et-Loire for the department of Ain, and with it the larger and more mountainous region of Rhône-Alpes.

Doubtless encouraged to accumulate by the nearby mountains, the cloud has steadily increased over the last two hours and it now moves above me with frantic purpose. Solid dark grey flights of cloud scurry west to east in regimented order; it is as if they are sorting out their final military positioning before they deliver a substantial payload of rain. Perhaps they are picking a time for maximum effect. Someone somewhere is going to get very wet indeed pretty soon. Maybe they have me in their sights, unfinished business as it were.

My arrival in the region of Rhône-Alpes is heralded by the first chirping crickets that I have heard on the journey so far, and with this single sound, the threat of any deluge from above is instantly forgotten as visions of the sunny south of France come to mind, even though the real *Sud de la France* is still several hundred miles south of here.

Here, as on so many miles of my trip, agriculture predominates, and once again I find myself surrounded by undulating grasslands. Here the grass is being munched enthusiastically by cattle the colours of milk chocolate and Cornish cream; they seem to be the standard breed for this area, replacing the ubiquitous off-white Charolais that I saw further north. Tiny mustard flowers, bright and cheerful as ever, are generously scattered across the fields while the red splashes of poppies growing wild at the roadside stand out like happy floral beacons on this overcast and increasingly dark afternoon. A large dip in the landscape offers several miles of easy cycling as I pedal rhythmically through level open farmland that is dotted with small patches of mixed woodland. Occasionally I pass a garden-sized plot of land that has been cultivated with vines, but other than these occasional nods to human activity, people and buildings seem to have disappeared from the planet.

As I approach the River Reyssouze and the little town of Pont-de-Vaux, I spot a large bird of prey standing in a field only fifty yards from the road. Chunky, powerful, and larger than a buzzard, I pull over for a closer look and hopefully a photograph. Without warning two extremely large and aggressive dogs startle me; the animals have been concealed from my view by the impenetrable fir hedge that separates the road from a garden. My heart nearly leaps out of my chest when their heads suddenly appear, snarling and barking and drooling just feet away. My heart rate only subsides when I realise that the massive creatures are securely penned behind a high close-mesh metal fence. Their fearsome growling continues until both the raptor and I have been scared away. Both red and black kites flourish in southern France along with honey buzzards, and when the raptor takes to the air barely fifty feet from me I can see its dull white tail is spread out in a broad fan shape. Unfortunately other than realising it is not a kite I am none the wiser as to the species.

Pont-de-Vaux campsite is devoid of tents, neither are there any caravans or motorhomes. A single chalet appears to be occupied by a family, but otherwise I seem to be quite alone here; even the proprietor appears to have gone AWOL. Having pitched the tent I set off into town having been persuaded to do so by a sign that informs me that Ville de Pont-de-Vaux has a *Port de Plaisance*, or marina. The sign is illustrated with a detailed line-drawing that shows an appealing scene of some pleasure boats and a river, so I set out to discover the marina and what else the town has to offer. Pont-de-Vaux proves to be a small and pretty place where I come across half a dozen cabin cruisers and a few rowing boats secured to the bank of the canal, which links the town to the River Saône. Dozens of other boats are berthed in the adjoining marina.

A short distance beyond the marina several well-spaced anglers are dotted along the river bank. Each is using a wooden tackle box as a seat; they all look deep in concentration as they watch their rod tips and colourful floats with intensity. Other than the anglers there are few people here, even the travelling fair that has taken up residence in the town is not drawing the people in with its noisy and colourful charms. Perhaps it's too early in the day and this evening will be busier for them. In the meantime the fairground contributes colour and jolly music to the atmosphere of the town.

Back at the tent a packet of 'just add water' couscous is emptied into the saucepan-cum-bowl together with a large jar of Mexican chilli sauce. It is an odd meal that will win no plaudits, but you know what, it is hot and filling, which is all I ask for. Main course out of the way, my evening's dessert is a few of those very inexpensive chocolate mousse puddings, which the French seem to enjoy so much. Several generous swigs of wine conclude my feast. *Voila!* Refuelling is completed.

The last two hours of daylight are spent writing up my journal and finishing the wine. I bet you think I'm having a leisurely time of it, don't you? Well, you would hope so, wouldn't you, but restricted headroom means writing is done prone. This causes a bent neck, tender elbows, and after a while some difficulty in moving. Eventually the discomfort caused by being stationary in an awkward position for too long forces me to bend myself in half in order to exit the tent for some respite. Once outside, a few minutes of limb stretching reboots my circulation, after which I use my newfound mobility to check that the bike is secure. While I am at it, I check that the guy ropes are still taut and none of the tent pegs have worked loose.

It is almost dark now, the wind is picking up, and the air is warmer, much warmer than it was several hours ago, which is not what I would have expected. Change is in the air, as they say. Zipping up the door of my cosy little home should keep the wind at bay; that said, at the back of my mind the thought lingers that the tent offers pretty flimsy protection, if I am honest with myself. With that in mind I place my wind-up torch in one of the pockets sewn into the wall of the tent before turning in for the night. Fingers crossed that the weather will not deteriorate too much overnight.

I conclude this particular Monday evening by recording that today has ended a rather meagre twenty-nine point seven miles down the road from Chalon-sur-Saône. A very short day indeed but there have been no more punctures and I'll settle for that. The bike has now carried me 581 miles since leaving my Devon home. This is the same distance, as the crow flies, as cycling from London to Copenhagen. A check of the barometer shows a pressure of 1,011; this surprises me as I expected a reading of under 1,000.

Thirty minutes later I check again. The barometer has now fallen to 1,008. Fair warning of an unsettled night ahead, methinks?

## Day 19 – Tuesday 4th May

## Department of Ain:

## From Pont-de-Vaux to St. Maurice-de-Gourdens

Without warning a violent sound hauls me from the bliss of deep sleep into a dark world. It is a world so black that in my confused state I cannot be certain if my eyes are open or not. These first moments of being semi-awake are alarming and disorientating in equal measure. A ferocious wind is roaring outside.

After a few minutes, my sight slowly becomes accustomed to the subtle nuances of darkness between the shadowy place to my right, where I can just about make out the pannier bags, and the featureless pitch-black void above my head. Slowly, the sudden shock of being woken up subsides, my heart stops racing, and my head clears enough for me to begin to take stock of what is happening around me. It is the middle of the night but I've no idea what time it is. My flimsy Vango 200 tent is on the receiving end of a battering from the elements. My little home really doesn't deserve this; neither do I, come to think of it. My tent was so very inexpensive that I wonder how on earth it's withstanding such a pummelling. Now that I am more alert and thinking straight, I chastise myself for being such a skinflint when buying equipment. I know now, as I lie here waiting for the fabric to be ripped apart, that it would have been so much more sensible to have put my hand rather deeper into my pocket and bought a proper mountain tent. But the middle of a storm is no time for regrets and what-ifs, and whatever fears I have about how robust or otherwise my tent will prove to be, for now at least, my little shelter is hanging on.

A full-blown storm is an unbelievably noisy place when you are living outdoors, what with the wind howling and the campsite trees creaking painfully. Add to this hullabaloo the urgent slapping of the tent fabric as it's stretched taut by the wind then released in an instant, only to be pulled back again with a sharp snapping sound. Of course, I can see nothing of what is happening outside, but the noises alone are more than enough to leave me feeling that it could all go wrong sometime soon. I would be lying if I didn't bear my soul for a moment and admit to feeling more than a bit vulnerable, with the sound of the wind and the flexing of the tent, to say nothing of the creaking trees above me. Something seems sure to give. But then again, let's not get carried away, let's have a bit of realism. I know by the law of averages it's not likely to be the tree above me that loses out to the storm, and the tent is still hanging on. To be fair I have quite enjoyed being alone in a small dark tent – it's a rather soothing experience. Most nights have been quiet, the silence broken only by the whisper of a light breeze, the gentle pitter-patter of falling rain, or the occasional small mammal outside the tent. It is not so tonight.

In the pitch black of the night, the features inside the tent are barely discernible so I resort to using my fingers to feel for the stitched seam that I know runs horizontally along the tent walls. I know it's to my left somewhere and after a bit of fumbling about I find the seam where the groundsheet and sidewall meet. It's about eight inches off the floor. I follow the slightly raised texture like braille until my fingers locate the sidewall pocket, which contains my torch. A brief wind of its handle and the inside of the tent is suddenly illuminated. My watch reads exactly two o'clock.

The tent is distorted above my head by the broken stay, but I can't say that it's any more bent than it's been for the last few nights, certainly nothing to fret about. The tent wall to my right, that's the bit behind the panniers that runs up to the roof, is stretched so tightly by the wind that it may as well have been starched. The fabric is bowing inwards an alarming amount. How is it even doing that? The nylon is taut as a drum, and with its compressed side wall the tent is now even smaller. But you know what, the fabric's undamaged and hanging on, and I'm comforted that I took the time to check the guy ropes were well set before I turned in last night. A good move, it now seems.

I'm fully awake now but still a bit on edge as I lie still, listening to the cacophony that bombards me from all sides. There is little chance of returning to sleep, what with the noise of the storm outside and the sight of the wind rippling and stretching the tent around me. It might sound a bit odd, but it is absolutely fascinating watching the tent flex. Not only that, but I have unwittingly fallen into the trap of having set myself the rather pointless task of trying to identify the individual sounds that make up the storm. Why would anyone do that? It's the middle of the night, for goodness' sake, why does it matter what noise is what? Inside the tent I'm dry and cosy and I'm warm enough, and I have absolutely no idea why the individual sounds of the storm are important to me right now, but they are.

Suddenly it is daylight. I must have slept for five hours solid. It's seven-thirty and the wind doesn't sound quite as strong as it did during the night. Hopefully the storm is well on its way to passing through. Even so, I would be lying if I suggested this is the sort of weather I had hoped to wake up to. I am in no rush to set off today – what's the point? So I do the sensible thing and stay in the sleeping bag where I go through a visual check of each of the seams that hold the tent together. I check slowly and methodically, all looks fine but I double check just to be sure. Next I peer at the two corners near my feet, then the groundsheet; slowly and precisely I look for torn material or frayed stitching. As far as I can see all is well, although I can't inspect the corner behind my right shoulder as it is hidden from view by the panniers. As far as I can tell my little tent looks to have held firm. Quite a relief, I would say. I've given it some thought and decided to set off on my travels in spite of the weather, but first things first and that means breakfast, even though it is nothing more than dried apricots and chocolate. Breakfast is eaten inside the tent before I venture to look at the world beyond my green and orange fabric dome.

After unzipping the top of the door, I stick my head into the porch for a quick glance around. It all looks fine so I peep outside the tent where I am drawn to the sight of the tall slender poplar trees that edge of the far side of the campsite. The poplars are bending spectacularly as the wind whistles through them. The trees sound as if they are in discomfort; it's a rather unsettling noise. A widespread devastation of leaves and severed branches clutters the grass, which was so tidy just twelve hours ago.

I am struck by just how chilly the air is. It's raining of course, but less than it was, which is good news. To counter the cold, I set about a limited unpacking exercise to locate some additional layers of clothing. It strikes me that Pont-de-Vaux is far closer to the Mediterranean Sea than the North Sea. It is the month of May, for goodness' sake, and all things being equal I really should be wearing a tee-shirt, shorts, and factor-something sun cream. Not today, I'm afraid; this is a long trousers and waterproofs day if ever there was one. My 'keep-the-rain-at-bay' overtrousers seem a sensible idea right now and under my Gore-Tex jacket I wear a fleece for good measure. A 'bobble-less' bobble hat and fleece gloves make up the ensemble. It is astonishing that I am forced to layer up this far south at this time of year.

Today's bike ride starts in a very bumpy way because the wheels have absolutely no chance of avoiding the bits of tree and the other windfall debris that covers the ground like a fitted carpet. The road out of town is exposed to the wind and busier than I expected, and even though it is still quite early lorries pass me regularly; each is towing an inevitable cloud of spray. If you think this is a hostile and unpleasant environment to start the day you would be correct, and yes, I do need my wits about me. Much to my relief the lorries are not going fast and without exception they overtake leaving plenty of room. It is a courtesy I very much appreciate. To make life simpler for myself I adopt a trick that I first tried near Chalon-sur-Saône where I discovered that it is far easier to cycle through clouds of spray with my glasses removed. I don't have handlebar mirrors; they would be useful but I never thought of them, to be honest. I know vehicles are going to overtake me but I never know exactly when so most startle me. This is anything but relaxing cycling, so when the first minor road presents itself, it is a joy to leave the main road and return to the quieter pace of life offered by the rural lanes of France. The wind persists, of course, as does the rain, but thankfully my trip has returned once again to being an adventure rather than an exercise in self-preservation.

Several long rows of mature poplar trees grow at right angles to the lane. The tall slender trees are bending from midnight to ten o'clock, a rather alarming angle. Apparently, poplar wood is odour free, which is why it is used to make the little circular boxes that Camembert and other soft cheeses are supplied in. Poplar wood is also used for storing fruit as it is food safe; on the other hand the wood is pretty useless as firewood because it splits and sparks as it burns. Have you ever wondered why poplar trees are such a common sight across France? Ubiquitous in places, it seems. Well, this has little to do with fruit or cheese. Poplar trees are fast growing and tradition has it that when a landowner has a daughter, he plants a grove of poplar trees and by the time she is to be married the trees will be mature and the timber can be sold to provide a dowry.

In England I would write off a very windy day such as today as just that, a very windy day, but can I say that in France? Is today just another windy day or is this a very different beast altogether?

The Mistral Wind is created when an anticyclone of high pressure occurs over the ocean about four hundred miles northwest of here. It usually centres in an area off the Bay of Biscay to the north of Spain. At the same time, a corresponding but opposing area of low pressure occurs two hundred or so miles to the southeast of here, off the coast of Italy, around the Gulf of Genoa to be precise. In order to equalise this imbalance of pressure, the wind draws down across the French landmass from the Bay of Biscay towards the Gulf of Genoa in the Mediterranean Sea, and because of the particular features of the landscape in this part of France the wind is funnelled between the Alps, which lie just to my east, and the Massif Central to my west. The Mistral blows mainly in winter and spring; it is a cold and violent wind that accelerates down the Rhône valley on its way to the Camargue and the sea, and its ultimate destination in the Gulf of Genoa. Mistral Winds usually top 40 miles per hour, but they can exceed 110 and can last for days. This morning's wind ticks all the boxes for the time of year and location; maybe this is the Mistral Wind and not just another windy day, how exciting!

By way of some happy accident the little rural road I am now pedalling along, selected completely at random simply to escape the lorries, you will remember, cuts a corner off my route and by doing so reduces it by six miles. I have no idea how I failed to spot the short cut when planning my route but thanks to my need to avoid the traffic I have found it anyway. Six miles shorter and assisted by a healthy tail wind – this is developing into a rather good day after all.

It starts as a speck in the distance, but only a minute or two later and I can just about make out another cyclist. It looks like he or she is coming towards me, then as we close ranks on this straight open road it becomes clear that not one but two bikes are heading my way, side by side on this otherwise empty road. The French couple on bikes are local people on the second day of a journey that will take them, over the next three months, from their home in Lyon to Russia. Naturally we chat about the cold and windy weather, and they confirm that this is indeed the Mistral, something they experience most years. After a few minutes of chatting, we set off in opposite directions, parting company with smiles, handshakes, mutual wishes for a good adventure and of course calls of, *'Bon courage!'* I am relieved to be travelling with the Mistral behind me and not cycling against it, which is the tiring fate of the couple from Lyon. I hope for their sake the wind doesn't continue for several days, but from what they tell me it may well.

Wind-assisted cycling requires a lighter touch to clock up the miles, and over the next couple of hours I put twenty-five miles between last night's campsite and the town of Châtillon-sur-Chalaronne. The town is an attractive place built next to a small river that has an ancient and rather fetching open-sided market hall. Once called Châtillon-sur-Dombes, the town discarded its historical name but not its place within the Dombes, which is the area of France I am now entering.

The Dombes (pronounced *Domba*), is an undulating plateau in southeastern France that's bounded by the three major rivers of the area – the Ain, the Rhône, and the Saône. The ground underpinning the Dombes is made up of a layer of boulder clay that was deposited here by glaciers millennia ago. The clay is largely impervious, which results in around eleven hundred shallow lakes dotted across the Dombes. In addition to these natural lakes a large number of manmade pools were dug around five hundred years ago because at that time, fish farming was more profitable than growing crops. Commercially this switch of trade was prudent but it came with a lethal downside: the still waters attracted mosquitoes and the whole of the Dombes became dangerous as malaria flourished. Treatment for the condition was non-existent at that time and the disease took its toll. Today, fish species including pike, carp, bream, and eel still exist in commercial numbers and they remain an important source of income both as a food source and because anglers visit the area in search of specimen fish. In turn the fish attract resident and migratory birds, and this brings ornithologists to the area.

I enter the Dombes on the northern edge of the plateau at an altitude of a thousand feet or so. The area is laid out twenty miles in front of me and a similar distance east to west. The Mistral tail wind has reduced in strength as the day has gone on but it still offers anyone on a bike useful encouragement. Thankfully the buffeting that was so challenging at the start of today has gone along with the cold temperature and my warm clothing. The hills, for now at least, are a feature of the past. What a difference a few hours can make.

Looking at my map through its window in the handlebar bag I can see that the Dombes is represented as a place of few contours. It is generously peppered with ponds and lakes, in fact on paper it looks to have rather more water than land. This is exactly why it drew me to plan my route through here in the first place. The Dombes is one of the areas of France I have been most looking forward to visiting.

Geographically I had expected something similar to Norfolk or Suffolk in appearance.

The Dombes, rather like the fens of eastern England is an aquatic landscape that provides an increasingly rare and important habitat for wildlife and birds. Five miles or so of easy cycling into the Dombes and it strikes me that I have seen none of the windmills I assumed would be commonplace here. Of course this could simply be down to the frequency of tall reed beds that hug the roadside and restrict my view. Exciting fauna are not far away, and I experience an exciting and unexpected encounter: An hour into traversing the Dombes and I round a corner just as the lane dips between shadowy meadows and small fields. The dip is hidden from view by the blackthorn bushes that now flank the lane. One moment I am pedalling along, concentrating on the lane ahead as it opens up in front of me, and the next my eyes are drawn to a recently ploughed field to my left. It is a particularly small field bounded by impenetrable hedges and there, right in front of me, standing in the fresh furrows are eight, nine, no – at least twelve statuesque birds, each as tall as a large child and far larger than any bird I have seen outside of a zoo. The elegant creatures stand together just twenty yards from where I'm gazing at them over a small gate. The small flock has a distinctly military look: red-orange bills polished to perfection, black shoulders pulled back, and smart white fronts with not a feather out of place. They are waiting to go on parade, I would wager. I have never come across wild cranes before and it is a genuine privilege to share some time with them, especially as they have not been startled by my presence. Perhaps they are waiting for me to climb the inspection dais for their march past. Seeing them is the highlight of the day by a very long way.

The campsite in Villars-les-Dombes looks a little uninviting when I pull up outside the entrance, although to be fair the season has yet to get underway and several sites that I have stayed at have had a 'not-quite-ready-yet' look about them. Reception appears closed but I've found that this is not uncommon outside certain hours at this time of year. Beyond the entrance barrier I wander around the site and locate the toilet/shower block, which is open, but there is no sign of anybody here. I could probably camp free of charge but I am not at ease with doing that, as this is someone's livelihood.

So, as it is only mid-afternoon, I decide to press on, and who knows, if I keep going I may yet clock up a decent mileage for today. The idea has considerable appeal as it will offset the time that I lost due to the triple puncture; extra miles today will edge me a step closer to having a spare day in the bag. As I leave the site a cheerful French postman passes me on his bicycle. The *'facteur'* is resplendent in his blue uniform and yellow-banded cap, which he has set at a jaunty angle. The cap and his beaming smile make him look entirely happy with life, a round peg in a round hole if ever I saw one. His *'La Poste'* bicycle is vivid yellow, cumbersome, distinctly old fashioned, and overladen with its side panniers and oversized front basket. We smile as we pass each other and I wonder, given our overladen bikes, which of us looks the most comical.

A few minutes after leaving the campsite I come across a tourist information office where a lady tells me I should expect rain tomorrow and then little change for the next three or four days. Her information completely contradicts an earlier text from home, which cheered me up no end by telling me the stormy weather was on its way out and that sun will soon replace rain. *(I had absolutely no idea until I returned to England that most of the positive weather forecasts sent from home were purely fictional; they had been invented simply to bolster my spirits.)*

To give you an inkling as to where I am in France, or at least help you visualise my whereabouts, it may assist to know that two and a half hours ago when I crossed into the northern edge of the Dombes I was at a point fifty miles due west of Geneva in Switzerland. I will exit the Dombes fifty miles to the west of Annecy in the French Alps.

It is mid-afternoon when I chance upon the ancient town of Perouges and what a wonderful little place it turns out to be. A little stone town where the simple act of walking allows me the rare treat of stepping into a bygone age. Made up of a delightful jumble of crooked old buildings, Perouges is perched on a hilltop elevated above the Ain valley some twenty miles to the northeast of the grand city of Lyon. I spend a delightful hour pushing the bike through the winding cobbled streets and soaking up the quaint architecture of this historical little place. A line of teenagers is being reluctantly herded through the narrow streets by a brace of frazzled teachers. Thick dark coats over black hoodies is the dress code of the day for the majority of the youngsters as they trudge along head down; their reluctant silent amble gives the unmistakable impression that this is the very last place on earth they wish to spend the afternoon. After the youngsters have moved slowly on, this little gem of a town is abandoned to me and me alone it seems, and considering that Perouges is only a short drive from the two and a half million occupants of nearby Lyon I feel very fortunate to be here today, for this wonderful old place must get very crowded on sunny days and weekends. Today may be dull and cloudy but my time in Perouges has brightened up the day immeasurably.

Leaving Perouges on the D65 road, the bike and I head off towards the village of St. Maurice-de-Gourdans where an hour or so later locating the campsite proves to be anything but straightforward: the site is accessed down a potholed side road, which in itself causes little difficulty. The challenge comes when I am faced with barriers blocking the road and a *'Route Barrée'* sign that directs me to an alternate route. Unable to circumvent the roadworks I dutifully follow the *'Déviation'* directions for half a mile before coming to a second *'Route Barrée'* sign. This one points me back exactly the way I have just come. Someone's little joke, perhaps?

Back at the original sign the only option is to move the metal barriers aside and press on until I arrive at the campsite. I find it less than a mile down the road. I am a little bemused when asked to pay six euros and two cents for my pitch and then thirty-one cents for a shower jetton; perhaps some local tourist tax has resulted in the charges not being rounded up or down. By the time I have booked in, explored the site, and selected my pitch, the wind has picked up considerably. Unfortunately the stronger wind coincides with me trying to put the tent up. Let me just say that I would understand entirely if you thought

I was hamming it up a bit when I claim that I had to wrestle the tent to the ground, but in all truth, it isn't far short of a wrestle and at one point it must have looked for all the world like I was trying to restrain a massive flounder flapping across the ground.

It's a good job nobody's watching this pantomime. To subdue the flapping tent my tactic is to place pannier bags on both front corners. Without this ballast I have little doubt the tent, which only weighs in at three pounds, would simply be carried up, up, and away in the style of the indomitable Mary Poppins. With the front end of the tent pinned down by luggage I lay the bike on its side so the seat and handlebars anchor the back of the groundsheet. Once the bulk of the tent is restrained in this way I am able to secure the edges of the groundsheet by firmly pegging through the eyelets. I double peg each of the four corners by inserting two tent pegs in the shape of an 'X', a technique that worked well for me half a century ago when I used to camp on the high moorland on the Lake District fells. In those days that was just called 'camping'; nowadays it's been elevated to 'wild camping'. Next the fibreglass rods are put together to form a long, thin, continuous pole, which is inserted into fabric loops of the outer tent. The second rod is then assembled and together they'll provide rigidity and shape to the domed roof. Finally, I tension the whole structure by tightening the guy ropes starting with those facing the wind. A final check of the pegs just to make sure they will hold. Job done!

This has actually turned out to be a very satisfactory day when I think back to the roaring wind of last night and the cold temperature this morning. On reflection I am very glad to have pressed on. It would have been very easy to stay out of the weather by sitting it out in the tent today. Had I done so I would have missed the cranes, I may have missed Perouges, and I would not be looking at a cyclometer that has recorded fifty-seven miles since breakfast.

# Day 20 – Wednesday 5th May

## Departments of Ain and Isère:

## From St. Maurice-de-Gourdans to Meyrieu-les-Étangs

Sleep was pretty good last night in spite of the best efforts of a barking dog in the thirty minutes before I eventually dozed off. This morning, I have awoken to the cheerless sound of rain lashing against the outer tent. Inside the sleeping bag I lay still listening in vain for something uplifting from the world beyond my green and orange surroundings. The most prominent sound is the occasional passing vehicle as wheels slosh through puddles. Suddenly I remember the loud clap of thunder that woke me in the middle of the night; thankfully the sound has not been repeated so perhaps the height of the storm has already passed this area by.

Right now, I must answer a question I have asked myself on more than one occasion at about this time of morning since I took up living in a tent three weeks ago: Do I stay where I am and keep dry, or do I press on and get wet, and by the sound of things outside, very wet? I briefly weigh up the pros and cons but it is not a difficult decision to get on the bike, as I have on all other wet days. I gained a spare day yesterday by cycling nearly sixty miles, hard won but well worth doing, and I have no intention of throwing away those efforts for a day in St. Maurice-de-Gourdans, however delightful that may be. Half a bottle of water and a whole packet of Jaffa Cakes sorts out *petit déjeuner*. It's a snappy breakfast that allows me to crack on: Lemon Jaffa Cakes, mmmmmm! How dare the French suggest we British eat to live whereas they live to eat. What's the matter with them?

Once decamped I secure everything to the bike rack with bungee cords before wiping the seat and handlebars as dry as I can. Pre-departure checks of the chain, tyres, and brakes are done before I climb over the crossbar and cycle away from my pitch. I pause briefly to thank the campsite staff, two of whom brave the foul weather to walk with me to the entrance and wave me off to calls of *bon courage et bon voyage* as I pedal off into the teeming rain.

It's nine-fifteen on a wet Wednesday morning and the little road south from St. Maurice is quite empty. Steady rain makes for poor visibility and were it not for the constant *ssshhhiiisss* from my tyres as they greet the wet tarmac the world would be a silent place. I cycle through the village of Loyettes without stopping, not even to pause on the stout granite bridge to gaze at the swollen Rhône as it flows purposefully beneath. The fizzing sound of the tyres on the wet road is a constant companion, which I find surprisingly encouraging.

Next, is the town of Pont-de-Chéruy, a bustling place that forms part of the larger community of Charvieu-Chavagneux. Navigation is very tricky now that I am amongst the satellite communities of Lyon; by some margin this is the most built-up area since I pushed the bike across central London three weeks ago.

Somewhere amongst the heavy traffic, the poor weather, and the bad visibility, I have completely lost my bearings. Usually I would fall back on the rudimentary but effective tactic of keeping the sun in roughly the same position relative to my intended route, but the sun is not visible today and I end up becoming quite lost for several miles until I come to the hamlet of Panossas, where I have the good fortune to find myself back on track, although I have no idea how I managed it.

Ten miles further on, at L'Isle-d'Abeau the route ahead is effectively blockaded by a motorway and several arterial routes that converge here. The motorway is far too busy to even think about crossing, and even if it were traffic-free the high concrete barriers on either side would require more than a knee-buckling heft from one person to lift the loaded bike over them. It takes me a full hour to find a safe way to put these intimidating highways behind me, but eventually I do, which allows me to devote the rest of the day to the much more pleasurable task of pedalling through open countryside looking for signs to villages south of here. Any village roughly in the direction of Meyrieu-les-Étangs will do me very nicely as Meyrieu is where I hope to camp tonight.

After a while the hazy view clears a bit and I pull in to look over a field gate towards a range of hills in the distance. Low cloud and mist partly obscure the view ahead but the hills fit with the terrain on the map and provide me with a much-needed clue to the way I should head.

It is five p.m. on the dot when I roll into Meyrieu-les-Étangs. First impressions are that it is a pleasant if modest village of around a thousand inhabitants. The name *Meyrieu-les-Étangs* hints that it will be pretty here should the haze lift. '*Étang*' is the word for a small shallow pond or lagoon; alas, any such ponds are hidden from view today by the weather.

Having put up my tent on the ten-euro pitch I have a shower, which although adequate enough falls short of the deluge of hot water that I was hoping to experience. Ideally, in my view, a shower should be hot enough to redden my skin but stop short of causing discomfort. Warmth may not feature on Maslow's Hierarchy of Needs but after a day in the rain it is top of my list of requirements.

A hazy lifeless sun hangs low over the trees beyond the campsite and if I'm too slow to react I will miss the half-hearted appearances it occasionally makes. The milky sun is far too weak to permeate the skin of the tent so its green and orange interior is rather gloomy and cheerless as I haul the panniers and handlebar bag inside and position them for the night. Fortunately, the panniers are no more than damp; they've been protected all day by the stretch-over hi-vis covers, which I've now removed and left to drip in the porch. Once the luggage on the tent floor has been sorted into some sort of order it's time for me to reach deep inside a pannier and grab a family sized can of ravioli and a thick stubby baguette, just the job!

As I've mentioned before, unzipping the door between the inner tent and the porch extends the usable length of the tent by about eighteen inches. This provides the perfect place to set up the storm cooker, and, come to think of it, a place to dry my shoes while I'm at it. The cooker would be fine outside in the rain but I'm not, well, not after a day of being rained on. I mean you'd have to be an idiot to enjoy that, wouldn't you? So here I am lying in the tent, with my head sticking into the bijou mini porch, looking up at the lopsided roof caused by the broken strut. Outside the rain is now lashing the tent in short, squally bursts but I don't care, I really don't. Camping in the rain can be a joyless experience, as everybody that's tried it knows, but not inside my tent, because although I know there are just a few microns of material between me and another good soaking the sound and sensation of the weather outside is oddly pleasurable, akin to sitting before a blazing log fire in some country pub after a long winter walk. It's rather soothing watching the steam rise up from the Trangia and smelling the background whiff of meths mixed with the aroma of food being cooked. It takes me back decades and is rather nice, in an old-fashioned 'billy-no-mates' sort of way.

Keeping a close eye on the cooker is essential right now because the wind has decided to change direction just so it can play cat and mouse with my little home. I don't think there's any need for that, really. Strong gusts distort the tent skin and push the porch fabric a few inches closer to the hot cooker. It's a calculated risk cooking inside the tent, I suppose, but I reckon the danger is minimal. The nylon can only stretch so far and by my guesstimation it can't stretch quite as far as the cooker. Also the meths burner concentrates the temperature very much towards the middle of the pan so there is far less heat at the edges of the cooker nearest to the fabric. I reckon that even if the tent touches the edge of the pan it might melt a bit but I really can't see it going up in flames. Anyway, if I am wrong some wag will probably hint at it on my epitaph – 'went out in a blaze of glory' or something along those lines. In the meantime I really do need to keep a close eye on proceedings, as much as anything because the steam from the pan is condensing on my glasses, and this isn't ideal when I need to watch what's going on. The upside is that it's toasty and warm in the tent now and as that hasn't happened very often, I'll take being cosy while I can.

Cooking is over in a jiffy and without the misfortune of my tent combusting. This, I think we can all agree is a bonus. I wolf the meal down straight from the pan while sitting cross-legged precisely in the centre of the tent, the optimum position to take advantage of the small area of headroom under the apex of the low roof. The canned ravioli doesn't really cut the mustard as its taste and texture are both substandard. It would have been returned had I bought it in a pub or restaurant, but the meal is hot and filling and provides all that I need as fuel; eating to live, as the French would say. That's one to the French.

After considerable perseverance and ingenuity, the rain has eventually found a way inside my porch. To be fair, rain in the tent comes as no surprise whatsoever. Doesn't rain always win in the end if you are camping? It's a long-standing law, as far as I know.

I have an analogy vis-a-vis rain and camping and it goes like this: Anyone who has lived in a country home next to open fields or close to a hay barn or a farm will know that whenever a field mouse decides that living in a barn or a field is a little too rustic for its liking it will take it upon itself to exchange the barn or a field or whatever for something more comfortable – fact. At this point the rodent will decide to infiltrate your home, and once it has made that decision the outcome is entirely inevitable no matter what preventative steps you may take. The mouse will always win, and once it has moved in it will bring its furry mates. Exactly the same logic can be applied to rain and a tent; rain will always try to encroach your inside space. Given half a chance it will drip on your face in the middle of the night, but sometimes it is sneakier than that and will silently seep in via some hidden corner. The first you'll know is when you discover the pile of clothes you had to leave on the floor because there is nowhere else for them are saturated and cold. Obviously these are the very clothes you intended to wear once you wake up. Anyway, you get my drift, the outcome is precisely the same; the would-be intruder, rain or mouse, will always prevail.

Thankfully for me, today's rain seems satisfied just to get into my porch. If that is where its ambitions end, we can both call a truce and it is welcome to stay. To be fair, having experience of both, encroachment by rain is far easier to ignore than a field mouse, so that is precisely what I intend to do. I am going to bed now and the rain can get on with whatever it wishes to do in the meantime.

It may only be seven o'clock but I am already zipped up in my sleeping bag and lying on top of the inflatable mattress. This is by necessity as the blissful heat from the cooker has long gone and an unseasonal cold has started to creep inexorably into my body. Barring the night in Pay-de-Calais when my water bottles froze solid, tonight looks set to be one of the coldest so far. By nine o'clock my feet are freezing and I'm not sure what else I can do about it because I'm in the sleeping bag. I'm fully clothed including socks, and I can't double-sock as I am wearing my last dry pair. Hopefully the temperature will plateau out soon. It's now dusk outside, which means it's virtually black inside the tent. Rain still beats against the fabric but my attitude towards it has changed; no longer does the rain conjure snug thoughts of a warm pub fire, not at all, this rain is just a loud, distracting, and at times quite an irritating noise. On the plus side I can't help but marvel at how well my under-thirty-quid tent is performing in its most recent battle with the elements.

The wind-up torch has proven itself to be a surprisingly good bit of kit, which is more than adequate for a short time. On the flip side regular winding becomes a bit of a chore that I can't really be bothered with so I do end up staring into a dark and featureless space, and with nothing else to concentrate on I find myself picking up on the almost imperceptible way that the sound of the weather outside increases in pitch and volume over the next couple of hours. The storm is cranking itself up into a bit of a tis-was, sleep eludes me (annoying!) but on the plus side the dripping rain seems satisfied to remain in the porch.

If there is a weak point in the tent, I'd expect it to reveal itself tonight, the way things are going. I find myself thinking about what would happen should the second fibreglass support rod snap. One's held together with gaffer tape as it is. But a more concerning prospect is that the storm will weaken the stitched seams and tear the fabric, which would be the end of a little home that, in spite of its flimsy construction and modest dimensions I am now quite comfortable living in. I would have to buy a replacement. *In extremis* I would have to consider a *chambre d'hôtel* for tomorrow night. I know I can do nothing about the storm now but in the morning I must text home and ask for a weather update. *(Remember if you will that while I was in France I thought weather forecasts from home could be relied on – wrong.)*

I still can't sleep so I get the map out and pore over tomorrow's route in the dim cone of torchlight. Still the storm prevents me from sleeping. Tonight is becoming extremely tedious as sleep evades me; it drags on, and on. You can only look at a map in the middle of the night for so long.

Suddenly, and set against the intimidating surroundings of a pitch-black tent in a raging storm, I am startled to realise someone is outside the tent and trying to get in. Well, that's what it looks like to me – surely not! My heart is racing as I unzip the door; it's the middle of the night, and it's the middle of a storm, but a person is outside, I'm pretty sure of that. Against the hazy dim light from a campsite lamppost a hundred yards away I can make out a crouched and bedraggled silhouette. The indistinct human shape is set against a curtain of rain that sweeps in front of the street light. Normally I would invite any windswept guest in to take respite from the weather but with no space this is not an option.

It is none other than the owner of the campsite, who must be absolutely drenched after his trudge across the soggy field to offer me shelter at the height of the storm. I struggle to understand what he is telling me at first, what with the sound of wind and rain. My initial thought is that something dreadful must have happened; damage to his house, perhaps, or an imminent risk of flooding more likely. Thankfully this is not the case. The owner saw my torch inside the tent and has come over purely to check that I am all right and to tell me that he is opening the guest lounge all night in case I need to seek shelter from the extreme weather. Wow! What a gesture. I am greatly touched by his generosity of spirit and concern for my welfare, and I shall certainly take up his offer should the storm beat the tent or me into submission.

About two thirty in the morning, I am woken after less than an hour's sleep by people talking in a nearby caravan. Now that I'm fully awake I unzip the porch door to walk to the toilet block but to my complete horror I discover my shoes are full of water. This is not just damp footwear, my shoes are quite literally filled with water: I left them in the porch overnight but hadn't taken into account that the distorted shape of the outer tent would funnel rainwater into both shoes. This is far beyond what will simply be uncomfortable to wear, there is a good inch of water inside each shoe. What else can I do but open the tent and empty each shoe onto the saturated grass outside?

Remember the *Sunday Times* that I bought at Chalon railway station? Well, I have carried the unread sections with me and now is the perfect time for several pages to be crumpled and stuffed into each shoe. It may be a long shot but as there's another five or six hours before I need to get up, the paper will wick away at least some of the water, and maybe, just maybe, the shoes will be a little more wearable by the morning. Well, that's the hope anyway, we'll see what transpires. How ironic that these are Gore-Tex shoes, purpose built to keep water out. Perhaps Gore-Tex is just as effective at keeping water in; I will discover that in daylight. In the meantime, I return to sleep completely forgetting that before I saw the shoes I needed to leave the tent.

# Day 21 – Thursday 6th May

## Departments of Isère and Drôme:

## From Meyrieu-les-Étangs to Hauterives

At seven-thirty I wake up suddenly and check out my footwear before doing anything else. I am barely awake, on my hands and knees heading for the porch. What's going on?

I feel like a child at Christmas hoping to be lucky enough to get what I really want – dry footwear. I unzip the pouch to discover the newspaper has done the job of wicking better than I hoped for. Both shoes are still damp and cold, of course, but not soaking; it's Christmas after all!

It is time to take stock after the storm so all my belongings are evacuated to the laundry room directly opposite my pitch. It takes several trips but as nobody is around nobody is inconvenienced. Long counters lining both sides of the laundry room are perfect for laying everything out at waist height. I grade all my possessions: Soaking, Wet, Damp, and Dry. Once everything is graded into heaps, I set about improving my lot. Tasks range from towelling the storm cooker dry, to wringing out a jumper unwittingly left in the porch near the shoes. Everything is re-packed according to how much water it retains. One pannier is filled with wet clothes, which I shall deal with at the next campsite laundry I come to. The other pannier contains dry items like the Trangia, cooking utensils, first-aid and washing kits, and my few dry clothes. Before leaving the laundry room I use it as a makeshift breakfast bar – drinking a litre of fresh orange juice will make the bike a bit lighter if nothing else.

With my bike loaded and the pitch checked I have just one question remaining before I'm ready to go. How to avoid my feet being cold, damp and numb for most of the day ahead. Luckily, I have come up with what is, even by my standards if I say so, a remarkably inventive solution. The campsite is still deserted when I try out this bit of fashion wizardry, and although my idea is pure genius I am glad there's no-one to witness the scene that now plays out. Visualise if you must, a proud Englishman hopping around the laundry room inserting his socked feet into plastic bags. This is the ignoble state I have been reduced to by last night's weather. Big plastic shopping bags, a damp-proof course for feet. Absolutely brilliant, if you ask me.

Inwardly, I am rather chuffed with this masterstroke of early-morning inventiveness. Let's be honest, who wouldn't be? To any strangers looking on I accept that I may present as a somewhat odd and possibly alarming sight as below the knee I do have more than a passing resemblance to one of one of those prized rare-breed chickens with feathers sticking out of the bottom of their legs.

You want more details, don't you! Who wouldn't? Well, you'll be relieved to know that the translucent bag selected for my right foot is not too obvious (I fool myself into believing). The other bag, however, is a rather unfortunate lime green colour so less easily hidden. Then again, the lime bag is not just any shopping bag, it is a 'Marks and Spencer' shopping bag. That said, I am quite aware that M&S bag or not, bagging my lower legs has simply completed the final touches of my transformation into a hobo. I'm not without pride, you know, so I stuff as much surplus plastic bag as possible up into each trouser leg. Maybe it doesn't look too bad.

Before leaving the site I visit reception to thank the owner for going beyond the call of duty to offer me shelter.

Today's short thirty-mile hop follows country roads from Meyrieu-les-Étangs to Hauterives. I'll have the Vercors mountains to my left and the Rhône valley on my right. The Vercors reach 7,600 feet and form a lofty line between the Rhône valley and the city of Grenoble. I will pedal over the fringe of the Vercors but not over the highest mountains. Nevertheless today's climbs will undoubtedly test my fitness and if I don't find the gradients too arduous, I may well feel confident enough to take the higher-level road south, through the ancient towns of Romans, Crest, and Grignan, before the bike and I re-acquaint ourselves with the River Rhône at the Roman town of Orange.

Although cold, the rain has stopped for now. This is a relief as my cycling mitts and leather gloves are still much too wet to wear even though I wrung them out with such enthusiasm that I watched the colour from the leather dye disappear down the campsite sink. I've cycled far enough since leaving Devon to know that without gloves the breeze will turn my hands cold and strip feeling from my numb fingers. Stiff, unresponsive fingers don't operate brakes well and this is not a reassuring prospect at the start of a day dominated by hills. Anyway, it's time to make progress: my pre-departure checks are done and my plastic-bag gaiters looking splendid – and not at all unlike regimental puttees, if I may say so. It's time to set off.

Today's winding route sets off through a landscape of small fruit farms set amid rolling and forested scenery. Bullrush-encircled ponds have settled in every available hollow in this landscape, it seems. Some of these '*Étangs*' are an acre or two in size but most are very much smaller. One of the ponds is for sale – a rather rough and ready 'a vendre' sign has been hung from a tree to attract the attention of passers-by. The lake would be just perfect for anyone with a small caravan, a passion for tranquillity, time on their hands, and a fondness for course angling.

Although pedalling warms up my torso in no time at all cycling is a still bracing affair as I pedal towards town of Beaupaire. On the outer edges of the town a mobile food van comes into view – it demands immediate attention.

*Le Cabanon à Patates* is run by an enterprising and friendly young couple and we trade four chicken legs cooked in turmeric for two-and-a-half euros. The food is handed to me in a paper bag; it feels so good to cradle the warm bag in my palms for a couple of minutes while we chat about their business and my journey. They asked me to take a photo of them through the open side of the food van, and fifteen minutes later I aim my front wheel towards the hills and the town of Hauterives.

Soon the gradient increases and I'm forced to push the bike. It may be the month of May but ahead of me hills are capped with snow. Thankfully the snowline looks to be well above the height I expect to climb to. A burst of purposeful cycling shifts my mind away from the unpleasant throb of chilled fingers.

Regular signposts along the D538 point to the towns of Hauterives, Romans, and Valance. Further south still lies the great cultural melting pot of Marseille. If ever there's a clear indication I'm close to the 'South of France', surely a sign to Marseille must be it. The 'South of France' is colloquially known as *Le Midi*, as in the Canal-du-Midi, but exactly where does *Le Midi* start? Apparently, there is no 'official' start to *Le Midi* although the little town of Valence is considered by many French people to be where it actually begins.

Rainwater fizzes off the tyres as I cycle through a nondescript if bustling little town that I failed to notice the name of. I do, however, spot a neon sign suspended above an apothecary shop in the main street. The flashing green sign reads five degrees. Five degrees! Come on, this is the South of France, what's going on? It's now just an hour shy of noon, only three weeks to the start of June and seven weeks from midsummer's day, and yet with the wind chill factored in it's around freezing here. It's ironic that lots of research influenced me not to set off in June or July. I set off in April expecting that northern France would be cool and I would avoid cycling in the summer heat of Provence. Well that hasn't worked to plan, has it?

Rounding a gentle bend after exiting Neon Sign Town, I come to an unexpected and amazing sight. In front of me is the most colourful and bizarre house you could imagine. The large garden surrounding the house is fenced off by scaffolding; the poles form both the vertical posts and the horizontal four-bar fencing that each post supports. Every inch of every pole is painted with rings of bright colour; in every six-foot section there are around twenty hand-painted bands – green, white, orange, maroon, yellow, then red, blue. Imagine that over several thousands of feet of metal poles, but the fence is just the warm-up act to this gloriously eccentric display.

Between the fence and the house lies a garden randomly littered with items dabbed with colour. A blue bench here and a red garage door over there. How about an industrial-sized knife-sharpener, painted of course; there are absurdly large metal flowers, a dozen or so tin baths, metal fuel cans, oil barrels, children's pedal cars, and every single item has been painted with lines and dabs of colour, hundreds of dabs on the bigger items, and tens of thousands of colour dabs overall. A large sign is positioned at the start of the display – it reads *'Salut les Routièrs Christian'*, or 'Hi, Christian Lorry drivers.'

The house has not been spared adornments and it would be wrong not to mention the painted canoe that's wedged high between the chimney stack and a satellite dish. Dozens of other items are suspended from trees. By far the most impressive is a model aeroplane that is raised above the garden on a plinth of scaffolding. I say model but the plane is a good ten feet long and painted in a random series of colour dabs, naturally. The items and colours are never ending but my observations must be or I shall never get away from here and I do have a few more miles cover today, after all.

The valley floor levels out and cycling becomes more relaxed for the next few miles, but all good things come to an end, as they say, and as the valley tapers to meet the hills ahead the road gains elevation and once again I am forced to get off and push. The next fifteen hundred feet is hard won as I alternate between pedalling and pushing as the hill allows. The exertion causes me to huff and puff, until, with the gradient finally behind me I can rest a while at the summit where I completely drain a litre of water. Who knew a bottle of water could taste so sweet?

My rich reward from the forested hilltop is the giddy enjoyment of freewheeling for several miles. Light touches on the brake levers are necessary to limit the risk of me losing control and being flipped over the crash barriers into the ravine below. Although I've had to push the bike several times today, including up six hairpin bends, the effort has not felt at all excessive when I think about it. My earlier concerns about today's hilly route have proved largely inaccurate, which brings a smile to my face, as does the thought that my 'damp-proof-course-for-feet' has worked a treat and nobody seems to have noticed.

'Chateau Camping' in Hauterives is a very spacious site set within the landscaped grounds of a chateau. The elevated site is conveniently close to the centre of town, which I hope to visit later.

The campsite owner comments on the cold weather and kindly offers to leave the TV lounge open with a request that I lock it and put the key through the letterbox before leaving in the morning. The campsite shower is fantastically hot and afterwards I feel thoroughly warm for the first time in days. The delightful sensation springs me into action and by five p.m. the tent is sorted out and I'm heading into town. I've decided against cooking my own food, or put another way, I feel like a treat.

In Hauterives centre I come across a pub-cum-restaurant with lots of customers. Inside, the simple pleasure of being surrounded by other humans feels like a treat in itself. A *'pression'* costs me two euros, which has been the going rate for a pint of draught beer throughout France. My beer and I take up residence at the one remaining empty table where I am surrounded by lively *joie de vivre*. The prospect of a few beers here and some French food, ideally a local dish, will make a wonderful finale to another interesting day on the bike.

The waiters don't seem to have noticed me yet but I'm in no rush, so out comes my notebook and I make a start on writing up the events of today.

I order a second beer at the bar and ask what local dishes are available. Like a stormy day on a summer holiday disappointment descends when the barman offers his apologies, *'Je suis vraiment désolé,'* and tells me that no food is provided in the evenings and they are closing at six – ten minutes from now! Thankfully he understands when I ask him not to continue pouring my second beer.

Notebook packed away, I walk further into town until I come upon another hotel. Inside, this one has a somewhat old-fashioned look like so many traditional hospitality establishments across rural France; often this is a good thing as many businesses are family run, quaint, and appealing in a charmingly outdated sort of way. But this particular hotel is sombre and a beer sets me back three euros. An extra euro is no big deal but the fifty per cent increase and dreary surroundings are enough to dissuade me from looking at the menu. Beer finished, I set off down the road looking for an alternative. Alas, my quest falls short of expectations and I find myself wandering around the empty town centre of Hauterives. No pubs and no restaurants, a pizza from a takeaway it is then!

Nine and a half euros for quite the largest pizza I've ever seen seems a good deal to me. The pizza is extremely well-insulated with several layers of metal foil inside a thick cardboard box so it's still hot after my walk to the campsite. I may not be able to enjoy my evening meal in a lively restaurant but it's a great pleasure simply to enjoy my meal at a table, in the TV lounge.

I've now pedalled seven hundred miles since Calais; it feels like a satisfying distance. Had I driven the same distance on the motorway I would have been at journey's end on the shores of the Mediterranean long ago. With just over a week to go I reckon I may just about crack the thousand-mile barrier, which has a good ring to it. Journal stashed away, I lie in the sleeping bag listening to the world outside the tent but all is silent – no vehicles, no wind, no people, not even the sound of birds. Best of all I am not listening to the sound of rain clattering down on the tent. Sweet dreams!

# Week Four

*Day 22 — Friday 7th May*

*Department of Drôme:*

*From Hauterives to Chabeuil*

This morning, I break with routine and set off on foot looking for breakfast. The grass through the chateau grounds is wet with dew as I follow the little-used downhill track through the Monterey Pines. Hundreds, perhaps thousands of tan-coloured cones are scattered under the trees. The cones are fist-sized and so numerous that I can't avoid crunching them underfoot as I walk. Why, in a land known for its superb bakeries, has it taken me until today to hunt out a boulangerie? A mystery of epic proportions and a display of inexcusable foolishness on my behalf. Better late than never, I suppose.

In no time at all I stumble upon a small boulangerie hidden up a narrow cobbled lane. This bijou family bakery may be tucked away out of sight but how could anyone fail to be netted in by the wonderful aroma that wafts out of the open door and drifts down the lane in the still morning air? Irresistible! I am drawn towards the smell of fresh bread as surely as any homing pigeon to its loft.

The boulangerie-patisserie offers all anyone would hope for: croissants on shelves, sheaves of baguettes standing upright in wicker baskets, seeded loaves neatly stacked, and as old-fashioned bakery tradition dictates, there is the lightest dusting of slippery flour on the black and white squared-tiled floor. Above all the nostalgia and charm it is the warm rustic smell of artisan baking that makes the greatest impression on the senses. Piping hot croissants at less than a euro each are quite irresistible. Within seconds of leaving the bakery a puff of steam rises from my croissant as I take one from the bag and bite into it. The croissants have to be enjoyed right now, standing here, in this ancient little street while they are still hot.

I discover much too early in the day for my linking, that there's nothing quite like a punishing six-hundred-foot climb up hairpin bends to start day twenty-two with a bang. This change of terrain occurs soon after leaving Hauterives and it certainly has my heart and lungs going ten to the dozen. I've absolutely no idea what I am trying to prove this morning but I pedal the whole way up, albeit at the expense of screaming calf muscles. Thankfully, like all trials the hill-climb eventually ends, although once I'm stationary the effort of the ascent forces me to pause, rest my forearms on the handlebars, and lean over the front of the bike gasping for air. Not for the first time I wonder if I've overdone it a bit. It is not until my heart rate returns to near-normal that I find the energy to pull the water bottle out of its frame to rehydrate myself.

It is as I am slouched over the handlebars that I notice a snake on the grass verge; it's a good four feet long and undeniably dead. The snake is dark olive green with short dashes of pale yellow covering its entire body from tail to head. The snake may well have been dressed by the occupier of the painted house. I have no idea what species it is but I have never seen such a snake before. It looks more tropical than European so I take some photos for future research. *(On returning home I discover the reptile is a green whip snake. The species is harmless and resides in the southern half of Europe and on some Mediterranean islands.)*

At fifteen hundred feet, the high point of the road is not great, not even a true mountain, but it's quite high enough unless you're sat behind a steering wheel with a gear-stick to hand. The crest of the hill rewards me with far-reaching views over range after range of low hills. Ahead, patches of woodland are scattered over a landscape that for the most part is divided into small pastures. Next to the road, a field provides grazing for a small herd of tan and white cattle; they are so close I can hear them munching as I cycle by. They don't look up as the grass is more interesting to them than some travelling stranger. Quite right, too. It's warmer now, twelve degrees to be exact, and the sky ahead gives me confidence that the weather should be set fair for today. Accordingly I exchange trousers for shorts whilst standing at the side of the road. No onlookers, no gendarmes, no harm done!

After another good swig of water, the bike and I set off along the upland road that winds its way along the crest of a wooded hill. Several bridges carry the road over fast streams tumbling down from the mountains. At one bridge I pause and look into the rocky ravine. The clear mountain water gushes far below between light grey rocks. A solitary white egret fishes in the eddies. This surprises me because egrets are more at home in lowland waters, saltmarshes, and estuaries, or so I thought. Downstream from the bridge the water has picked up the pace in its haste to reach the valley below. On the mountain side the water foams over large white boulders before tumbling with happy gusto down a series of cascades. These may be modest hills but there is nothing shy and retiring about this mountain torrent. Carefree cycling, surrounded by highland scenery, and warmed by the first sunlight in many days is just what I need after the recent rain. Traversing the Drôme is a joy on a morning such as this, especially as the road falls over a thousand feet in the next six miles. I wonder if there's a more rewarding or intoxicating pleasure than sitting astride a bike and gliding down from the top of a hard-won hill.

Using the pedals as my footstool the bike freewheels unhindered by me and in total silence along this beautiful empty road where mature trees grow on both sides. The massive trees seem to be looking down and checking my progress as they stretch their branches high above me. The trees reach out to each other like a sabre arch at a wedding, and with the light breeze swaying the upper branches it's as if the trees are encouraging me with applause as I pass under them. Centuries of growth have created this beautiful foliage tunnel and the trees are especially enchanting today with the flickering sunlight leaving a golden sheen on the pale green leaves and the thick chalky grey trunks.

Plane trees such as these originate from Turkey and history has it that timber from plane trees was used to build the Trojan horse. To many people, myself included, plane trees are more evocative of France than anywhere else. In France the trees flourish in village squares where they provide shade for boule players; majestic plane trees line the grand Boulevards of Paris, and as I pedal under these plane trees I simply cannot imagine being in any other country.

A rolling landscape of farmland surrounds me now that I have come down from the hills. There are few trees now so the view opens up to show a line of low, flat hills capped by white rock in the middle distance. The hills, about an hour away by the look of it, are my next challenge, I would say.

Clues that the land hereabouts has been shaped by mankind for aeons can be seen by looking at the detail: Firstly, the fields here are small; unusually small, come to think of it, and they've been created wherever a more or less level parcel of land pops up in the rocky terrain. Most of these little fields, and there are plenty of them, are edged with low walls of unfinished stone. Only the lower part of these walls remains intact, that said, I can still make out the precision and effort that went into their construction all those generations ago. Most of these limestone walls have long since lost their tussle with nature and are hidden under squat thorny shrubs and a drapery of dry grasses. Large patches of lichen cover some of the larger stones, and as some lichen organisms grow just a few millimetres a year, the patches here indicate that these walls are centuries old. Stoney land such as this must have offered little but torment and broken backs for anyone trying to grow crops, it's all hard texture and scant soil from what I can see. Most of the fields look long-abandoned now; people must have found easier ways to sustain themselves. Well, you would if you could, wouldn't you?

Here and there this drab pale-ochre wilderness is lifted by an intense burst of colour from a patch of yellow flowers. In the shaded field edges tall wispy plants exist in thin rows and add a vibrant splash of blue to the dry land. These flowers may not be crops but they show that some plants can thrive here. Fauna too, it seems, when I spot a pair of frolicking butterflies skipping over the landscape before pausing on a tumbled-down section of sun-bathed wall. Then, just as I am about to set off a small lizard allows me a brief glimpse of its emerald body before disappearing under the dry rocks.

A couple of miles on a pure white horse trots from an adjoining meadow towards me. The animal is prancing in a very frisky way with a carefree mane and its tail swishing from side to side. The horse is obviously delighted to see me. Well, let's be realistic, it's delighted to see anyone, absolutely anyone. I simply fit the bill. The horse shows off as it canters across the field and stops next to me for a moment before sauntering along the weathered spars of the wooden lath fence that separates us. The animal shakes its head and snorts to attract my attention. It is impossible not to smile at its efforts and spend a few minutes with the animal. I offer the horse a handful of long dry grass from the verge but the splendid animal isn't interested in the least, and why should it take second best when it has the exclusive eating rights to a wildflower meadow? I leave the endearing and spirited creature to its floral banquet and pedal away in an unhurried fashion. 'Dobbin' follows for a minute or two before announcing its departure with another snort and a shake of the head.

With surprisingly little transition the landscape changes from fallow parcels of stoney land to well-tended olive groves, the first I have seen on the journey. The olive trees have charcoal coloured trunks that are gnarled, stunted, aged, and deeply textured. The grove is planted in rows, each about fifteen feet apart and at right angles to the road. All the upper branches are wizened and twisted; they form a low, dark tunnel and unlike the light and airy arch created by the plane trees, the olive tree tunnel is barely head height, very dark, and quite foreboding to gaze into. The dark, twisted branches would illustrate a scary children's book to great effect. Looking closer I see that the fruit has already set and the first crop of juvenile olives is already pea sized.

The city of Romans lies within the Parc Naturel Régional du Vercors. Romans (or Romans-sur-Isère to give this historical city its full title) welcomes me with the beautiful sight of the glorious River Isère flowing sedately through the city like a broad silver ribbon. It would be good to halt here for an hour or two but the local campsite closed two years ago so I have little option but to press on.

The D538 road out of Romans is wide and straight and busy. Conveniently it has a lane specifically for bicycles and mopeds and although narrow it's much safer than sharing the main carriageway with the other traffic. Several miles later I come to the village of Montelier, which has been awarded four stars by the prestigious *Village Fleuri* scheme and is very much worth seeing at the right time of year; unfortunately I'm a couple of months early for admiring floral displays so I pedal on to Chabeuil and my base for tonight.

The campsite turns out to be very large and well-equipped, and with a heated pool, waterslides, play areas, and indoor entertainment, this site is fully geared for lively family holidays. I won't use the facilities of course but I pay a premium to pitch my little tent, which is reasonable enough given what's on offer. I check out nearly a dozen muddy pitches before venturing away from the main campsite where I find a small area hidden away in a corner of the site. The entrance is much too narrow for motorhomes or even large cars so it's had little use. Maybe it's not really a pitch. Who cares? I don't because it's grassy, it's quiet, and it'll do me very nicely, thank you very much.

Once the tent is set up, I return to reception for a bottle of *alcool à brûler*. A bad move on my part as I probably have enough to cook for today and my request results in one member of staff telling me, in an unnecessarily excitable gallic way, if I may say so, that I MUST buy food from the campsite takeaway as open fires are strictly prohibited. Now, I've been on this planet long enough to suspect that this is, at least in part, a wheeze to get me to part with more of my hard-earned cash for a pizza, a burger, or something else near the top of my *what-do-I-not-want-to-eat* list. Accordingly, I try my very best to explain to the person that my cooker is just a very small camping stove that is not in any way *dangereuse*.

Although highly tempted, I don't over-egg my case by insisting that I always carry a fire blanket, water and foam extinguishers, and a hotline to the local *pompiers*. Buying on-site food will make this already expensive stay even more costly and I need to watch my expenses. As it is, I've noticed that prices are on the up as I close in on the tourist hotspots of Provence. An on-site pizza will push my costs here to around thirty euros. Thirty euros for the rental of a small bit of grass and some warm flavoured bread! Do I have 'Village Fool' tattooed across my forehead as an invitation to screw me for every penny? I don't think so.

One advantage of being alone in a quiet corner is that my sausage omelette is cooked without anyone knowing. I am not usually one for breaking rules but there are times when common sense must apply and this is one of them. Anyway, the French are a nation of serial rule breakers when it suits them. Do French farmers not blockade roads at the drop of a beret whenever they feel disgruntled with the European Union's common agricultural policy payments?

After finishing my omelette I set off to the bar for a beer and to catch up on my journal. Unfortunately, I abandon the idea when I come across a group of children who are simply bursting with the fun of being on holiday. Quite right, too; good on them, they are doing just what they should at that age, but they really are unbelievably noisy. Laughs and shouts I can cope with but not piercing screams and lots of them. No, too much high-volume exuberance in a bar isn't for me, I'm sorry to say.

By nine o'clock I've written five full pages back at the tent. Today's experiences from the warm croissants that started the morning so well to the uphill bends that brought me back to earth so soon after I set off. I have mentioned the snake that was dead, and the horse that was very much alive. A few lines are devoted to the tall and light plane trees and the low and dark olive trees. I wonder what will come my way tomorrow.

# Day 23 – Saturday 8th May

## Department of Drôme:

## From Chabeuil to Crest

Many days have involved less mileage than I expected, which is odd given that the whole trip is looking like it will end up a few hundred miles more than I planned for – the conundrum makes no sense to me. Anyway, today involves a very short ride to Crest, which is awarded absolutely no stars by the Michelin Guide to France. Surely this must be a bit harsh. I set off to decide for myself.

My travels start by backtracking three miles to Chabeuil to reconnect with the D538 for my onward journey. Thankfully time is not at all pressing and I have time to see something of the town before heading south. The main bridge offers me a pleasant upstream view and the perfect angle to photograph the town. Upriver from the bridge there is a second, rather ancient-looking arched bridge and to its right sits Chabeuil town hall with its castellated turret.

Another solo cyclist stops next to me and gets her camera out. Mariah is Dutch and has cycled here from her home in the Netherlands in a week. A week! What's that all about? Ridiculous, if you ask me: that's over one hundred miles a day. How do you even do that? In her case you do it by being young, cycling at pace, staying in hotels every night. She has a minimalist approach to luggage, so minimalist in fact that beyond a minute rucksack and two water bottles she has none. Not that any of this takes anything away from her achievement, horses for courses and all that. Mariah asks if I would use her camera to photograph her against the backdrop of Chabeuil town. A couple of passing Frenchmen walk over to us. They assume we're travelling as a couple, which is rather odd as I'm twice her age and far more decrepit. Maybe they think we're father and daughter. Either way they insist on taking our photograph. We all laugh when Mariah, in what sounds like fluent French, explains that we had only met a few minutes earlier.

The parting words were Mariah's as she apologised for not smiling for the photograph and explained that she hit a patch of wet mud a few days ago when cycling at speed and ended up bruised, grazed, and with a row of badly broken front teeth, hence her reluctance to smile. She added that the real annoyance for her is that she has a particular liking for French baguettes but isn't able to eat any.

We set off on our separate ways after much convivial hand-shaking and a rather loud chorus of *'bon courage'* all round. The Frenchmen resume their walk into town, Mariah zooms off towards the south of France, and I cycle off at the almost pedestrian speed of seven miles per hour.

After leaving the Chabeuil behind me I come to open countryside and eventually to an area of wildflower meadows that sparkle – yes, the fields really do sparkle as the sun catches flashes of red, blue, and yellow flowers as they are blown about in the strong breeze. Poppy, cornflower, and mustard, a repeat of yesterday's landscape in many ways but much improved by the bright sunlight that shimmers over the scented land. The whole outlook is very cheerful and come to think of it, very south of France. Spurred on by the warm sun I find myself putting the miles behind me at a fair lick. Strange, really, because I am not even pedalling fast. A straight level road and no stops helps me to tot up the miles even though my speed is still shy of ten miles per hour.

By late morning the sun has evaporated the final remnants of haze when I spot a giant wicker basket at the side of an otherwise empty road. The basket is four feet high, filled with vegetables, and placed at the end of farm track to advertise produce for sale. The display has been arranged with the greatest care and precision; the artistic pattern looks rather like a massive version of those beautiful Italian micromosaics made as nineteenth-century souvenirs for grand-tour travellers. I wonder if the artistry displayed has backfired a bit because the honesty box is empty and the display is completely untouched – I think I would be reluctant to disturb the perfect design by buying anything.

It's eleven-thirty on the dot as I cycle past the ornate entrance to Crest town and I have a decision to make: It's a lovely day, I'm on schedule, and I have more than enough time to explore Crest should I wish, even if it is not rated by Michelin. Alternatively, I can just crack on and get another ten miles in before lunch. Day to day necessities must come first so I pop into the Casino supermarket to replenish my supplies.

Once my shopping is done, I leave the bike secured and alarmed so that I can walk into the town unencumbered by its weight. A couple of hours and twenty or so photos later I've had a taste of the ancient streets of Crest and far be it from me to contradict the revered experts at Michelin, but I have to say they've got it wrong: Crest is a charming town that has tempted me so much that I intend to explore the place in more detail once I have found the campsite here.

Good fortune is with me because almost as soon as I decide to overnight in Crest I come across *'Les Corinthes'* while walking back to collect my bike. The site is next to the Drôme River and conveniently situated for exploring the town later. Eleven euros secures my pitch, and after setting camp and a quick lunch I set off on foot back over the bridge to see more of the town, which is billed as yet another *'Ville Fleurie'* but also *'Crest la Medieval'*.

Sometimes you just warm to a place. Crest is such a place for me and no discernible reason it just feels right here even though I'm not at all familiar with the town and I know nothing of what it has to offer.

Setting off in search of a castle-like building raised high above the town, I end up in a labyrinth of narrow, steep, and ancient passageways, and not for the first time it strikes me that losing your bearings in an unfamiliar town is one of the best ways to discover its more interesting nooks and crannies. Some of the alleys in Crest are spanned, twenty feet up or more, by sturdy stone arches that bridge the gap between the ancient buildings. I've seen identical arches in the ancient Greek city of Rhodes; the arches there were constructed centuries ago to make the buildings more resistant to earthquakes. Perhaps the land here is also unstable and these architectural arches provide the same support.

The castle suddenly appears in front of me as the alley I'm wandering up gives way into a small courtyard. High above me looms the medieval *Tour de Crest*, and I can see now that it's indeed a *'tour'*, or tower, rather than a castle. At fifty-two metres high the tower commands the limestone outcrop it's built upon – very fitting for the highest medieval tower in the whole of France. From its lofty position the tower is all that remains of a once huge fortified building that was dismantled on the orders of King Louis the thirteenth. It may be peaceful here now but in less enlightened times the *Tour de Crest* was used to incarcerate Huguenot free thinkers who opposed the king's regime.

After climbing a seemingly endless flight of limestone steps my expectation is dashed when I discover I'm not at the base of the tower but at a tower-like church, which boasts an oversized weather vane and a four-sided clock as its principal architectural features. The clock chimes as I saunter between the trees surrounding the small churchyard. Eventually, and somewhat out of breath, I arrive at the real *Tour de Crest*. The climb has taken lots of effort on my behalf but I am well rewarded by the panoramic view from the top.

Both the town of Crest and the sparklingly iridescent River Drôme are laid out below me in a magical toytown scene. Beyond the town miles of farmland are hemmed in by a barrier of rugged peaks on the horizon and from my eyrie-like position I watch cloud building from the west. A black skyline above the peaks looks ominous and threatening. After taking my fill of the expansive view and approaching weather front, I make my way down through a labyrinth of quaint alleys until I arrive at an open famers' market. Most the vendors are selling fruit and vegetables but cut flowers and local wine are also available. I leave with a brace of large, misshapen, and slightly muddy genuine field mushrooms, a world away from those forced to grow in some dark polytunnel. The mushrooms are handed to me in a brown paper bag that reminds me of shopping as a small boy, hand in hand with my late mum. I very much enjoy the unexpected memory the experience brings back to me.

Old narrow alleys converge on the marketplace like spokes but as I have no idea which one to follow, I just choose a zig-zag path at random. On the way down I find myself walking under lines of brightly coloured washing hanging from wires stretched between the buildings. The washing lines are three storeys up and operated by a pulley system strung between the houses. The pulleys have surprisingly hefty wooden handles, which give a clue as to the effort needed to haul heavy, wet washing into position. However much this is just a simple example of everyday life, it is a rare sight nowadays, which adds a charming touch of nostalgia to the town.

Several of the houses in the alley have been painted. Some umber, several ultramarine, and others terracotta. A single pink one stands out. The bright hues are entirely in keeping with the ancient and somewhat whimsical delight of Crest, a town that I find myself liking more and more as the day goes on. Crest has filled my afternoon with interest and the very least I can do is pay it an honest compliment.

Perhaps spurred on by the elevated washing lines, back at the campsite eight-and-a-half euros buys me one hour's use of the washing machine and dryer. The once distant rain starts to fall silently around me and not for the first time I use a laundry room as an indoor kitchen.

A handful of eggs, a packet of lardons, and the brown-bagged mushrooms are cooked together. Unfortunately, the mushrooms seep colour into the whole meal, but however unappetising it looks, and it does look pretty shocking to be honest, it is unquestionably tasty.

Within an hour of eating the rain eases so I return to town to write up my notes after what has been a very pleasant day indeed. Crossing the bridge over the wide, clear waters of *'La Drôme'* coincides with a spotlight of sun shining through a hole in the clouds. The beam of light illuminates the front of the *Tour de Crest* making the tower stand out boldly against the sombre black sky behind it. The shaft of light makes the tower stonework sparkle, and Crest (which some say is named after the old Roman word for crystal) truly lives up to its name.

It defies all logic that I seem to have ended up in another town where the bars close in the early evening, but all is not lost, thankfully, because I've discovered I possess hitherto hidden talents for seeking out ale at the end of a day on the bike, and after a bit of a trek my efforts are rewarded when I find a bar that is open. Well, almost. The bar has no customers, half the chairs are upended and stacked on top of tables, let's say the place is not an inviting or promising sight, but Monsieur Le Patron invites me to stay until he closes at eight, which is ideal for putting pen to paper in comfort and silence and doing justice to a brace of *pression* beers. *(Pression literally translates as 'pressure' and in the context of beer it means draught.)*

I note nineteen miles of cycling for today, the shortest daily mileage since I wheeled the bike off the ferry, but it all adds up, I suppose, and my total mileage is now seven hundred and fifty-two miles. I may crack eight hundred tomorrow, either way I think I'll get wet as the watch barometer has fallen steadily all day; it's now at under a thousand, the lowest reading for more than a week.

On returning to *'Les Clorinthes'* the proprietor, who seems to have been lying in wait, beckons me into reception to warn me that I must take great care in the coming days as it is going to be exceptionally stormy for the time of year. He explains that torrential rains have caused flooding near the city of Nice where over a hundred cars have been washed away. One hundred and thirty KPH winds have closed Montpellier airport and the ferocious weather is set to continue across southern France. The proprietor is most earnest in expressing his concerns, which he repeats to make sure I understand just how grave he considers the danger will be in the coming days.

I thank him for the warning and walk back to the tent deep in thought. I thought I'd already experienced my fair share of bad weather what with the rain in Burgundy, Mistral winds, and odd overnight storms. My initial thoughts are to press on and put my faith in good fortune. After all, the storm may head off over the Mediterranean and miss me completely, and above all else I must catch the bus in Montpellier eight days from now. Of course, there's a fine line between blind optimism and reckless folly. Surely, with luck on my side, the heavy rain and strong winds will be no more than an unpleasant consequence of travelling in the open air. That said, I think this is a situation that needs more consideration.

Back at my little tent the weather is still benign, nevertheless this seems an appropriate time to check the tent, poles and guy ropes. What more I can do for now?

# Day 24 – Sunday 9th of May

## Departments of Drôme and Vaucluse:

## From Crest to Grignan

I am pleased to report that the weather caused no problems overnight and I've woken up completely refreshed and ready to press on south after a very decent night's sleep. In theory I suppose I'm heading into the eye of the storm but it really doesn't feel like it.

The D538 leads me out of Crest. It's been my road of choice since leaving Beaurepaire fifty miles north of here. Sunday starts dry and overcast and whilst I'm enthusiastic about the day ahead there's a clear disconnect between my mind, which is determined to make progress, and my reluctant legs, which don't seem at all keen to put in the miles. So, my sabbath starts on a slow burn with limbs not yet up to the job of pedalling. It's all a bit odd, really, because since leaving Calais I've progressed from a wobbling novice pedalling twenty miles a day, to a moderately able cyclist not fazed by fifty miles with a heavy load. In fact, I would go as far as to say that the bike and I are now as one; each day we help each other to the end of the road, as it were. Well, not so today, I'm sorry to say, and to make matters worse the road is not proving to be a team player either. It has no sympathy for me or the bike with its bumpy surface and steep inclines.

As I enter the village of La Répara-Auriples it begins to rain, steadily at first, but soon the drops fall with great enthusiasm. Thirty minutes on, it's pouring down and my thoughts turn to my 'waterproof' panniers. I hope my clothes will be dry at the end of today – I don't want the eight and a half euros for drying clothes to have been spent in vain.

The rain intensifies and the sky darkens as this steeper section of road demands that I get off and push. Even with only sporadic traffic this is a good time to switch lights to flashing mode. Poor visibility, low cloud, and constant rain make this an unpleasant morning but for all that, it's not cold and I am grateful for that.

The first col tops out at fourteen hundred feet; here the wind has shredded the thin layer of cloud that lies between the col and the valley – thin white tatters remain between me and the toytown farm buildings on the valley floor. It's a beautiful view that cheers me no end, especially as the landscape ahead is billiard table flat and the road across the valley floor is dead straight. That's my sort of road; the day's about to improve.

The road alternated between left and right on the steep downhill sections. Negotiating corner after sweeping corner is exhilarating even at the modest pace I'm setting. The fun only ends when I pop out from under the low cloud into the village of Puy-St.-Martin.

A noise from my Nokia phone is a rare event and it's fortunate I heard it as I often turn it off to save battery life. Anyway, as I have to stop to read the text, I grab an impromptu drink at *Les Platanes*, a roadside bar in Puy-St.-Martin. Today is a hot drink sort of day if ever there was one, but I'm always reluctant to order coffee on the continent as it seems disproportionally costly more often than not. So, cold or not, beer it is.

In front of the pub the paved seating area has been pushed upwards by the exposed roots of a large pollarded tree. Pretty cast-iron tables and chairs sit on the uneven surface under attractive umbrella-shaped awnings with red and black stripes.

Today really is a day for sitting indoors and the prospect of warmth does tempt me, but I'm far too wet to go into the pub. Watching the world through the curtain of rain that pours down from the awning above, plus a few minutes of inactivity, makes the chill creep further into my body. Outside there are no other customers for me to say *bonjour* to, so I entertain myself by watching the stream of rainwater scurrying frantically down the roadside into the village. On other days Puy-St.-Martin may well be full of cheer.

The first icy sip confirms what a ridiculous idea ordering even a small beer is on such a day. What was I thinking? Anyway, I put my brave face on, take hold of the glass and down the cold golden liquid in one go. Unsurprisingly this triggers a vigorous shiver, a rush of blood to the head, and a sharp cold-induced pain across my forehead. I have to wait a few minutes for these unpleasant side-effects to settle before I can set off. Yes, drinking it down was unwise but at least I can get back on the bike and warm up a bit now.

I cover the next four miles at pace to generate body heat. At the head of the valley the road climbs to the village of La Bégude-de-Mazenc. Here, having paused since I left the pub, the rain not only resumes but quickly goes through the gears from mizzle to drizzle to what is known in the northeast of England as *'plothering down'* (huge drops of rain with no wind). I power into the downpour, head down until the exertion becomes uncomfortable.

Metal barriers warn of the drop at the roadside and for the first time I can see the height I've gained since leaving the pub. There are even views to be enjoyed although this is no weather for sightseeing. Rainwater trickles off my cycle helmet and into my eyes. Add this to my numb hands and face and I'm wondering if I should have stayed put in the tent today. But I'm here now. I've made my own luck so I'll just have to put on a brave if wet face on and crack on until the weather changes. Whinge over!

All is not bad, you know – I'm a thousand feet up and sooner or later the top of the hill will appear and reward me with a downhill ride. Another mile on and I'm surprised to discover that on the way up the lee side of the hill has sheltered me, and my unexpected reward on reaching the top is to be battered almost senseless by the wind. Where's the justice in that, I ask you?

The wind at the summit is consistently inconsistent, predictably unpredictable, and this causes me a real problem: A constant strong wind is a challenge I can battle against; I can lean into it, at least I have a chance, but here the wind fluctuates from a steady force that I can make progress against, to the occasional powerful gust that I struggle to stand up to, and if I were cycling would probably swipe the bike from under me and send us both crashing to the ground.

Did I mention that it's raining heavily? Well, it is, of course it is, and for the umpteenth time I wipe water from my face. This is an entirely futile gesture as my hands, along with everything else, are saturated, and trying to keep water out of my eyes is a repetitive pointless exercise. (If I'm not sounding bitter, it won't be long.) Anyway, it's just struck me that maybe this is the storm the campsite proprietor warned me about.

Just as I'm thinking to myself, *When did I last see a vehicle?* a pick-up overtakes me in a cloud of spray before pulling to an overenthusiastic halt a hundred yards further on in a scattering of roadside grit. The driver runs towards me beckoning with some urgency that he wants to give me a lift.

With his blue denim jacket, trousers, and boots all speckled with plaster, this good Samaritan obviously works in the building trade, and with very little help from me he picks up the bike, complete with panniers, and lifts the whole lot over the tailgate and deposits it, none too gently, into the open back of his pick-up. It weighs a ton! How did he even do that?

We drive for several miles through an upland landscape obscured by low cloud and torrential rain to the rhythm of swishing windscreen wipers and a loud radio until we arrive at the point where he must turn off to reach his place of work. Before we stop this knight of the road offers to drive me to Grignan. I thank him profusely but decline his kind offer so he can get back to work. He lowers the tailgate and we unload the bike together. *'Bon courage!'* and, *'Merci beaucoup!'* are bellowed into the wind in unison. Unfortunately, neither of us could understand much of the conversation in the pick-up what with the noise of the overworked engine, the windscreen wipers, the music, and the weather. The driver really didn't have to stop in this atrocious weather and he certainly didn't have to get himself soaked by lifting my bike into the back of this pick-up. What a gentleman.

Before resuming my travels, I check that both the panniers are attached to the lugs on the bike frame. The bike was laid on its side and bounced around a lot during our rather hectic drive so it would be no surprise if something has come adrift or broken off. After a quick once-over, everything looks fine. Grignan, here we come.

The wind eases considerably on the more sheltered downslope. This should be a cause for cheer but I suddenly feel very deflated when I realise that by accepting a lift, I have voided my aim of cycling every mile from the English Channel to the Mediterranean Sea. The feeling of disappointment is quite out of proportion with the fact that I simply accepted a ten-minute lift, quite unsolicited, from a well-intentioned local, nevertheless it does leave me feeling that I have let myself down. What's done is done, as they say, and I guess there are no hard and fast rules to my little adventure; my aim remains simple, to pedal across France from north to south, from coast to coast. and if common sense is applied, I shall still achieve that goal even after the little help I have just received.

Fizzing along through streams of surface water and down a series of sweeping bends is a very exhilarating run, which lasts until the tarmac levels out as I make my final approach to the little town of Grignan. My first impressions are of a compact and ancient town elevated above the valley floor and surrounded by fields of lavender. There's not a flower to be seen this early in the year but what a wonderful place this must be in a couple of months when Grignan floats on a sea of blue flowers amid the heady fragrant aroma produced by acres of the lavender herb.

Grignan sits on the Tricasin Plain. For many years this was thought to be a reference to three castles but the current academic thinking is that the name actually refers to the *Tricastini*, a Gallic tribe who occupied this area during Roman times. Either way, this is a very ancient place of human habitation, and I am drawn to stop a mile short of the town just to gaze over the patchwork of lavender fields and small vineyards that encircle it. Grignan is a collection of ancient buildings huddled together; the high walls of its interlocking houses create buttress-like defences to the outside world. The town is built on a massive natural rock plinth elevated above the surrounding plain. Looming high above the town and all before it is the castle. An elevated fortress in some form has existed here for over eight hundred years. The castle before me was rebuilt a century ago by Madame Fontaine, a local lady who spent her entire fortune restoring the dilapidated structure to its former Renaissance glory.

My arrival at Grignan coincides with the rain stopping, which I take as a good omen for my stay at *Camping Les Truffières*. The site is perfectly situated a mile or so from the centre of Grignan. The proprietor makes me a large coffee while I record my details in the registration book. I probably look more bedraggled and colder than I feel but I've perked up a bit now that I'm out of the wind and the rain has ceased. Either way the hot drink is very kind and extremely welcome. The site owner is widely travelled and we share a few stories while I warm myself next to the radiator. Once booked in, I pedal around the level wooded site until I find a pitch surrounded on three sides by tall slender trees; it is a pretty pitch much like all the others, and the only reason I picked this one is that a jay with the telltale blue edge to its wings landed nearby and seems quite unconcerned by the prospect of me taking up residence in its woodland home.

Within an hour a hot shower and dry clothes put me in just the right frame of mind to set off to explore the town. As I leave the site I chat with an English couple staying in a nearby caravan. The couple are keen ornithologists from Rutland who have seen several green woodpeckers and many jays on the site. If I am particularly fortunate, they tell me, a golden oriole is occasionally seen here. The paradox of the golden oriole is that although they are vivid yellow, they are extremely secretive birds and very difficult to spot.

Leaving the campsite by a gated side road I follow an uneven and deeply potholed track that is clearly little used and although just about fine for a bike I certainly wouldn't push my luck driving a car along it. The narrow track weaves its way through a pretty landscape. Short rows of gnarled olive trees grow in the small fields at the side of the track. Many of these little parcels of land have a long-abandoned look to them, crumbling walls everywhere festooned with wild poppies and weeds. That said, interspersed between the olive groves some of the other fields have been planted as miniature vineyards, just about big enough to produce the grapes needed to keep a family in wine.

The backdrop to this short cycle ride is the sight of the castle sitting high on its rocky pedestal. It seems to be beckoning me to Grignan while watching my progress as I approach the town, checking if I'm friend or foe as it will have done for countless centuries.

Grignan has charm in abundance; its streets bustle with life, and it is by far the most vibrant place I have chanced upon since the open-air bric-a-brac market in Montreuil-sur-Mer two days out from Calais. Grignan is crammed with so many people that to make any headway I have to dismount and push my bike through the narrow streets. This hubbub of humanity is not at all what I expected but I am more than happy to be a small part of it. Gathered in small groups, people are chatting and laughing, many with a glass in hand, families, neighbours, acquaintances, long-lost friends perhaps, people of all ages and backgrounds. By the look of it this is no normal Sunday and I must have stumbled upon one of Grignan's annual events.

Six in the evening and stalls selling all kinds of goods line the wider streets. There's no sign that these traders are about to pack up for the day, quite the opposite in fact; here in Grignan brisk business is still being conducted under bright canvas awnings. It all adds much colour and cheer to the town.

Outside the mayor's office twenty or so glass vases are lined up at waist height on a low rendered wall. Iris flowers, one per vase, are being judged by a short procession of local dignitaries. Nearby wooden tables are laid out with an assortment of fresh fruit and veg; each piece carved into an artistic pattern. The courgette with the intricate symmetrical pattern cut into its green skin would win first prize if I were judging. Above the entries a row of signs reads: Traille crayon (pencil sized), Tap-Tap, Coupe-frites, Eplucheurs (vegetable peeler), Mandoline, and Shopper. Unfortunately I have absolutely no idea what most of this is meant to mean.

After half an hour or so of exploring the town, I come to a small cobbled square in what proves to be a much quieter part of town. A neoclassical open-air bathhouse commands the centre of the square; it has a domed roof supported by a circle of sixteen Doric columns and its very apt local nickname is the 'Water Temple'. It all looks very ancient, Roman perhaps, but first impressions deceive as the bathhouse was in fact built by the town mayor in the nineteenth century. This matters not a jot as it all looks very splendid.

A cluster of people are listening to three South American musicians who have set up shop here and are doing a fine job playing panpipes and oversized guitars. A selection of dream catchers and bead jewellery is for sale, all spread out on a large rug in front of the musical ensemble. With people milling around and others seated at the outdoor café overlooking the 'water temple' I feel this is as good a place as any to padlock the bike to some railings, freeing me up to wander off unhindered to explore some more of this delightful town.

Away from the centre of town one passageway in particular takes my fancy: it is exceptionally narrow and runs between facing terraces of tall houses. The alley, which is curved and steep, is only accessible on foot and it's more of a clamber up it than a walk. I'm intrigued. The worn footpath was hewn out of the natural bedrock countless generations ago, and if I spread my arms out, my outstretched fingers can just about bridge the gap between the buildings. The houses closing in on both sides of me are built of stone blocks, textured and distressed with age in a pleasant, lived-in sort of way. Paint flakes on many of the windows and doors that I pass on my way up the alley; it all looks very quaint and not at all neglected or run down.

The alley reminds me that France has a knack for retaining the magical appearance of its older towns and villages, it is a uniquely French look rather than an acknowledged architectural style. *'Crumbly Chic'*, it could perhaps become known as? Well, whatever it is called, 'Crumbly Chic' exists in abundance here in Grignan and I find it very appealing.

Continuing up the stepped path makes me breathless; I can feel the texture of the uneven cobbles under my feet and it crosses my mind that in a tiny way I'm adding to the wear caused by thousands of feet over hundreds of years. In North Yorkshire this alley would be known as a *'Snicket'* or a *'Ginnel'*, and if you ever go to the enchanting Yorkshire fishing town of Whitby on the northeast coast of England, there are many such ancient snickets to be explored.

Plant pots have been placed all the way up, on the right, by proud residents, one pot to every fifth step. Further along, shutters and doors are painted in brighter colours than those lower down; painted some years ago, I would say, and they are delightfully crumbly-chic now, which is perfect because shiny new paint would look most out of place. Most doors have an ornate metal knocker; a chunky lion's head here, a cast-iron bunch of grapes there, and just ahead a particularly splendid fish knocker, the rich olive-green colour on its scales acquired by time and weather acting on the copper alloy. Eventually the slender alley opens out into a wide flagstone courtyard that feels particularly bright and airy after the restrictive cosiness of the pretty 'crumbly-chic' snicket.

Immediately below Grignan Castle I pause to catch my breath, like so many before me, on a bench provided for this very purpose. In front of the bench, and forming part of a metal fence placed to prevent walkers from falling over the edge is a large cross. The ornate wrought-iron cross is mounted on wood and marks the start of the *'Chemin-de-Ronde'* or parapet walk. Having allowed a few moments for my heart and lungs to recover from my exertions, I set off along the level parapet path. Dusk is falling now but even in the fading light I see the Tricasin plain laid out before me. Beyond the flatness of the plain the land heaves itself up and transforms into a range of distant hazy mountains.

As I gaze over the parapet it is not the enchanting twinkle of fairy lights that draws the eye most, it is the sea of roof tiles. Few of the houses below me are constructed to the same footprint or shape; this is not a place of repetition, it is a place of individuality. Some rooves are startlingly higgledy-piggledy, most are small, surprisingly small, and some are set at rakish angles to each other. The covering of pantiles are mostly red, but some are burnt umber, others ochre, and they seem to be fighting each other for space. Individual rooves almost touch in places, hiding the little alleys under the sea of rooftops converging from all directions. There is no geometric order here and the chaos is a visual delight. Directly in front of me are dozens and dozens of dumpy square chimneys, and after a while of taking in the detail I realise that there are no large windows, not anywhere, not one.

I am mesmerised by this little medieval town of Grignan, which has come alive below me. Just when I thought the magic was over the view is transformed by the final embers of the setting sun as it lays a wash of pale tangerine over the rooftops. I'm left to sit and admire the glorious creations of man and nature. Could anything be better than this? I doubt it.

I have become so engrossed with this place (perhaps you can tell?) that I've completely forgotten to eat! This is a first! And it needs to be corrected forthwith. So, down the hill and back among the townsfolk I go. The festivities are still in full swing and if anything, the town seems livelier than earlier with the addition of illuminations and music. Soon after retrieving the bike I prop it against a wall at the first eatery I come to. Fortunately for me, one side of an outdoor picnic table that abuts a busy little street is available. A man having coffee nods his approval when I gesture that I would like to sit opposite him. I'm surprised at the feeling of relief that comes with sitting down.

Thankfully the waitress speaks perfect English. Apparently, the café is doing a trimmed down menu as it's carnival day so the choices are – *Pizza, Panini, Salades, Sandwiches, Tartines, & Boissons*. My panini with an embarrassingly huge wedge of apple tart and a beer are all served quickly just as the man opposite me gets up to leave. Writing my journal while eating is a skill I've developed in recent weeks but today's entry is short and notes little more than thirty-three miles of cycling and a few more in a pick-up van. I shall pad it out back at the tent. Looking up from the journal I see people are leaving the carnival now that it's dark, emptier, and quiet comes to Grignan surprisingly quickly.

The waitress walks over with a man who has great difficulty walking and asks if he could sit at my table as this is his usual place. She speaks to him in French and points to my bike before introducing him to me.

The waitress is on a break from her university studies and joins us both once the café is quieter. The three of us sit at the table together and spend the next half hour talking about our respective lives. I learn from Camille that Pascal was involved in a dreadful car accident some years ago, which cost him the use of his right arm. Walking is slow, awkward and uncomfortable as he has only partial use of his legs. Pascal has limited use of his left arm and some fingers on his left hand, but only with difficulty. Conversation is difficult and I feel acutely embarrassed that I simply cannot understand most of what Pascal says. But what comes through above anything else is that Pascal is an engaging and determined man with a lively expression and a ready smile.

After a while Pascal slowly raises himself up from the bench seat. He steadies himself with his elbow on the picnic table in order to remove something from a trouser pocket. His difficulties are most uncomfortable to watch so I insist on paying for the coffees in the hope that this would allow him to sit down again. Pascal smiles at me but persists with his struggle for several minutes until he's successful. Every movement is a challenge that leaves me humbled and feeling truly ashamed when I think that I moaned to myself when facing obstacles on my travels. Watching Pascal makes me realise that I haven't got any idea what obstacles really are, not the slightest idea.

Pascal secures one side of his open wallet to the table with the back of his permanently bent wrist before beginning the excruciatingly slow process of manipulating his other fingers to extract a card from the opposite side. After several minutes of effort and concentration Pascal indicates that he would like Camille to show me a card. The laminated card bears a photo of Pascal, and Camille explains to me that it's his membership card for the local Pétanque (boules/bowls) club. Pascal was part of the team that won the local cup. I may have only just met Pascal but looking up from the card and seeing his beaming face makes me appreciate the profound significance that this little card holds for him. It is such a pleasure to learn of his success and to see the pride that Pascal enjoys by sharing his extraordinary sporting achievement with me.

My time with Camille and Pascal is over too quickly but it's getting late now so I must press on as the route to the campsite is unclear in my mind. After bidding my farewells I leave Grignan and its fading celebrations behind. Once clear of the town I cut through the olive grove track hoping it's the one that the proprietor told me about. Moonlight is all that illuminates my way and as the surface is uneven, potholed, and hard to make out, I push the bike rather than risk a painful tumble. Roadside walls feature as indistinct silhouettes and in places trees completely block out what little moonlight there is. I have to take care on these inky black sections of road. It is all a bit disconcerting, to be honest. As I near the campsite I'm suddenly very tired. The effort used against the morning's wind and rain and on the steep alleys of Grignan have caught up with me. That said, I hope I never forget that whatever I do, it will pale against the effort Pascal puts into everyday life.

I pause briefly and turn around to gaze back towards Grignan for a final time before I enter the wooded campsite. The profile of the town with its castle illuminated by the moon and set against the indigo of the night sky is a magical sight that I shall not forget. As I push the bike through the campsite gates I reflect on the mixed experiences of today; the foul weather, the good Samaritan, the unexpected delights of Grignan and its festivities, but more than all this it is the indomitable spirit of Pascal that will leave its mark.

# Day 25 – Monday 10<sup>th</sup> May

## Departments of Drôme and Gard: From Grignan to Orange

Sunlight streams through the green and orange tent walls and fills me with get-up-and-go for the day ahead. What a contrast this is to yesterday's wash-out. To speed up progress, breakfast is white chocolate and water because it's quick and my food supplies are depleted after the weekend. I could do to find a supermarket before the end of the morning or it will be Kendal mint cake for lunch. Sleeping bag and mattress rolled up – check. Tent shaken, folded, and stowed – check. Panniers attached – check. Map re-folded for today's route – check. Valuables bag clipped onto the handlebars – check. Valuables inside – double check. Water bottles refilled and secure in cradles – check. Tyres and brakes OK – check. Me – check.

I pedal through the wooded campsite quietly because I am keeping my eyes open for the elusive golden oriole. It didn't show up but then again, I didn't expect it to. Neither do I see any of the owls that hooted so loudly during the night.

The weather lives up to its early promise and by eleven the temperature has risen to a balmy sixteen degrees – what joy, this is more like it for the south of France. Today is the first day in seven that it isn't pouring down or threatening rain and I can't tell you what a joy it is to be dry and warm and following the lovely D71 road as it takes me through the village of Chamaret. Today's route follows a quiet road with no steep gradients; mile after mile has been easy cycling under the bright sun. Just what's needed after yesterday.

The human body is a wonderful thing, when you think about it. Its ability to reinvigorate itself is truly astounding. Yesterday I felt completely washed out at the end of the day and lethargy this morning would have been no surprise, but no, my body's having none of it; eight hours' sleep, and a small snack for breakfast, and I'm ready to go. The bigger picture I find even more remarkable when I think that three weeks ago I'd not cycled much more than a dozen miles, and never with heavy panniers. Then just for good measure, I completely neglected to practice before setting off and decided to train myself on the job. Day one was a slog and night one brought cramp that triggered self-doubt and thoughts of a sneaky retreat over the flatlands of the Benelux countries. And yet, a little more than a week after leaving Devon my body had risen to the task. Forty miles was cracked one day, then fifty – what a confidence boost that was. And then once, just once, I nearly cracked sixty miles. Who'd have thought? Not me, that's for sure. And now, after three weeks of pedalling, and a few days loafing in Chalon-sur-Saône, I am well into my stride. I don't know that I'm a proper cyclist yet but I'm getting there, I'm sure of that.

Today the bike and I are taking a straight tack pretty well due south, which means pointing the front wheel along an imaginary line roughly five miles east of a cleft formed by *Le Rhône*. The great river has nibbled away for millennia at this landscape and over time it has eroded itself a convenient wedge between the Alps and the Massif Central. The river broadens to the south of here and acquires the splendidly aristocratic-sounding title of *Canal de Donzère-Mondragon*. Unfortunately the truth is far less charming as the name relates to the Donzère-Mondragon dam and hydroelectric plant. From that point the river is deeper and navigable enough for larger vessels to ply their trade between inland towns and the Mediterranean Sea.

Today I'm set on covering the fifty-odd miles to the Avignon along the *Route Touristique des Côtes du Rhône*, at least for some of the way. Avignon lies within the region of 'Provence'. The name alone puts a spring in my step. Provence is such an evocative place, don't you think?

Pretty villages, olive groves, vineyards, lavender of course; all of these are already more frequent sights now that I have edged further south.

An hour out of Grignan the untended road verges are enriched by thousands of crimson poppies, their wispy translucent petals waving gently to encourage me as I pedal by. A little later a gnarly clump of prickly-pear cactus makes me realise just how far south I am as I pedal into the town of Suze-la-Rousse between ranks of plane trees. The mature trees make an impressive sight with their stout trunks and smart grey plates of smooth bark. A square turreted castle is built high above Suze-la-Rousse and fortress casts a massive shadow across the road where the air has still to be warmed by the morning sun. The town is disproportionately smaller than its castle and minutes later I am cycling out of Suze-la-Rousse and leaving its impressive medieval defences behind me.

Four Norwegian cyclists have propped their bicycles against a fountain in the central square of the next village I come to. They're pondering over a map as I approach them but seeing a fellow cyclist they pause their deliberations for a chat. The two married couples have flown here, with their personalised bicycles, for an off-season cycling holiday in Provence. Today is day one and they've pedalled out from their hotel in the city of Orange to get a taste of the area for their week ahead. We discuss our respective cycling plans before being joined by two young Australian women who overheard us speaking in English. The pair are from Sydney and have flown halfway around the world to organise a marriage in Provence. None of us are surprised when the bride-to-be tells us her wedding is taking a great deal of organising as she's never been to France before and only speaks English.

I continue heading towards Orange on a quiet and deliciously picturesque road that weaves its pretty way between small stony fields and the pretty rural houses. Along much of the way a wonderful fragrance hangs in the still air from wild herbs. Could this be anywhere else but Provence? I doubt it. Portions of land remain as *garrigue*, that rough low scrubland found along the Mediterranean rim where the tall broad-leaved trees of further north have finally given way to heat-loving plants and squat bushes, which thrive in these more arid and stoney soils – juniper, holm oak, prickly pear, and of course wild herbs.

Orange has UNESCO World Heritage status and is the third largest city in Vaucluse. I hope the thirty thousand people who live here like history because Orange is acclaimed for its Roman architecture. My first notable sight in Orange is not Roman remains but a statue of a praying mantis in the form of an enormous metal sculptures that sits in the middle of a roundabout. Other than because it is a native species I have absolutely no idea what its significance could be.

A mile on and my architectural expectations are met when I find myself cycling towards the *Arc de Triomphe d'Orange*. Far less iconic and a great deal smaller than its Paris namesake, the arch here is by no means small and, dare I suggest, it's better in some respects than its more northerly big brother. For one thing, this *Arc de Triomphe* is not penned in by concentric lanes of manic traffic so it can be enjoyed more leisurely and without the distractions of passing cars or crowds of people. Also absent are the forceful street vendors that sell souvenirs under the landmark in Paris. This triumphal arch may not have the same initial 'wow factor', but in many ways, I prefer it. I need to take a closer look.

The original arch was constructed here on the orders of Emperor Augustus (27BC-14AD) to honour the veterans of the Gallic Wars. His successor, Tiberius, reconstructed the arch to celebrate his victories over the Germanicus tribes of the Rhineland. *(What was it with these Roman emperors? It was all me, me, me.)* A thousand years later, during the Middle Ages, the arch formed part of the medieval city walls. The walls have long gone but the Roman arch remains, in marvellous condition except for some pot marks in the stone left by medieval crossbowmen who used the arch for target practice; I doubt you'd get away with that for long if you gave it a go nowadays.

Five minutes down the road I make short work of pitching the tent and washing some clothes, which I drape over the tent to dry in the warm sun. The only other person using the site acknowledges me with a nod and a wave as he replaces the empty gas bottle in his caravan. This is a quiet site with no on-site restaurant or bar; facilities are limited to a tennis court and a *'sanitaire'* block, so I set about making the best of it by settling down to the job of writing up today's notes and examining my route for the coming days.

Day twenty-five ends as I reflect on what a good day it's been. I've met people from the very north of Europe and others from the very south of our planet. I've enjoyed great scenery, the smell of wild herbs, and a close-up view of a two-thousand-year-old Roman arch, complete with ancient artillery marks. I may have cycled less than thirty miles since leaving Grignan this morning but I've passed the eight-hundred-mile barrier. That fact alone makes me rejoice or *'se réjouir'*, as I understand they say in these parts.

# Day 26 – Tuesday 11th of May

## Department of Vaucluse:

## From Orange to Avignon

I awaken from slumber that was doubtless helped no end by last night's monster baguette, some apple pie, and an over-generous quaffing of rosé wine. I have no idea why I bought rosé wine, I don't even like the stuff.

It's the eleventh of May and our youngest daughter Katie is twenty-one this very day. She is at university in London and we've arranged a get-together to celebrate a few weeks from now. Katie will doubtless enjoy a cake this evening, and I'm going to start the celebrations early with the remaining three-quarters of a delicious *tarte aux pommes*. After my tasty if unconventional 'Happy Birthday' toast I am ready to leave Orange by nine.

The sky has the sombre appearance of a black crumpled duvet and within half an hour of setting off I feel the first raindrops. Putting my Gore-Tex coat on before any deluge is an easy decision, but waterproof overtrousers are a trickier matter altogether: what with removing shoes and hopping about to keep your balance, and fighting material that clings to wet legs just to put them on. Worst of all, overtrousers are hot to wear – no ifs, no buts, I will be hot, uncomfortably hot. But they'll keep me dry, of course, and that sky does look pretty intimidating. So, am I going to wear waterproof trousers this morning? Absolutely not! Living on the edge? I would say so.

'Murphy's Law' and 'Sod's Law', everyone's heard of them but who knows exactly what they are and which is which? I certainly don't. Well according to an esteemed Emeritus Professor of Mathematics from Imperial College London: Murphy's Law dictates that *'what can go wrong will go wrong'* (eventually). Whereas Sod's Law requires that *'something will always go wrong and when it does it will go wrong with the worst possible outcome'*. Today I am on the receiving end of Murphy's Law and my decision to rely on wearing shorts with legs *au naturel* proves to be incorrect as quickly as you can say 'what a fool'. And as if to prove the point that *'what can go wrong will go wrong'* (eventually), the rain starts to fall with the output of a moderate sluice. I spontaneously muttered under my breath to myself, something along the lines of, 'Not this rain again,' although perhaps I said it a little more briskly.

The rain is torrential now. I'm drenched, and I'm not exactly happy about the situation, let me tell you. 'Soggy legs' may be a lesser-known medical condition but it's the one I am suffering from right now. My symptoms, in case you are the least bit interested in my welfare, are that my upper legs are cold and they are wet, and the material of my shorts is sticking uncomfortably to my thighs like the tentacles of some long-dead octopus. And to cap it all, both of my shoes are completely waterlogged because the rain is running down my calf muscles as if they are downpipes from the guttering. I wager I'll have trench foot by teatime the way things are going, and the conspiracy does not end there because my socks are now enthusiastically in on the act and have taken up the chore of wicking the downpour from my legs in such a way as to ensure that as much rainwater as is scientifically possible ends up inside my footwear. Getting close to Sod's Law now, I feel. I hope I don't sound bitter.

Right now, my shorts cause me a great deal of concern, if I'm honest. In fact they are causing me the most concern of anything on the journey so far – except perhaps for the startling moment when 'Monsieur Marcel-Le-Whatever' bent down in front of me and enthusiastically fondled my calf muscles after the TV chariot racing in the pub up north. Enough of that. It's the visual aspect of the shorts that cause me the most concern because when I look down at my waist, I am looking at an exact re-enactment of the truly horrid predicament I suffered last week as I pedalled along the Burgundy wine route outside Beaune. I may not have mentioned it at the time because a byproduct of that particular day's rain was that it caused a moment of such acute embarrassment that I have had to keep it to myself ever since: To wit: my shorts are khaki, you see. But, once they are rained on, especially if, as I was, you are sitting on a pushbike in what is in effect an outdoor car wash, the material, (most notably in the vicinity of the crotch, I should point out) transforms itself from pale khaki into a dark brown colour as it becomes wet. I'm sure we can all agree this is unlikely to be a good look. To be fair to my French friends, I am quite certain that any gallic passer-by who may have seen me outside Beaune – providing they had even a microgram of sympathy – must have thought: *Oh, mon dieu, cet homme souffrait d'un énorme problème incontinence*, which is not the impression any self-respecting Englishman wishes to leave in France. My enduring wish is that hordes of smug Burgundians do not still talk in mocking terms about the day they saw '*Le Rosbif*' wet himself!

Towards the end of the morning hailstones, fired from a Gatling gun by the feel of it, provide an unexpected surprise! I know this will be hard to take on board, but believe it or not, the experience is less fun than it actually sounds: being peppered by hailstones while forcing a bike into the face of a cold wind is a time of torment and pain, nothing more and nothing less, but, while it may not sound like it, this is actually my lucky day because the cold rain has made my legs and hands numb to the point of being anesthetised. I really can't feel the impact of the little frozen pellets as they hit my exposed legs.

My forehead and face are another matter entirely and periodically I am forced to stop cycling and turn away from the worst of the weather, which blows straight at me as I pedal along.

After shielding my face just long enough for some feeling to be restored to my flesh, I set off again wearing what I imagine to be a slightly odd, probably frightening, and certainly rather glum expression. It is entirely possible that if someone looked at my face right now, they may well think I'm smiling at them in a rather inane and slightly demented way. In reality, of course, my facial contortion is simply the effect of the cold weather, which has caused every facial muscle to malfunction and distort as it would following a visit to an overenthusiastic dentist. And let's be honest, who hasn't met one of them?

In just a few minutes, pedalling has become an exercise requiring extreme caution. This is because a generous smattering of hail has left the road surface very slippery and care is needed to avoid the ignominy and likely pain of being upended as the wheels slip from under me. Luckily for me, fifteen minutes later I can rejoice wholeheartedly that the hail was short lived and the rain has abated, at least for now.

Unquestionably the Rhône valley is the avenue of choice for wind in these parts. The river valley lies three miles to the west and right now it seems that the Mistral is back for a second shot at me. The headwind reduces my momentum so much that it's a struggle simply to keep the front wheel pointing ahead, and when, as happens occasionally, a particularly vicious gust of wind snatches the wheel to the side I'm robbed of steerage. You wouldn't think this was possible – a spoked wheel, even with its handlebar is hardly a solid object. How can my front wheel and valuables bag possibly offer such resistance to the wind? Somehow, against all logic, the wind secures enough purchase to create a yawing motion, which I find all but impossible to make headway against.

This is energy-sapping stuff so I grab the chance to leave the main road and follow a farm track downhill through vineyards. Minutes later the bike and I are sheltered from the wind; this is more like it. Thankfully my folded map has been protected behind the polythene window on the handlebar bag, and after rubbing off the beaded rain I can make out an unclassified road running alongside Le Rhône River. The track I'm on doesn't feature on the map but hopefully it'll meet up with the unclassified road sooner or later. If so, I should be able to hug the riverbank until I reach the dam or *'barrage'* marked on the map, after which the route should take the bike and I all the way to *Île de la Barthelasse*, and the campsite I need in Avignon.

Barthelasse island was formed over much time by the gradual and entirely natural merging of a string of smaller islands in the River Rhône and at over 1,000 hectares *Île de la Barthelasse* claims to be the largest river island in the whole of Europe. The next two miles of pleasant downhill cycling end as I round a corner and emerge from dense woodland to be confronted by the River Rhône.

Ah, the Rhône, the mighty Rhône, the majestic Rhône. What a sight it is set out before me, all vast and moody. I go with the flow for half an hour with the river on my right until I come to a very dilapidated bridge, which was obviously a very beautiful and stylish structure once, but sadly all that remains now of the long and slender '*Le Pont des Arméniers*' only hints at its original elegance and splendour.

Prior to the bridge opening in 1926, cable-hauled ferries provided the river crossing but the irregular nature of the old ferry service made the transport of goods, particularly at harvest time, and the carriage of passengers unpredictable. Sometimes it took pupils hours to walk to school when the ferry wasn't running. '*Le Pont des Arméniers*' is a suspension bridge that in its heyday was very advanced. The bridge spans five hundred feet of river, it has a metal frame and a wooden deck, and what a splendid sight it must have been in back in the day. Not so nowadays – the bridge makes a forlorn sight as I look down the long, narrow gap between the support cables to the far bank. Now a mere framework remains, a skeleton of metal supports and some twisted metal sections, all corroded – a bridge made unsafe by the passage of time and decades of neglect.

Virtually nothing remains of the original wooden decking. The timbers, green and black with decay have all but rotted away leaving just a few slats to hang down towards the water. Some swing gently from side to side above the river; they resemble bunting but without the cheer. Ironically, the bridge is listed as a historical monument. Hopefully this status will one day trigger restoration before the whole thing collapses into the Rhône under its own weight.

The bridge may have been neglected for decades but not so the local environment, which has benefited from long-term investment and care. Once again this place is home to an exceptional variety of native plants and wildlife. Sixty species of bird, twenty species of fish, and several species of animals, including the beaver, now call this place home. I stop awhile hoping that some creature will make a show, but none do.

I continue on the bumpy track as it meanders under overhanging trees beside the river. It's quite beautiful here, although after a couple of miles on the track it morphs into a slip-road and then a dual carriageway. Tranquillity is lost on the outskirts of Avignon. What a culture shock it is to exchange a deserted overgrown track for such a busy highway. My arrival in Avignon coincides with the rather unexpected sight of top-end car showrooms, hypermarkets, and commercial premises. This unexpected fanfare of modern life is the opposite of my rather romantic, and to be fair unrealistic hope of cycling into a wondrously historical city unchanged for centuries. Spanning several lanes of traffic, a large gantry suspended over the road invites me to turn right towards *Avignon-Centre*, the *Pont D'Avignon* and *Palais des Papes*.

Avignon bridge and the papal palais are sights of world renown and both are places that for reasons I can neither remember nor explain I have wanted to see for decades. Shortly after leaving the dual carriageway my surroundings are transformed for the better when I am once again reunited with my good friend, Le Rhône.

The river flows purposefully through the centre of Avignon where it is edged by a wide path beyond which lies a wide grassy public area. Taken together they proved a delightfully light and airy promenade. To my right Pont D'Avignon of the famed song *Sur le Pont d'Avignon* juts into the river. The real name of the ever-so-famous 'Pont d'Avignon' is actually *Pont Saint-Bénézet*. The bridge is very charming but incomplete as only three of its stone arches remain, and so it ends rather abruptly well short of halfway across the river.

As befits one of the largest and most important medieval Gothic buildings in Europe, the papal palais looms imposingly over the riverside embankment and all before it. It's a massive and rather austere building, and more of a fortress than a palace by the look of it – either way it cannot fail to impress onlookers with its bold towers and colossal walls, which are topped with a glittering gilt statue of Christ.

I'm keen to visit later but for now I'm at ease with the simple quiet pleasure of pushing the bike along the riverside path and soaking up the views and history that make up Avignon.

After a while I come to a bridge that leapfrogs my half of the river onto Barthelasse Island. Camping Bagatelle and a youth hostel occupy the same bit of land on this massive island. Once I'm settled in, I will be perfectly placed for exploring the city. Both booking-in receptionists are incredulous that last night's pitch cost eighteen euros. They announce with a smile that a night here is six and a half euros, which seems very reasonable for such a tourist-centred city.

Having booked in I set off on my now routine pitch-hunting exercise. Tents are few and far between for this is the land of gleaming double-axel caravans and swish five-star motorhomes. Row upon row of these opulent wheeled palaces are parked on stony pitches; a few owners relax outside on luxuriously padded reclining chairs with all the modern conveniences anyone could possibly require close at hand. I, on the other hand, peg down my simple nylon abode at the end of a row of four modest tents. The tents here are humble, but mine is by far the smallest, which is a fact I'm rather proud of in a nonsensical sort of way. Philip, my new neighbour, is at the site for several weeks, it's something he does yearly because he works on the lighting arrangements for the Avignon festival, a notable event that much to my shame I've never heard of. Philip explains that the festival is similar in popularity, content, and size to the Edinburgh Fringe.

By mid-afternoon it's time to retrace my steps back across the river. The bridge provides me with a distant view of the vast stone frontage of the papal palais while on my left Pont D'Avignon juts into the upstream river. Midway across the bridge (this one is *Pont Édouard Daladier*), I halt and lean against a stone parapet observing the panorama in front of me. By squinting my eyes, I blur out the intrusions of modern life. Now, with soft-focus and a bit of imagination I find myself gazing at the medieval scene set out before me. In its day the formidable block of ecclesiastical buildings ahead was by far the largest manmade structure for hundreds of miles. I try to imagine the impact such a sight must have had on the penniless pilgrims who flocked over this bridge in the fourteenth century. They must surely have been stunned by the impressive sight before them, which would have left them with absolutely no doubt of the awesome power, the unchallengeable authority, and the wide-ranging influence of the Avignon papacy.

Tall narrow turrets sixty feet above me crown the crenelated entrance to the papal palais. The turrets bear more than a passing resemblance to church organ pipes, rather fitting for ecclesiastical architecture you may think, but through my eyes the building looks just as military as it does religious. This may have been a building of faith, but not a faith to be messed with, certainly not in medieval times.

Surprisingly few people share the huge open courtyard with me; the occasional couple here, a small family group there, and others talking to a row of street vendors selling rather accomplished artworks displayed at eye level on tall wooden easels. The artists are positioned in front of the palais around the perimeter of the square; their work is protected from the bright sun under crisp white awnings with scalloped edges. It all looks very classy and a cut above your average outdoor market. Taking centre stage is a large and brightly painted carousel, which if there were more people here would surely be drawing the crowds to its colourful vintage charms and jaunty fairground music.

I set off to explore some of Avignon's ancient alleys and although I've wandered around similar places several times on my coast to coast journey across France, somehow the experience is richer here; the sun seems brighter, the colours more vivid, and the contrast between shadow and light is as intense as the Avignon sunshine. But of all the fascinating alleys and buildings here, and there are lots of them, it is the papal palace that impresses the most and draws me back for another look. Building started in 1335 and the palace was completed in just twenty years, which is a remarkable feat given its size. Recalling a visit some years ago to the Vatican, I notice striking visual differences between the centres of papacy here and in Rome. Visually Avignon palais is a defensive castle, what with its cloister fortified against attack, its towers, and its castellated roofline. Add to this the sheer size of the place and it really looks as if it means business. The Basilica and St Peter's Square in Rome are much softer on the eye, more welcoming, ecclesiastical rather than defensive, so I shall keep my eyes open for an information board that may explain the need for the more adversarial style of construction used here.

Walking up a massive stone ramp gives access to the upper levels of the palais, from where a splendid panorama is presented over treetops towards the river and its many bridges. Beyond the Rhône the wooded slopes of Mont Andaon are home to a large stone castle that's so huge, that even from a mile away I can see that its colossal walls linked by circular stone towers look quite impregnable. I discover later the place is called *Villeneuve-lès-Avignon* – it's referred to as Avignon's twin sister, a complex of palaces, convents, and fortresses, which together form one of the finest groups of medieval monuments in the whole of Europe.

My afternoon has flown by, so much so that I leave much of the palace unexplored as I need to hunt out some food. I pass no shops on my return to the tent and the cafes I see are aimed squarely at tourists willing to pay beefed-up prices, but they are not for me, not today.

Once back at the campsite I discover that the youth hostel offers an inexpensive range of meals. The hostel is catering for one hundred and fifty young guests this evening, which I take as a positive sign in that I figure teenagers will not take small portions lightly. Quantity if nothing else should be good. Luckily for me the heads-up from reception staff about the descent of hordes of young people on the dining hall alerts me to the obvious dangers associated with such events. Accordingly, I decide to eat immediately. In all honestly, I would much rather delay eating for an hour or so but by eating now I should avoid the horror of eating with a swarm of teenagers who will doubtless arrive as an excitable and chaotic mob with little control of either their limbs or the volume of noise they'll generate.

I hand over six euros for tagliatelle bolognese; not exactly French cuisine but it's slightly preferable to pizza or hamburger and chips. I carry my small beer to a table in the far corner of the large dining room;

here I'm conveniently close to a door to escape the hordes, nothing more than astute planning if you ask me. My meal is substantial rather than tasty, but credit where its due, the food was hot, it didn't empty my wallet, and it was served with plenty of garlic bread and a generous bowl of freshly grated Italian cheese. Pretty good, I would say. Best of all the young people have all gone AWOL and whatever's happened, their absence has allowed me to stay in the café until nearly dusk and write pages of notes.

As I leave I spot some people standing under some low-hanging trees on the embankment. A few are pointing across the water towards Avignon city while others strand in silence. They all seem engrossed. Curious, I walk towards them the until the trees open up to reveal the stunning view over the river of the papal palais bathed in the light of the setting sun. The sight is absolutely captivating; the massive stone 'organ-pipe' walls that were so sombre and imposing earlier are now painted golden orange and the Rhône has been transformed into a wide ribbon of molten gold flowing sedately past us in the foreground. Clouds of gunmetal grey hang over the palais and this palette of deep tangerine and graphite transforms it into a gothic building illuminated by fire. I can't imagine what a 14th-century pilgrim would make of such a sight. Surely they would see such a moment as highly symbolic and drop to their knees in devotion and awe.

Inside the tent it's too gloomy to write until the wind-up torch is cranked into life. It allows me to get the job done, in a fashion. The light lasts only a while between wind-ups so my notes are short, rather like the distance I pedalled today. Twenty-one miles to be exact. That being said, my total is now eight hundred and thirty-four miles, which is rather more than I expected to cover for the whole journey.

# Day 27 — Wednesday 12th May

## Departments of Vaucluse and Bouches-du-Rhône: From Avignon to Arles

*Mon Dieu!* My plan for today, in as much as there was a plan, was to march at pace to the meals room, where, by judicious application of elbows and gusto I would fend off the anticipated mass of rampaging teenagers in order to stake my claim to a warm croissant or whatever a nation of amphibian munchers start their day with.

'*Petit déjeuner*' — what's all that about? You have to question any nation state that calls breakfast 'little dinner'. I mean, come on, at the very least it shows a remarkable lack of imagination. Consider a 'Full English', if you will. The clue's in the word FULL. It's not difficult, is it? Alas, I arrived too late for breakfast, so this morning my plan goes for a ball of chalk before it has even begun. This is unfortunate because I am ravenous. I blame James.

I bumped into James, metaphorically I should say, while building up a head of steam as I walked with purpose for breakfast, as I've just explained. Naturally enough my mind was completely focussed on my anticipated early morning spat with the young unwashed.

Like myself, James had travelled to Avignon from England, from the Isle of Wight to be precise. Amazingly he paddled the whole way. Now, with the end of his journey through France within reach he intends to take his kayak round the coast of southern France towards Italy, where he will circumnavigate the boot before paddling off into the sunset towards Greece.

James' journey started in January, but not this January, he left seventeen months ago! He told me that the temperature during his first weeks had dropped to minus ten overnight. Initially the pointed bow of his kayak had sliced its way through the surface ice on the canals of Northern France, but as the ice built up his little boat had been unable to force its passage and he had to halt his journey until the canals thawed. James is also camping, but he's having to wild camp most nights because his canoe necessitates him finding campsites close to waterways. We could have chatted about our respective experiences of solo self-propelled travel all morning but we both had places to go.

Pedalling over the Edward Daladier bridge gives me my final view of the papal palais before I follow the west bank of the Rhône to avoid cycling along the dual carriageway out of town. A mile or so on, it's clear that although this is not a dual carriageway, I'm on a ring road and at this time of the day it's just another frantic road where the whole world's in a rush, it seems. This is no place for me – urgency forms no part of my agenda this morning.

After less than a mile and with self-preservation uppermost in my thoughts, I cut my loses, about turn, and cycle back towards the papal palace, then for the second time today I bid farewell to Camping Bagatelle which passes on my right before I come to the second bridge of the day, which links Île de la Barthelasse to Villeneuve-les-Avignon. Once over the bridge I exchange the main road for the picturesque and much quieter D2. My escape from the city is complete.

South of Avignon is floodplain country. Beside me flows the Rhône, which is much wider now than at any time since the river first became my companion one hundred and twenty miles north of here at the little town of Loyettes. The vast river flows close to the road against what looks to be its usual riverbank, the Rhône doesn't appear to have taken on extra width as a result of the recent rain. Overflowing or not, the river makes full use of the wide flood plain and the far bank is many hundreds of yards away. If James is out there in his kayak somewhere, especially if he's close to the far bank, I doubt I'd spot him from this distance. Better him than me, I fear; with its swirling eddies and currents the river looks foreboding and dangerous, especially under today's dark sky. As if to underscore the point, the silence of the countryside is interrupted by the clap of distant thunder.

Historical weather data reveals that the month of May should bless Avignon with an average of eight hours of sunshine a day and eighteen degrees. Once, in May, thirty-four degrees was recorded in the city. I couldn't do with anything like that, such heat is not for cycling, but fifteen to twenty degrees would be just grand. But it's not so today and by the look of things ahead the weather gods are going to short-change me again.

Le Rhône is a rich earthy brown this morning, like liquid milk chocolate meandering to the sea. The great river still looks determined and unstoppable as it did some miles back in Avignon, where, while not quite baring its teeth the much narrower Rhône was forcing a path to its destination, just as it was doing yesterday when I was trying to keep up with its flow, it was a personal challenge I set myself for a bit of fun as I tried to match the pace of the natural debris washed down by the rain further north. I expect James will have weighed up the river this morning and launched from La Barthelasse only if he judged it safe to take to the water. The brisk flow near the campsite will have had him surging along, a far cry from kayaking down a languid canal. Hobson's choice, it seems to me: too much speed in Avignon, or the unseen risk of colliding with submerged branches in these slower, chocolately waters. The Rhône's not for me, I'm afraid. Pedalling, not paddling, is the way to go. *Bon courage, James, and Godspeed*, I think to myself.

The Alps are behind me now, over my left shoulder and back towards the northeast. Ahead, my travels stop just short of the Pyrenees, the last mountain range to the southwest of here. Perhaps pushing the bike is behind me forever now; if so, it's not something to mourn. The sea is just fifty miles to the south, which is a sobering thought.

A slice of yellow sky sparkles brilliantly and marks out the distant horizon. The thin sliver is especially bright against clouds of burnished dull silver, and though many miles ahead, the unexpected promise of sunshine later today cheers me no end. Better still, the wind gently places its hands on my back and gives me an encouraging shove, the first for several days. What a pleasure it is to feel the breeze billowing out my foresail. This is relaxing cycling indeed, steady as we go.

With the river on my port side the need for navigation is redundant, so I potter along without a care in the world and find myself wondering just how many times my pedals have turned in total; tens of thousands? Maybe even hundreds of thousands since I cycled away from North Devon. A calculation for another day if I remember, just for interest. Ahead of me the river marks out a sweeping right-hand curve into the distance. Scanning its surface I realise there are no boats, in fact I've seen no vessels, large or small since leaving Avignon, which makes me question if James is even out there.

Suddenly an almighty bolt of lightning flashes above me. It strikes from nowhere and is immediately followed by an enormous and prolonged explosion. No time for *'one-monkey, two-monkeys'*, the simultaneous eruption of light and sound is much too close for that. Terrifyingly close, to be honest. The unexpected noise makes me flinch violently. Squeezing the brake levers is an involuntary reaction, as is ducking down. My sudden movement makes my foot slip off the pedal, which causes the bike to lurch to the left. I'm still in one piece though, which comes as a bit of a surprise. Instinct and self-preservation have kicked in, in the few seconds before I stop at the side of the road. Leaning forward, I can feel my heartrate surging as I rest my chest against the handlebar bag to catch a breath and allow myself some time to stop shaking. After composing myself for a while I lift my head but nothing ahead is damaged. I look to my left and my right then behind me but nothing looks out of place, then I realise that if it's a storm more lightning may follow. I scan all directions for more threats although I have no idea what I expect to see or indeed what I am going to do about it. *Why isn't it raining?* I wonder to myself. That was a close call.

The event causes my mind to jump back many years to when the family and I were driving from Bude in North Cornwall to Holsworthy, a market town just over the county border into Devon. We had just driven past a local landmark called Red Post when a lightning bolt struck out of the blue, like the one I have just experienced. That bolt impacted into a field about a quarter of a mile ahead of us in a brilliant flash of light; the bolt pierced the grass in a shower of sparks and smoke. For us it was a remarkable and unique sight. No sparks today, I am pleased to say. The noise, the flash, and the surprise were quite enough for me, thank you very much.

With my elbows still resting on the handlebars I feel reassured and very exposed at the same time, then it strikes me that it's still not raining, which seems odd. In preparation I unpack my waterproofs and bungee cord them to the top of my luggage for easy access. I cautiously set off and for some time find myself scanning the horizon and looking up at the clouds, but there's nothing to alarm me, the attack has passed. The bright sliver of sun to the south is larger now and beckoning me towards it. It's a comforting sight.

To my right a stand of bamboo eight feet tall flanks the tarmac. The breeze swishes the tall grasses vigorously as I pass, to teach the bamboo a lesson for robbing me of the view, I fancy, and for stealing my wind propulsion. Still, it was good while it lasted. Another four miles, another thirty minutes, and the clouds are slung above me like sultry low hammocks. Suddenly they start to release rain in enormous droplets. This is not yet heavy rain, although I fear a drenching's coming my way. In the meantime it's fascinating to watch the rain as each large drop plops onto the grey tarmac road leaving a blotch the size of a golf ball. With my waterproof jacket in readiness on the pannier behind me I continue to cycle in shorts and tee-shirt, but the temperature has dropped markedly now and it would be chilly were I not cycling. The rain pauses as I arrive at the town of Tarascon.

Two road signs mark the entrance to the town: The first informs me that I am now entering the Catalan/Basque region; the second bears the Ville de Tarascon coat of arms, underneath which the words: '*Ville sous vidéosurveillance*' are written. The sign has a bit of Orwellian *1984* about it. I mean, it's not exactly *Comité National pour le Fleurissement de la France*, is it? And I have to say it has a rather unwelcoming feel to it.

Heavy rain begins to fall without even the courtesy of a watery preamble. How rude! The streets of Tarascon are all but deserted as I cycle along and the dismal weather dilutes much of the town's obvious charm. I pause to take sixty euros from a conveniently placed bank machine and in the few minutes it takes me, the rain has repainted the matte grey roads shiny black. At the intersection of four cobbled streets I come upon little restaurant; its bright illuminated windows look inviting on what has turned into a rather dull day. Outside a trio of customers are seated under a large burgundy-coloured *'brasserie'* awning. They're being attended to by a moustachioed waiter wearing a blue and white hooped top; he looks archetypally French, if only he had a beret.

A menu blackboard on the wet pavement reads: *'Menu à 15,00 euros'* is available *'du Lundi midi au Vendredi midi'*, which is ideal as today is *Mercredi*. Am I tempted? I would say so.

Once inside I discover that a host of diners have opted for indoor seating and most tables are occupied which is a good sign in any restaurant. Interior decoration is an eclectic mix of framed items adorning the walls in a gloriously haphazard and busy fashion: I count nine separate specials boards, all written in chalk, each offering a different selection of the day's gastronomical offerings. A large print of 'Girl with a pearl earring' by Vermeer hangs in its frame, at a charmingly jaunty angle, and there are innumerable certificates of excellence which I assume are for culinary work and hospitality. Perhaps the real highlight of this frenzy of wall decoration is an incongruous amateur painting of a tree, the branches are covered with orange and pink blossom and there is a vastly oversized finch of some species clinging to a branch, the bird is vibrant yellow and makes up a good third of the painting. Let's just say it is bold and draws the eye!

The visual cornucopia continues with at least two dozen indoor plants; most grow in coloured pots suspended at various levels against the walls, some are secured by thick wire, while others are balanced on small bespoke shelves. Some plants are very large indeed and appear ready to submit to gravity at any moment, either that or the wall may give way. Whirring at speed above all of this and revolving perilously close to a pair of tall glass chiller cabinets are several large and very garish gilt-coloured ceiling fans. Varnished wooden tables with rattan seating completes the dining room. The whole place is extremely quirky, it is a feast for the eyes, and I like it very much indeed.

The waiter guides me to a small table in the centre of the restaurant and advises me that for an extra four euros wine will accompany my lunch. No contest then, wine it is. I order the *salad Ardechoise* to start, *entrecôte grillée* (plus *frites/legumes*) for the main. My pudding will be selected later from the board headed *Dessert Maison au Choix*. My table has been precisely set with a crisp blue tablecloth and a matched napkin together with a jug of iced water. The large glass of red wine, a basket of fresh bread, and the three-course meal are most enjoyable, making my entirely spontaneous decision to stop here a very good idea indeed, especially so because for the hour and a half I've been here, rain has hammered it down outside and my departure coincides with it ceasing. Now that's what I call a result!

After lunch I continue along the same quiet lane that brought me into Tarascon. I was in no rush when I arrived in town and I'm in even less of a rush now that I am leaving. My pedalling is relaxed and unhurried in a mellow autopilot sort of way that you would expect after a decent meal and a hefty glass of red.

Joy of joys – periods of afternoon sunshine become longer, reminding me how close Spain is, and as if to underscore the point several farms are not named using the French word '*ferme*' but are called '*mas*' from the word '*masia*', used specifically in eastern Spain and the Catalan area in preference to '*finca*', which is the more general Spanish word for a small farm. As I approach the city of Arles, I remember campers in Avignon who advised me to avoid the busy historic city centre; accordingly I skirt Arles to the campsite at Pont-de-Crau.

It's twenty-three-degrees, sunny, and bang on five o'clock when I wheel into Camping Roserie. After booking in the owners offer to recharge my phone and camera batteries for just half a euro each, which sounds like a bit of bargain and is very helpful indeed. Once the tent is sorted, I pop off to the nearby 'Giant' supermarket and come away with a twelve-inch cherry pie (which proves to be excellent), a baguette (which is exceedingly good – of course it is, I'm in France) and some ham (which was worse than mediocre so I just binned it). Suddenly it's nine o'clock and I have absolutely no idea where the time's gone. For the next hour I'm serenaded by the first movement of a distant thunder storm. As concertos go it's a rather gentle melody, no more startling than Beethoven's eighth, *'The Pathetique'* – and in complete contrast to the afternoon thunder and lightning that hit me with the fury of Verdi's *'Day of Wrath'* at full blast.

I've decided to take a day off tomorrow, my first since leaving England twenty-seven days ago other than the enforced halt in Chalon-sur-Saône waiting for a new tyre. After 868 miles it's time for a day of leisure.

# WEEK FIVE

*Day 28 – Thursday 13th May*

*Department of Bouches-du-Rhône:*

*Arles and its vicinity*

You will be delighted to learn that I have decided to entertain myself royally on my day of repose by going for a bike ride. But before I actually set off, allow me to mention an interesting encounter with the French weather:

Well, it was sometime after midnight and pitch black. The deep rumbles of thunder and occasional flashes of lightning were captivating at first, after all it was some way off and who doesn't like a good storm? Then the front closed in and once it'd spotted exactly where I was, it unleashed itself with fearful vengeance on the world beyond my tent. It was hit and miss at first, but then the storm got its act together and focussed its aim perfectly. What I've come to realise with storms is that familiarity brings complacency once you've experienced a few decent ones in a little tent. That's not to say the storm didn't cause my heart to surge a few times, but the thunder wasn't that bad, it can't have been as I drifted back to sleep. I must have irritated the storm by not reacting with the timidity required so it had a bit of a strop and lobbed what sounded like a military-grade thunder-flash my way. This would be about 3:30, a direct hit and nothing less than a major assault on my senses. The loud bangs and piercing flashes of light were, in my state of deep sleep, nothing less than horrifying – and to be honest with you I'm amazed it didn't trigger a massive cardiogenic shock and with it the premature end of my little jolly on a bike.

Today started tranquil enough; I guess the storm's passed Arles by in its hunt for another victim. Talking of storms, I'd better I adopt post-storm assessment mode: I'm on my back looking up at the vaulted nylon three feet above me. The colours are muted so it's probably overcast outside. My check is methodical, front to back, side to side, edge after edge; only a few drips of rain have penetrated so nothing to report back on so far. By rising onto my elbows, I can examine the darker corners of the groundsheet – it looks fine. Then I track the stitching up the sides to where they converge above my head. No telltale signs of water ingress from seams that have been overstrained, I'm please to say.

Once again, I marvel at the resilience of my little tent, which however flimsy it may appear fends off the rain for a hobby. Sometimes it does so all night, and let's not forget the tent has endured half of this adventure with a fractured support rod held together with gaffer tape. In all truth I'm in awe of my little tent, which, as if in homage to the short-reigned last of the Plantagenets, King Richard III, stands proud with its crooked back, and just like him it holds firm against allcomers for as long as it can. What a majestic little tent, what a noble little tent.

A fresh sunny day is revealed when I unzip the tent door, which is quite a surprise given the dullness inside. After breakfast I trim luggage down to the minimum needed for a day out: My camera, passport and cash are all stowed in the handle bar bag, one rear pannier is left inside the tent and the other is stripped bare except for a few tools, a spare inner tube, my Gore-Tex jacket and waterproof overtrousers, and last but not least the remaining third of the cherry pie. Carrying two litres of water is a given.

Before leaving England the bike and I struck up a pact that come what may we would look after each other throughout out little adventure. Since leaving Devon I have become as one with my cumbersome friend the Velo. The bike feels the same about me as far as I know, although it hasn't bothered to tell me. We have worked in harmony for hundreds of miles with never a cross word, not even when we get soaked. What a team we are.

On reflection our partnership had a bit of a rocky start. At first, we didn't know each other and we were awkward in each other's company and I was new to this cycling lark, which didn't help. I wobbled a bit and stumbled my way through the gears until I eventually came across one that seemed appropriate, and to be honest I huffed and puffed regularly and took to salty language more than once, but harsh words were never directed to towards the bike, you understand. Overall, I think I've kept my part of the bargain: My cycling has improved as we've progressed together, I am fitter now and I have lost weight, about a stone and a half in fact, so the bike has less to carry now. I suppose I may have let the side down by being a bit slapdash with maintenance. My daily preening of brakes, gears, chain and tyres has fallen by the wayside as familiarity and a steadfast belief that the bike will just get on with it have crept in. I don't think I have taken the bike for granted; I hope not.

And as for the bike, well, what can I say? The bike is a star, and a most splendid companion... (but listen up because I have to whisper now) I've been a bit concerned about the bike's health, particularly this last week. I mentioned back in Chalon-sur-Saône (that place with the closed bike shops) that a couple of rear spokes had snapped. Well, since then I haven't really checked the integrity of the wheels. Naturally I removed the broken spokes because if I'd left them all snapped and protruding, sure as eggs are eggs the revolving wheel would have sent one of the snapped spokes into my calf like a twelve-inch hypodermic, and being skewered in such a fashion really would have produced a flurry of salty language, let me tell you, but all that was back in Chalon. More recently (and I really am having to talk *very* quietly now) the rear wheel has started to groan in recent days. More of a grind than a groan, really, but I can see nothing wrong so how can I help? I hope that doesn't sound heartless. And so, to today. Well, today's just another day out for two good pals, and on this sunny Thursday morning, the yoke of excess luggage has been discarded. How liberating it is for me to be pedalling the *velo* unladen. More importantly the bike is enjoying it too. I reckon it will tell me so by grinding less.

By combining some nifty navigation and a stroke of good fortune I somehow avoid the Arles-Marseille motorway that runs between the campsite and my first port of call. Beyond the motorway is a marshland known as the *Marais de Meyranne*, which is home to the Canal d'Arles and the Pont Van Gogh. The canal is providing sport for anglers this morning. They're out in three small rowing boats a hundred yards apart, each containing two fishermen. I have no idea if these are lucky anglers or not, but as they are standing up in little rowing boats surely whatever luck they have is being used to stop them overbalancing into the canal. Unnecessarily precarious if you want my opinion, but whatever rocks your boat, as they say.

On the 28th of February 1888, Vincent Van Gogh arrived in Arles. He made over three hundred paintings and sketches while he lived here; amongst them were many versions of *'Le Pont de Langlois aux Lavandières'*, which he painted near the very spot I'm now standing. The most famous of these paintings is called *'The drawbridge near Arles'*. The original bridge was built by engineers from the Netherlands and Van Gogh was drawn to paint the bridge because the scene was so reminiscent of his homeland. Nowadays the bridge has been replaced by a replica, which although not wholly accurate is still worth a visit.

My departure from Van Gogh's bridge coincides with the arrival of twenty or so Citroën 2CVs, several Triumph TR6 cars, and a very splendid Porsche Panhard. All are beautifully restored and instantly attract the attention of the few people by the canal, who like moths to a lamp flutter over to have a closer look at the classic cars. After a quick nose at the vehicles, I leave them to it and pedal into the city where I secure the bike outside the tourist information office, freeing myself up to explore the city on foot. As always, it feels a little odd walking round without the bike, which has become something of an extra limb. I hope the *velo* doesn't feel left out.

*'Place de la Républic'* (every town worth its salt has one in France) is an open space situated in the heart of the city. The square is surrounded

by the fine civic buildings of Arles including the grand town hall or *'mairie.'* Town halls, even in the smallest of communities, are easily identified by the Tricolour fluttering proudly above the entrance at the mandatory forty-five degrees.

The civic buildings of Arles may be impressive, but it's the elegant four-sided fountain that draws me to the centre of the square. The fountain pours water from the mouths of classical bronze faces into a stone basin, while above the nozzles, four bronze lions with faces tarnished by time and verdigris keep guard over the Place de la République. The fountain doubles as the hefty base for a tapered stone obelisk, which looks very grand and at fifty feet tall is by far the most dominant feature in the square. The backstory of this Egyptian obelisk is that it was found in the city's Roman amphitheatre and moved to the square in 1676.

After leaving the square I cross the Rhône over the Pont de Trinquetaille. This bridge, like so many other places in Arles features in a Van Gogh painting.

It is late morning now, sunny and warm with not a puff of wind. Strolling through Arles is a delight under the deep azure sky and history is everywhere I look. Several roads such as *Place du Forum* and *Rue des Arènes* indicate long Roman habitation. Arles was the second most important city in the region after Marseilles and a popular posting for the elite, particularly Constantine, whose son Constantine II was born here. Two millennia ago, Arles, although not coastal by any means was closer to the sea, and in the first century BC, under the leadership of Gaius Marius the city was linked to the Mediterranean by constructing a canal, which enabled the Romans to use Arles as a major port, as indeed it had been by the Phoenicians five centuries earlier when the coast was very much closer.

Arles Roman Amphitheatre is small and intimate and has a very different feel to others I've visited. A footpath encircles the stone structure and as you walk around it you feel that the more modern buildings, themselves many hundreds of years old, have wrapped themselves around the ancient structure. It's as if they're hugging a well-loved but rather geriatric architectural centrepiece. I find that visiting the amphitheatre in Arles to be a very different experience to when I admired the much larger examples in Rome or Aspendos. There is no open space around this arena, whereas at Aspendos in Turkey visitors approach the amphitheatre across a vast arid plain. Rome's Colosseum, on the other hand, is set back from the villas on the Palatine Hill by a wide tree-lined boulevard. Wonderful ancient places such as these don't lend themselves to ratings and I don't have a favourite as such, but let's just say this amphitheatre is particularly pleasing. It's homely rather than overbearing, intimate rather than intimidating, and I rather like that. I decide against visiting inside the monument as much as anything because I want to explore what lies beyond the city.

Three and a half euros is the very fair price I pay for a seeded baguette bursting with prawns. I take lunch in the open air on a bench overlooked by a row of pretty houses in a cobbled backstreet. Nobody passes as I sit in the hot sun: just me and my lunch, not a soul in sight. Amazingly there are no sounds, not one. How can that be in a city, even a small one like Arles?

Beyond Arles a row of far-off trees separates the farmland from distant hills that appear as a hazy purple line in the shimmering sunlight, and not for the first time on this journey I could imagine myself in some bygone age before signs, pylons, and modernity, just for a few moments.

A distant car horn bursts my peaceful bubble and signals that it's time to return to Place de la République for a reunion with the bike, which I'm sure will be pretty keen to be released from its shackles after catching its breath in the warm sun for a bit. I fancy the bike will be well up for an afternoon out.

Just clear of Arles eleven flamingos fly low overhead in a wonky 'U' formation. The birds are an improbable shape when airborne, what with their long slender wings positioned amidships, their long spindly necks and head jutting forward, and their even longer thinner legs pointing aft. Their flight is leisurely as they head south towards the wetlands and saltpans of the Camargue. Who knows? With luck I may make their acquaintance there tomorrow.

The soil is dry and barren wherever I gaze. A few crimson patches of roadside poppies are the only relief in a landscape where low thorny scrub is king and everything is the hue of sand. A few miles on, and suddenly, as if someone has just turned a switch this parched place changes to a landscape of purple and green. The carpet of dull thorn bushes has been edged out by thistles, acres and acres of purple thistle heads with their wispy little bonnets tied under their chins. It's all very pretty. A canal bisects the landscape, its ruler-straight water carpeted with bright green duckweed as far as the eye can see. Eventually the canal tapers and disappears into the distance without even the hint of a bend or even waving goodbye.

Ten minutes further on and I come to an area of flooded land that's divided into small squares, salt pans perhaps, but I'm miles from the coast so maybe these pens have been hollowed out the rock to raise fish. On the far side a low outcrop of limestone flanked by trees and bushes is set against a vivid dome of blue sky.

The rocky escarpment is shown on my map as the *'Aqueduc Romain'*. Back in the day, sixteen 'overshot' wheels existed here in what was then the greatest known concentration of mechanical power in the whole of the ancient world. The mill complex has long gone, of course, but the narrow cleft cut five feet deep into the limestone ridge and once used to carry the water needed to power the wheels, remains. The cleft is still impressive, although it's better not to think too deeply about the price extracted from the slaves who were forced to hack the rock out.

A road sign points me to the Moulin de Daudet and beyond it the town of Fontvieille. The road leading to Daudet's mill winds its way up a wooded hillside where large white cubes of chiselled limestone edge the road and offer some protection against ending up in the dry gorge below. The gnarled pine trees set back from the road are well-spaced and ankle deep in a spongy carpet of ruddy brown pine needles. It's an attractive place here, especially so as a pleasant heady aroma wafts over the wooded hillside as I cycle along. I am higher now and the light breeze that blows gently through the trees makes pedalling more comfortable than earlier in the hot valley near the ruins. Scattered eucalyptus trees share the hill with the pines and provide much of the aroma along with a mixture of wild herbs that I am unable to distinguish; the smell is deep and complex and rather like being in one of those wholefood shops where produce is displayed in open wooden bins and the fragranced air tempts you to buy a selection. This is just what I expected in Provence, I guess. What a cracking day out this is turning into.

Daudet's windmill is set back from the road on a small hillock of exposed rock. Its elevation matches the tops of the trees that surround it. The base of the mill is a short squat tower constructed from large stone blocks hefted from this very hillside. It's been built to last a thousand years by the look of it; it's the only windmill I have ever seen that could repel boarders. Its blades are intact, or at least the four wooden lath frames are and the windmill tower has a conical top lagged with vertical wooden slats painted a deep russet brown. I can't tell if the mill still rotates with the prevailing winds.

*'Daudet's windmill'* is really 'Saint Peter's windmill' and it last functioned as a mill in 1915 after more than a century of operation. Alphonse Daudet describes the mill in his acclaimed book *Master Cornille's Secret* and as a consequence it's been turned into a snug museum and named after the author. After leaving the windmill to the other visitors I get back on the bike and coast through woodland dappled by bright sunlight. Freewheeling gently through the trees towards Fontvieille with the hot sun and natural aromas for company is simply delightful.

My velo may not be having such a good time, I'm sad to say, what with its rear wheel rasping and grating intermittently. It sounds most uncomfortable and is quite an alarming to hear. I take it slowly of course but I wish there was more I could do more for my trusty hard-working friend. It seems odd to me that the sound is louder now that the bike is has been relieved of its two heavy panniers. The noises seem to emanate from the middle of the rear wheel but beyond guessing that it may be something to do with ball bearings or whatever secrets the gubbins inside the hub perform, I really don't know. What I do know is that the hub is beyond my technical ability to have a go at fixing, so with only few days to go I'll have to push my luck, press on, and hope the bike will forgive me. What else can I do?

I prop the bike against a hefty tree slap bang in the centre of Fontvieille. The bike and I have found it extremely hot under the direct sun and I for one need no encouragement to sit outside a bar in a comfy wicker armchair in the very welcome breeze that has now sprung up. As for the bike, I've made sure it's in the shade but as I have no nosebag or water, I just have to hope that shade and breeze will be enough. I spread the map across the table I'm seated at and lean back in the comfy wicker chair to take in the sight of the town square which is laid out in front of me along with a glass of ice-cold beer. An hour later, after a second beer, and a relaxing hour in the sun, it's time for me to head off, somewhat lethargically, for the campsite. Everything lends itself to a leisurely return as neither the bike nor I have anything to rush for and the weather and scenery are both distinctly 'South of France'. An hour out of Fontvieille, having pottered seven or eight miles through a sparse and open landscape a heavy downpour pops up from nowhere and catches me out. I hadn't noticed the wall of cloud creeping up behind me; a bit underhand if you ask me. Particularly large drops of rain start to fall, the road changes from bone dry to soaking wet in seconds, and as rainwater gathers pace a little stream appears along the edge of the little road. Both sides are flanked by bamboo to a height of eight to ten feet. The tall plants, the black clouds, and torrential rain all make the road darker and then darker still. It's 'lights-on' time I would say.

Heavy rain persists and an erratic wind picks up. Gusts shake the tops of the bamboo vigorously as I pass; the movement is spectacular and accompanied by the sound of leaves thrashing around and a clicking noise as the hollow stems knock together. The sight and sound of these natural bamboo wind-charms is an unexpected joy. Without warning someone above turns the tap off, the rain stops just as suddenly as it started, and I remember that I've left my towel and some other bits and bobs of clothing draped over the tent to dry. Obviously, what was only damp this morning will now be saturated: the best laid plans of mice and men and all that.

A few miles on and the temperature cranks right up, and again I'm cycling through little wisps of steam as the sun gets to work drying the tarmac. At Pont-de-Crau I discover there's been no rain while I have been away and my towel and clothes are as fresh and dry as I could have hoped for. Ideal.

I walk to the bank machine so my trusty bike can enjoy some peace and quiet while I'm away – a hundred euros should see me to the end of my trip. Back at the site I give the wheel a visual once-over and although there's nothing to indicate the rear hub is near terminal collapse, I can't ignore that its groans of complaint have been louder and more frequent as today's progressed. Time for some TLC, I think. The panniers are unclipped and laid on the grass and the bike's flipped onto its handlebars and seat. Spinning the back wheel shows it's wobbling a full half an inch out of true on every revolution. This is one badly bucked wheel, it's as plain as day. And I can see more missing spokes. It's not a reassuring sight.

But here's the thing: the bike is still a bike and the wheel is still a wheel, and they still function together. Yes, the bike may be a bit rickety but aren't we all? The rear wheel won't improve by itself, any idiot can see that, and if I'm honest with myself I know it may not hold out – but then again if I'm careful, and if I trust luck, and if I nurture the bike by taking it slowly, well, the rear wheel could have miles of life in it yet. I only need it to last another two and a half days. That's not too much to ask, is it?

Now, here's a bit of mechanical skulduggery for you to think about: But before I astonish you with the details of what I have just come up with to help the bike, let me be the first to admit that while I may not have had a stroke of brilliance for a while, when I have one, I really have one, if you know what I mean. Anyway, a brainwave has just come my way, out of the blue, who'd have thought, just when I needed one most. I hope I've not inflated your expectations too much, because the idea is only small – small but brilliant, mind you – and it could very well turn out to be the saving of the bike and me.

Listen up: Using some careful jiggery-pokery with a screwdriver, a pair of pliers, and a handful of fingers I have disconnected the rear brake. Yes, you heard it here first and you heard it correctly, I have just disconnected the back brake, completely disconnected it, it is no more, as they say. That's the wobble sorted – in an instant. Naturally I am praying to God that the French, being the guillotine-happy race they are, do not have the gallic equivalent of Section whatever of the Bicycles (Safety) Regulations 2010, because the last thing I would wish for, or need come to think of it, for is some wet-behind-the ears, overenthusiastic, trainee gendarme to stop my bike for inspection and for me to have to fall on my sword about having disconnected the brake cable. I would probably spend days, or even years in the Bastille, and nobody would want that, would they?

Anyway, enough of all that, because joy of joys the bike is no longer upended and being fiddled with. Naturally, I whizzed the wheel round at near terminal velocity as a spin-test and I'm pleased to report that my once buckled back wheel can now turn its wobbly self unimpeded. Ideal! Well, it still wobbles, of course it does, but we're not going to worry about that, are we? It wobbles in a rather happy-go-lucky, 'fairground ride' sort of way that's somewhat pleasing to the eye, if I may say so.

'But you've not really fixed it, have you?' I hear you suggest.

Of course I know that (what type of a fool wouldn't?). I'm aware that the problem is masked rather than fixed, and yes, I AM fully aware that my velo will fail any health and safety inspection imposed upon it by some Gauloises smoking roadside gendarme, but let's have less of the down-sides, just look at the benefits:

This velo has less than a hundred miles to go and there are no hills of note between here and the sea. Distilled down it only has to survive another twenty hours of pedalling. Surely that's not too much to ask. I reckon a wing and a prayer might see us through, and let's not forget that when I'm sat on the bike the dodgy wheel is completely hidden;

out of sight out of mind and all that. If I were to get some ear plugs the problem would disappear completely. Voila! Head in the sand or not, that's it, job done, decision made, we are going to wing it and time will tell. Ideal! Simply ideal!

It's early evening, all is quiet and still, and rain is falling silently against the tent. I'm lying in what has become a familiar if uncomfortable position, crumpled as usual, under the low roof of my little bendy home. Because I'm folded in half – and not for the first time, I should remind you – I have pins and needles in my arms and circulatory problems that any doctor worth a stethoscope would tell you are not far short of thrombosis-inducing. You guessed it, haven't you? Yes, I am lying on my sleeping bag writing my notes.

Putting my journal and pencil aside for a minute allows me to lay on my back, regain some movement, and listen to what's going on outside. In reality this means listening to weather and there's not a lot of that going on just now. Well, not in the noisy, scary, *'blow-your-house-inside-out'* sort of way I listened to twenty-four hours ago. You may never have thought about this – but a small tent is not exactly full of visual stimulation if you are camping solo. The mind wanders, it's inevitable really, and so my thoughts return to family, to England, and to returning home quite soon, and also to the simple pleasures of day-to-day conversation and company, and to enjoying the home comforts that I swapped to learn the rather basic skills needed for touring with a bicycle and a tent. If I'm sounding a bit nostalgic for home, it's because I am.

But what's this I see if it is not a miniature bauble of rain creeping into the tent uninvited? Very sneaky, nearly got away with it. A single drip has just landed where my head would rest if I were sleeping, then another drip near the door, more frequent this one. Seemingly the rain isn't satisfied that it soaked me this afternoon and now wants to get me when my defences are down, which is not cricket if you ask me. Anyway, I counter this watery invasion of my little shelter by reorganising my possessions so that I can sleep diagonally and avoid getting wet. This way the drips can get on with whatever they want to do inside my tent without interfering directly with me. Outside I am fair game for whatever weather comes my way, I understand that, that's the law, and I take it on the chin, but I am not going to allow the elements to beat me inside my little tent of all places.

So ends a twenty-seven-mile wobble round some of the lesser-known delights of Provence. At the end of today I am no closer to my destination, of course, but I've had a pleasing enough time of it on my day of repose – not only that but my grand total on the bike now stands at just shy of nine hundred miles and I'll happily take that. Right now, the barometer reads 1,025 millibars, so drips in the tent or not, I'm pretty optimistic about tomorrow's weather. More optimistic than I am about the durability of the rear wheel, come to think of it.

## Day 29 – Friday 14th May

## Department of Bouches-du-Rhône:

## Arles to Saintes-Maries-de-la-Mer

Last night the tent outwitted the rain yet again. *Bravo for the peapod tent!* I think to myself. I leave the site at exactly nine-thirty on the start of the fifth week of my jolly little jaunt peddling south through 'La belle France'. I stop briefly to say farewell to Monsieur Patron who vigorously shakes my hand, and to Madame Patronne who kisses both my cheeks, a kindness that causes me to suffer a brief and mildly embarrassing uncertainty at our parting: Is this a two-kiss or a three-kiss area of France? (And more to the point does anyone actually understand the rules of this oft-repeated ritual of French etiquette?) Anyway, after a bit of awkward cheek pecking, smiles all round, and enthusiastic calls of *bon courage!* I collect my recharged batteries and set off on a bike, which for now at least, has neither a wobble nor a grinding sound. Nor, come to think of it, a functioning back brake.

To my considerable displeasure extricating myself from Arles takes some doing. Near gladiatorial combat with heavy traffic just to clear the city is my less than relaxing introduction to the day ahead. This includes the N113 dual carriageway that's loaded with thundering traffic all rushing to arrive at Nimes or Montpellier ahead of everyone else. Why such urgency? It's not yet 10 a.m. With no hard shoulder the road provides not a smidgen of safety; this is a grin and bear it sort of road and there is absolutely nothing I can do but grab my bike by the ears, pedal with vigour, and hope that I am not some sad statistic about to happen.

To my considerable relief my uneven bout with lorries is stopped prematurely after the first few rounds when I throw the towel in and scuttle down a little slip-road that appears out of nowhere and coughs me up into the comparative tranquillity of a somewhat squalid zone of urban commerce. Suddenly I'm a bit lost but I don't care about that because I'm still intact, and I'll take being intact any day. Fortunately for me some workmen repairing the road point me towards a side road that leads away from Arles and towards the Camargue. Ideal!

Just when I think the manmade horrors of today are over, I come to an underpass made of concrete slabs. Dreary doesn't do it justice, the only relief from dank and grey is the graffiti on the walls and roof. The 'Tags', all angular, sombre and angry, cover the longest subway I've seen anywhere – the intimidating 'artwork' makes this a very nasty edifice that's utterly out of place in such a splendid city as Arles. I'm very glad when the underpass ends and I emerge from the gloom into the daylight of a well-tended housing estate and then a pretty canal embankment that leads me back to the countryside.

Just as I'm getting into my stride a loud twang from under the seat tells me another spoke has given up the ghost.

After checking the wheel, I unfold the map across the handlebars. A thick blue strip runs across the bottom – the first sea since I left Calais. This map is printed to much larger scale than the others I've used and the extra detail illustrates just how different the Camargue landscape is. Thin blue lines illustrate a complex network of narrow waterways; most are set out in a linear or grid arrangement. Larger bits of blue show open water and wetlands of various sizes, many of which are linked by irrigation ditches and canals. Scattered single-digit numbers tell me that elevation here is barely above sea level. Little tufts of blue grass, hundreds of them, mark the location of marsh – salt marsh I imagine. After a few minutes I've got the message that the Camargue is a very wet place, but if this is the natural state of play what happens after heavy rain when the Rhône deposits millions of extra gallons of water here? Is the Camargue then changed into one massive floodplain? And what if there's a sea surge? Is the land submerged by high tides? And what about the effect of spring tides? Or do big tides simply not occur at this latitude? If I remember correctly Mediterranean tides are very small and measured in centimetres, not metres.

I think I'm going to like the Camargue. For one thing the place names sound romantic and fascinating and add a layer of intrigue: *Marais de la Grande Mer*, for example, and *Marais des Saliers*, and how about the impressive-sounding *Étang de l'Impérial*?

After stowing the map behind its transparent window, I take on half a bottle of water in big glugs before returning the bottle to its cradle and exerting a little pressure on the right pedal. The bike responds and off we go together along a well-surfaced level lane where everywhere is peaceful except for the metronomic clunk from my rear wheel. Quite surreal, I suppose. Silence, silence, *clunk!* Silence, silence, silence, *CLUNK! Clunk!* Silence.

I try to forget thoughts of the failing wheel but it's difficult because I know my mechanical tweaking has done nothing but stop the brake blocks rubbing against the rim. The real problem lies in the hub and if the hub fails, my ability to cycle anywhere goes with it. It's tricky really because I shouldn't stick my head in the sand, nor can I allow myself to be too distracted by what may or may not go wrong – right now my sights are set firmly on reaching the Mediterranean Sea later this afternoon.

So, with less regard for my velo friend than I'm comfortable with I crank up the pace to a heady twelve miles per hour, which in my world is nothing short of zooming along. Don't get me wrong, I have no desire to rush past the enigmatic beauty of the Camargue or to take the bike for granted, but if the wheel's OK after a brief shock-test I'll have more confidence that the hub will last the course.

Much to my delight the Camargue is pretty well devoid of traffic, at least today. From my elevated position I can see an exquisitely pretty lake to my left. The near perfect circle of water is set within a halo of reeds that glint and flash as the stems are caught by the breeze and sun. More lakes follow, then tiny ponds, and between them patches of marsh catch the attention of wading birds. Another stand of bamboo blocks the view for a bit but it brings a faraway feel to the place, which I find rather exotic.

Instead of taking the most direct route to the coast I branch off west towards the town of St. Gilles. It's a little out of my way and I may not stop at the town but the detour keeps me on these appealing little byways and well clear of the busier D570 road.

The little town of Saintes-Maries-de-la-Mer sits on the southern tip of the Camargue with the Rhône Delta, western Europe's largest river delta by some margin, emptying into the sea on both sides of it. Now that I have crossed the Petit Rhône I enter the Department du Gard and in doing so I pedal from Provence into the Occitaine (now renamed Occitania). It's the southernmost administrative region of France excluding Corsica.

To my right the *Canal-du-Rhône-à-Sète* runs northeast to southwest, cutting a roughly diagonal line through the Camargue. Here the Petit Rhône flows parallel to the canal while my route takes to a narrow band of raised dry land between the two for the next couple of miles before I leave them both behind to find myself fully encircled by three hundred and sixty degrees of marsh, lagoons, and waterlogged fields. Here there is interest with every turn of the head: nearest to me a watery roadside ditch is full of clear still water, doubtless it's the habitat of countless amphibians, small fish perhaps, and water snails, water beetles, nymphs, larva, and the unseen oddities of nature that reside in such places, like sponge flies, flatworms, and leeches.

My birthplace is Kingston-Upon-Hull in the East Riding of Yorkshire where little waterways such as these are known as drains. They drain the land, of course, but the word 'drain' has other connotations and brings to mind unpleasantries such as water management and discharge. The word has never sounded appropriate to me; surely in the context of the countryside the word 'drain' does an injustice to these places of ecological wonder. Someone needs to come up with an alternative that sounds altogether more fitting and pleasant.

Over four hundred bird species have been sighted in the Camargue and I'm fortunate enough to see a few of them as I cycle along. First a heron; it looks different to the grey herons in England. Perhaps it's a purple heron? Ten minutes on, in a nutrient-rich lake waders sift for food with their long slender bills. Shiny oily-black plumage sets off their curved deep red beaks splendidly. Some sub-species of stilt, I think, but with no bird book at hand I can only guess. Species uncertainty disappears instantly with a row of brightly coloured bee-eaters. As vivid and unmistakable as any kingfisher, they're perched in a row on a cable above the lane. Around the size of a woodpecker, the birds are quite unconcerned that I've stopped less than twenty feet away. What an astonishing palette nature has used to create the bee-eater – deep teal and bronze, these birds don't wear muted colours, these are in your face, 'look at me' colours. The bee-eaters are a definite favourite for me, topped only by the field of storks as the wildlife highlight of my trip.

In the middle of adjoining field, a billboard the size of a lorry proclaims: *Camargue – Terre de Riz*. This is surprising news to me as I never realised that rice is cultivated in France. Who'd have thought? But it explains why the fields are such quagmires. Deep ruts churned by heavy tractors provide unmistakable evidence of field preparation, although the crops are not yet visible this early in the season. *Twang!* Another spoke snaps beneath me: *Keep calm and carry on!* as General Kitchener famously said. Surely if the remaining spokes follow his clarion call, they'll see today out – not too much to ask for, or is it?

Massive signs seem to be favoured in these parts. The next one reads *Parc Naturel Regional de Camargue*. Now that its official, it's fitting that I come across several white Camargue horses up to their fetlocks in water. They're pretty well free to roam where the fancy takes them, which pleases me. The horses are a distinct breed indigenous to the Camargue; the animals I'm looking at are all adults, which is easy to tell because Camargue foals are born very dark and don't turn white until they are four or five years old.

Silence, *CLUNK!* Silence, *Grind!* Deteriorating bearings? I would say so, but still up to the job I hope because I am still a dozen miles from the next town and that is a long way to push. There's no sign anywhere of *'The Brotherhood of the Camargue Horsemen'*. I know they sound like a dodgy spinoff of the Sicilian mafia but nothing could be further from the truth. The brotherhood are highly skilled horse guardians, cowboys of the riviera if you will, who've earned the trust of these semi-wild white horses. The brotherhood spends much of their lives caring for the animals and in return the horses help the men manage the Camargue's population of black bulls.

The Camargue is endlessly flat, which may not appeal to some people, but for me it has a unique appeal and if time allowed, I would spend longer here to savour the tranquillity and enjoy its wildlife. I've cycled miles and although I've yet to see another human I've had close encounters with wading birds, dragonflies, wild horses, bee-eaters, and stilts, and just when I'm absorbed in the wonder of this place the second flight of pink flamingos fly overhead in loose formation. The birds above are just twenty of the fifty thousand that live here each summer. Winters are mild in the Camargue but not quite mild enough for flamingos, so most of them overwinter in Morrocco, southern Spain, or even Turkey.

Ten miles ahead is Saintes-Maries-de-la-Mer. It's a small town with a very big significance for me as it will mark the completion of my coast-to-coast travels, although not of the end my bike journey as that finishes the day after tomorrow at Montpellier. Crossing the Petit Rhône for the second time today coincides with a 'Clunk' from the bearing and a subtle change in the Camargue.

Passing the occasional *Rizieres* is now a sight of the past as the proportion of land to water swings considerably in favour of liquid. To my left is the final spur of France before it terminates at the *Golfe-de-Beauduc*. To my right, the tall olive-coloured grasses give way and reward me with a panoramic outlook right across the Petite Camargue. Before me is an expansive patchwork of individual lagoons; each is prevented from merging with its neighbour, and ultimately becoming part of an expanse of water several miles long, by the thinnest slivers of land.

The D38 provides blissful solitude for the final few miles even though the road is responsible for carrying all vehicles in and out of Saintes-Maries-de-la-Mer. All is peaceful as I cycle the last few miles to the Mediterranean. In all honesty I need this peace and quiet just to take in that I shall soon be standing on the shore and looking out to sea with the whole of France over my shoulder.

The nearer I pedal to the coast the more unsure I become of how I'll actually feel when I arrive there. This has been a unique experience for me, a one-off trip, far more interesting and fulfilling than I could ever have dreamed of. Most wives, I suspect, would not have been keen on hubby going off on some jolly across France, leaving them to hold the fort, so I am grateful, deeply grateful in fact, that my wife agreed to me going off on my little adventure. Before retiring from work my job required me to be away from home to attend some conference or other for a few days. Occasionally I was away for a week or two but nearly five weeks away is a first so now feels the right moment to call time on my little escapade and to return the family.

Thoughts of home and family are forced to the back of my mind as complaints from the wheel become louder and more regular. Today started with: silence, silence, *clunk!* Twenty miles on it was: silence, *clunk!* Silence, *CLUNK!* Then, other than the occasional rasp, all went quiet for many miles until now, with the coast literally within sight, and the bike's reaction to its state of health has changed from an occasional grumble to an unmistakable cry for help: Silence, *CLUNK! CLUNK!* Silence, *GRIND! Clunk! CLUNK!*

I know I've pushed my luck and I do feel genuinely guilty because I know I've treated my two-wheeled friend in a rather slipshod and carefree manner these last few days. I have taken the bike for granted, I suppose, and I'm not at ease with that. Now, as I look to my left across the lightly rippled and sparkling waters of the *Étang des Launes*, I can't believe how fortunate I am to have a bike that has not only remained loyal but tried so hard for so long. It should have been on its knees ages ago; a lesser bike would have been. Note to self… Pack less if I ever do this again. Much, much less!

'*La Santi Mario de la Mar*', as the road sign puts it, comes into view as a thin line of low buildings on the horizon. Behind the small town a vast backdrop of azure sky reaches up to the firmament, and sandwiched between the town and the sky is a sparkling thin line of gold that is the Mediterranean Sea twinkling brilliantly in the afternoon sunshine.

Closer now and I can make out that most of the buildings in St. Maries have white walls and red-tiled rooves. The place has a Mediterranean look and why wouldn't it? There is only one structure that's more than two storeys high and that's a church tower that stands proud above all before it. It may only be a modest tower but it is the only prominent feature for miles. Pleasant heat from the afternoon sun warms my face and arms as I close in on Saintes-Maries-de-la-Mer and I can feel the refreshing breeze against my skin as I pedal steadily towards my goal. It's not often you can see the wind, but here I'm watching the effect of the breeze as it puffs thin whisps of dry sand across the road from the dunes to my right. For several mesmerising minutes, millions of grains of sand flow in long 'sidewinder' movements over the surface of the dusty grey road. Air-blown sand joins the escape from the dunes as the wind picks up for the last half mile to Saintes-Maries-de-la-Mer and the open sea beyond.

I'm close to the church now and I can see there are people on the roof, which strikes me as a bit odd. It's not a just few people engaged in maintenance or whatever but a couple of dozen. Thankfully the roof has a very shallow slope. Most of the people are standing on the tiles with perhaps a dozen more seated along the ridge tiles. From this distance it looks like some kind of protest, but civil disobedience on a church roof? Surely not. Whoever heard of such a thing? I guess all will become clear when I reach the town but for now my priority must be getting the bike repaired.

I make the tourist information office my first port of call as they're bound to know the best campsite and whether the town has a bike shop. Staff strongly recommend that I use a campsite a mile out of town near the breezy sand dunes I passed on the way in because the town's annual festival starts next week and people are already flooding in from across Europe. They caution me that the festival attracts people who steal and fight when drunk so I'll be better off a bit out of the way. 'Best of all' they tell me, is that I'll be leaving before the festival really gets going!

Dissuasion seems an unusual tack for tourist office staff to take when advising guests, but they seem genuinely concerned, apprehensive even, at the prospect of the imminent festival – I'm most intrigued.

It takes me five minutes to push the bike from the tourist office to the sea wall where the landward side of a wide wooden boardwalk is edged with small gift shops and the like. On the seaward side a waist-high wall separates me from a few hundred feet of sand and the sea. The limp surf is a long way back so perhaps the tide's out. After twenty-nine days of having somewhere to aim for it feels a bit strange to have finally arrived at the coast under my own steam.

Me, of all people! My youth but a distant memory, and a non-cyclist only a few weeks ago. I've done it, I have actually pedalled from the English Channel to the Mediterranean Sea, solo and self-sufficient for nigh-on a thousand miles. I'll tell you what, it's an outcome I wouldn't have put money on, that's for certain, in fact it's a bit of a surprise that I got here at all if you ask me.

What I am really amazed to be saying is not that I got to the end of my skinny eleven-foot map in one piece, surprising though that is. No, it's that having arrived at this point I only feel a small sense of achievement and none of the euphoria that I thought would be standard at such moments. Arriving here is not at all the emotional experience that makes me want to a whoop about or whatever people are supposed to do on such occasions. Yes, getting here is a milestone event, of course it is, even if it's just a personal one for me. But in all truth arriving at the Mediterranean is not what I expected, in fact it's a bit of a let-down. There's no point saying otherwise, so there you have it, my bubble has burst, as it were.

The bike and I lean against the pale blue railings that run along the top of the sea wall, and as I look out to sea I rub my hands slowly along the top rail and I can feel how the salt-air is encouraging the rust to break through the paint just as it does at Westward Ho! A few miles from my North Devon home. Surprisingly few people have been tempted to enjoy the beach today even with its fine magnolia sand that shelves imperceptibly to the sea. At the water's edge there's no surf breaking, just gentle wavelets that greet the sand without fanfare. To either side of the wall I'm leaning on, perhaps two hundred yards each way, a pair of breakwaters have been built from massive rocks. They reach out like the arms of a crab, which seems very fitting. All the while the sky's been clouding over and now a grey sky creates a grey sea, but it is warm enough and the breeze has eased and that's grand by me.

My contemplation is broken by the smile of a cheery beanpole of a waiter walking towards me carrying an empty tray. He works at the beachside bar behind me that I hadn't even noticed. He asks about the bike, the panniers and my journey, and if I'd like a drink. I explain that I've come from Calais and a cold beer would be most welcome. I'm beckoned to an outdoor table that faces the boardwalk. While I gaze out to sea and think about a journey now largely completed my feelings start to change: I am proud to have reached this little bar on the coast and to have done what I set out to do. Tomorrow the return trip to England begins, and soon I'll be back with family who I have missed enormously.

Beer is served in a frosted glass: Kroonenberg 1664, large, ice cold, and very welcome. To be honest I feel I've earned it in an unbecomingly smug sort of a way. Seemingly the sentiment is shared by the waiter who refuses my enthusiastic and varied attempts to pay. He wins by telling me that as I've not arrived by car, he is providing the beer at a special price that we can agree tomorrow and I'm left with no alternative but to shake the waiter's hand and graciously accept his generous hospitality.

Beer in hand, I look admiringly at my bike as it leans against the sea wall catching its breath. Over my shoulder I can sense the entirety of France behind me and it feels like the right time for me to update the family.

My text reads: *'2.15pm. Arrive at the Med at Saint Marie de la Mer. About 940 miles so far, looking forward to coming home in a few days XX.'*

A passing couple stop to chat and take a photograph of me with the bike and the sea as a backdrop; a good one for the album, hopefully. I'm tempted to have another beer as I'll never have this moment again, but I have a campsite to find and then a bike mechanic, so I bid farewell to the waiter whose inevitably response is a smile and, *'Bon courage.'*

Once he's out of sight I leave a brace of euros under the empty glass. He didn't quite win the negotiation after all.

Back on the saddle the only sounds are seagulls and *Clunk, CLUNK! Click, grind, clunk*. I cycle gingerly to the campsite, which covers several acres of sparse grassland and sand dunes just to the northwest of town. Dry marram grass of some sort pokes through the sand in small savage tufts. It's the same colour as the sand it grows in and although worn short by years of camping it's still needle sharp. I position the tent with great care to avoid the groundsheet being punctured by the shards. I'm not at all confident the sand will secure my thin metal tent pegs, but for now they seem to be doing their job. No wind overnight would be a good thing.

Assuming I can get the bike fixed I need to be in Montpellier two days from now. Forty miles on Saturday and a twenty on Sunday morning seems do-able to me, but first things first: I know the rear hub won't be a pretty sight when someone lifts the lid on it, and apparently an adult bike has between twenty-eight and thirty-two spokes per wheel. Nine of mine, nearly a third, are snapped or missing; that's an awful lot of broken wheel and it's time to get it sorted out once and for all.

I unclip and stow the panniers in the tent before setting off for Saintes-Maries-de-la-Mer. Unladen, the bike has developed a pronounced wobble that passers-by are sure to notice. I hope they don't think I've been on the wine. It seems peculiar to me that the wobble is much more severe now the load's removed, and come to think of it the grinding noise has disappeared completely, it's been exchanged for the wobble and I'm not sure if that's a plus or not.

I find *'Le Velociste'* within minutes of returning to town. The proprietor, let's call him *'L'homme de la bicyclette'*, inspects the bike and states that he'll have a look at the hub and replace the spokes. He'll do it immediately and would like me to return in one hour. This is absolutely splendid. Who could ask for more?

In the middle of town, a rather squat stone church with a stumpy tower sits unassumingly to the side of a small square. Undoubtedly, it's the church I spotted with people on the roof as I cycled across the last bit of the Camargue.

A group of twenty or so people are jostling in a well-mannered fashion waiting to enter a narrow flight of stairs. One thing's for sure, this isn't the main entrance to the church but it's the one attracting the most attention. I join the group without giving it a second thought as it seems the thing to do. The cluster of people I'm with enter the tunnel together and almost immediately I discover what an odd sensation it is to be propelled along as part of a flow of humanity gently held together by its own mass and moving as one towards the basement or whatever awaits us. Fortunately for us, whatever unseen hazards may lie ahead, coming a cropper on the worn steps is unlikely because we're all wedged together, being carried ever downwards as a noisy log jam of happy people. I've no idea what my new acquaintances are talking about, but whatever it is they seem excited beyond belief. A few others, mainly older folks, glide along in silent reverence – I notice that the animated chatter fades to a respectful hush the more we advance downwards.

The dimly lit stairwell with its arched stone roof and walls seems unusually warm for a tunnel, not that I have extensive experience of such places, you understand. Anyway I would have expected cool and damp, instead it's warm here and getting warmer as we descend. I put this down to the tight mass of people all crammed into an airless space moving at a snail's pace. As the end of the tunnel nears the air's hot enough to dry my throat and unless this is a sauna, which I doubt, I'm unclear as to exactly what awaits us because I can see nothing beyond a wedge of people and the stone blocks that face the tunnel. Suddenly the stairway opens up, the log jam unjams, and along with several others I lose my footing and stumble into a small room with a flagstone floor and a low vaulted brick ceiling. The room looks like an ancient wine cellar, my luck is in!

The room is bathed in an orange-yellow glow that emanates from the far end of the cellar as people pass to my left and double back towards the steps behind me – in need of an escape to cooler breathable air, no doubt. Their departure clears the view so I can see hundreds, no, thousands of small candles arranged on a semicircle of waist-high metal tables at the end of the room. Without prompting or discussion people sort themselves out to walk in an orderly anti-clockwise line round the room. In the far corner of this ecclesiastical hothouse stands the statue of a Madonna.

The Black Madonna has an enigmatic and compassionate expression but it is the wonder etched onto the faces of those gazing at the statue that I find most fascinating. The middle-aged couple in front of me reach out and gently stroke their hands over the statue, others stare in hushed admiration. The reaction of these people transfixes me until I'm gently nudged from behind by a swarthy man in his early twenties who leans over me in his impatience to kiss the statue – he is not alone in his adoration and several others do the same. This is unquestionably a moving experience for all, highly devout or less so.

Beyond the church, the warm outside air feels chilly after the intense heat of the crypt. I learn that next week's festival is primarily a religious event that draws thirty to forty thousand visitors most years. The feast of Saint Mary, after which the town takes its name, is centred on the ninth-century Romanesque fortress church I've just visited. Most visitors to the festival will be Roma Catholics. Apparently Saint Sarah, Sarah the Black, or Sara-la-Kali is the saint of the Roma people and as Saintes-Maries-de-la-Mer is the centre of veneration, the saint is honoured here every year with a festival that culminates with the statue being carried aloft to be washed in the sea. The procession finale, a few days from now, is attended by great numbers of Roma people who come here from all over Europe specifically for the pilgrimage and to renew old friendships.

Back at *Velocistes*, 'L'homme de la bicyclette' is all smiles when I arrive. He's mended my bike but it wasn't just the spokes that needed attention, as the rear axle and bearings were disintegrating into fragments and dust, making repair out of the question. My new wheel costs forty-seven euros but given the mechanical failure found I doubt it could have limped the seventy miles to Montpellier so it's money very well spent.

Specialist bike buses depart for England each week from southern Europe. Spaces are pre-booked many months in advance, in fact I booked this 'May' slot back in January – it was my Christmas present and it's not very often you get a bus ticket for Christmas! Had the wheel collapsed on the final leg I would have been in a right pickle but to be fair, the old wheel did me proud; it struggled for hundreds of miles since it discreetly started to fall apart in Chalon-sur-Saône. Those first broken spokes were half a journey ago. I know I've pushed my luck, and although I wasn't worried about the overall condition of the bike (had I been realistic I would have been) it's reassuring, comforting even, to know the bike is restored to full health.

Today seems to have been a long one but immensely satisfying nonetheless so I've decided to walk back to St. Maries later to treat myself to a celebratory 'mission accomplished' meal. My only qualm about doing so is that I can't fasten my bike to marram grass and there are no trees or fences to secure it to. Tourist information staff told me to be very guarded; the barman reinforced this by warning me not to leave anything unattended. He was most earnest and clearly thought that to do so would be a risk too far.

Part of me is reluctant to ignore these warnings but part of me is less cautious: When I left Devon I half expected to fall off the bike at some point, nothing spectacular necessarily but a tumble of one sort or another seemed a fair bet over a thousand miles. I thought my tent would prove too flimsy, and as for hills, well, certainly the bigger ones were bound to be too difficult. More than anything I had doubts about my fitness. I never practiced on the bike, wasn't I bound to seize up? But none of this happened, which goes to show that sometimes you've just got to trust to luck and crack on.

Soft sand oozes into my sandals as I stride over the dunes that separate the campsite from the beach. My valuables bag is slung over my shoulder. The warm sand would be a pleasing sensation were it not for occasional sharp pricks from marram grass shards as I make my way to the shoreline. The marram keeps me on my toes, quite literally. The *'get on with it'* maxim won the day; my panniers are in the tent and I've partly hidden the bike behind the tent which I've pitched in a hollow in the dunes. The town's about an hour's walk along the water's edge.

A dark cloudy sky hangs low over the dull sea. If I were inland somewhere, on moorland perhaps, it would feel sombre, but here the moody sky and the smell of the sea reminds me of home. A paraglider dangling under a copious red sail passes silently overhead but otherwise the beach is deserted except for the incongruous sight, some way off, of a man standing behind a table on the beach. The man is alone, motionless, and standing with his arms behind his back and his back to the sea. As the gap between us narrows I can see that the man is all spruced up in a dinner jacket and bow tie and the table has been formally laid with a crisp white tablecloth and twenty or so fluted glasses. Red roses and champagne bottles set the scene so I scurry by, not wishing to interrupt someone's special occasion.

Back in Saintes-Maries-de-la-Mer I discover a town busy with people even though it's nearly dusk and most shops have closed.

A nine-piece jazz band has set up in the square next to the squat church; the musicians are playing with great gusto and even greater volume. What an entertaining bunch they are with their jaunty hats and colourful shirts: a brace of trumpets, a percussionist with a full kit of drums and more cymbals than anyone could possibly need. Most intriguing are two very large brass instruments that are coiled around their keepers like shiny musical pythons. Behind the band a stone water fountain is topped with a bronze statue of Christ the redeemer. A bijou restaurant is almost hidden just behind the statue. Given that you can't hear yourself think above the music, the restaurant is perhaps the last place for a relaxing meal, certainly if you wish to talk to a companion over food, but I'm eating solo, and for anyone like me wishing to embrace the vibrancy of the little town it's ideal. That being said, I opt for an indoor table. Hearing is a precious sense, mine is none too good as it is, and however uplifting live music is, the band is loud beyond belief.

A waiter guides me to a small table next to a window and hands me a menu, which I am delighted to see is written in English, or more accurately 'local' English: Some of the more interesting offerings are: *'Mouse to fresh fish'* or *'Plate of cooked bull meats'* (both starters). Or how about *'Bull Pave grilled'* or *'Gardiane of Bull'* or even *'Rice Timbale'*? Personally, I could never be tempted by *'Trigh of Frog'* as a main course. If I'm honest I am slightly unnerved by the selection of food on offer until I come to the dessert section, where I am relieved to see that *'Catalane cream' (made house)* and *'Coffee and sweet things'* are both available – who could ask for more?

My starter is *'Soup fish'*, with *'Bolagnessed Spaghetti'* for my main. Timid choices, I know, but I'm hungry, I'm not feeling brave and I don't want to leave food I'm unsure of. The spaghetti is listed in the section intended for children and cowards, but at least I can fool myself into believing I've avoided bull of uncertain provenance or amphibians, which, to be quite frank, I would much rather watch in our garden pond.

Inevitably the restaurant needs time to prepare my food so I order a bottle of red: *Chateau L'Ermitage, Rhône 2008*, and put the time to good use by testing the acceptability of the wine while jotting some words in my journal. The wine is mediocre at first, but remarkably by the time I am midway through the bottle it has transformed itself into something rather good. Clearly the better vintage had sunk to the bottom of the bottle over storage. Remarkable! Half a bottle of wine and five pages of notes later my *Soup Fish* arrives piping hot, a little spicy and full of flavour together with a hefty slab of fresh crusty bread. What is unquestionably a great start to my culinary celebration is short lived as the *'Bolagnessed'* is sloppy in texture and tasteless, so much so that I'm dissuaded from ordering *'Coffee and sweet things'*. Who ever heard of a celebratory meal with no pudding?

With the sea on my left and dunes to the right I set off to walk two miles back to my tent. Dry sand creeps into my sandals and wraps itself around my toes. The sand's lost its earlier warmth and feels cool against the warm night air. Out to sea an oversized reflection of the moon appears as a creamy circle on the water until the wave that the moon's riding on loses its balance and the moon topples into the breaking surf. It shatters into a thousand sparkles like a broken mirror; it's a magical sight that repeats occasionally as I amble along the deserted beach. A warm westerly blows into my face from over the Pyrenees, the wind whistles as I make my way along the sand, in fact it outperforms the crashing surf, making the beach a surprisingly noisy place. The focal point for much of my walk has been the moon reflected on the sea, so clear and crisp and perfect earlier but now the breeze has erased the detail and wobbly strips of floating silver are all that remain on the dark shiny Mediterranean. It's rather sad but I can't explain why.

Even in bright moonlight the outline of one sand dune looks pretty well identical to the next so all I can do is look for a cleft between them and set off in that general direction, hoping to find the campsite. Then I remember the marram grass – vindictive stuff. I reckon it's lying in wait and out to get me again. True to form the unseen marram spears my feet within minutes of me trespassing into its territory; each prick makes me wince. I walk gingerly in expectation of the next sharp pain. My trek across the dunes truly is a stab in the dark. Well, several actually.

On top of the dunes the wind is stronger and louder, but not as loud as the croaking frogs. A chorus erupts from hundreds and hundreds of hidden amphibians as they welcome me back. They must be here in huge numbers yet I see none of them, not one. What a memorable moment this is, and a close thing come to think of it as it dawns on me that I may just have stumbled across the source of *'Trigh of Frog'*.

After a bit of aimless wandering amongst the dunes the outline of my tent emerges from the darkness. Did the frogs guide me for resisting *'Trigh of Frog'*? – I'd like to think so.

Back at my little home I note with surprise that the tent pegs have held against the wind. This pleases me no end, as does finding the tent in the dark, and my bike's still behind it.

DAVID PAUL ELLIOTT

# Day 30 – Saturday 15th May

## Departments of Bouches-du-Rhône, Gard and Herault: From Saintes-Maries-de-la-Mer to Palaves-les-Flots

It's six o'clock and the tent walls are luminous so the sun must be out. The only sound is an odd little noise that I've decided must be the breeze whispering over the sand dunes and caressing the marram grass behind the tent, but who knows? Maybe it's those frogs snoring, that's a nice thought to start the day on.

Once the tent's dismantled I give it a vigorous shaking to get the sand out, because as sure as eggs are eggs some will hide in the folds of the fabric and in the zip, just waiting to make the inside of my little house all gritty and uncomfortable next time I use it (and probably for time immemorial because sand's like that, you know, it never gives up).

Such a beautiful day tempts me to cycle back to Saintes-Maries-de-la-Mer to find a bakery for breakfast and something for lunch. Back on the open road I'm surprised to discover it's incredibly windy; the tent and I must have been sheltered by the sand dunes. It seems that cycling is not going to be free and easy after all today. Ten minutes after leaving the site I discover the bakery just off the main road in a pedestrianised part of town. The bike is propped against a conveniently placed metal grille that juts at right angles from a gift shop into the pavement directly opposite the bakery. Perfect.

As I'm pushing the boulangerie door open an almighty crash occurs, which causes me to spin round automatically: the metal grille and my bike have collapsed to the ground. The grille is six feet high by eight feet wide and made from hefty metal rods welded together to form a solid mesh. It seems over-substantial for displaying goods but I think that's what it's for. The almighty clatter attracts a fair amount of attention from the few people in the street and from everyone queueing in the shop. They're all looking at me with a clear expectation of some kind of action on my behalf. It's not all unreasonable because my bike was leaning against the grille when it collapsed so I'll just have to sort it out.

I take a few minutes to access the situation and examine everything: The bike, the metalwork, the shop front, and finally the pavement. Everything looks tickety-boo and I'm very relieved that no harm's been done. The bike's resting on top of the grille so I untangle it from the metal and wheel it aside before trying to lift the metalwork, but it's far too heavy for me to lift upright in order to slot it back into the support holes drilled into the pavement.

People have gathered round to watch but no-one offers to help as I struggle with the massive grille, even though a few of us working together could sort this out in a jiffy. By looking closer I can see that the metalwork was never properly secured in the first place. There are no hefty hinges or brackets fitted to the wall as would be needed to support the weight, the grille was simply held upright by two eight-inch metal prongs slotted into holes in the concrete footpath. The weight of my bike tipped the balance, of course, but the way the grille was balanced was a bit shoddy if you ask me, and unsafe.

I strain to lift the mesh again but it's an impossible task and nobody's the least bit interested in helping. The number of grumpy onlookers increases when the lady from the boulangerie joins them in a very agitated state and thrusts a pen and paper in my face demanding that I write my name and address. She's rather het up and overly excited for my liking especially as the only damage caused is a few scratches to the paintwork of my bike. I calmly decline to give the lady my details because however unlikely, I'm wary that doing so may trigger me being stopped at Calais and questioned about some trumped up damage allegation. I could give her a false name and address, I suppose, but that's not my style. It wouldn't be playing cricket, would it?

By now the congregation has increased to about twelve people, all of whom seem to know *Madam Baguette* or whatever she's called. I assume they're locals as they're all chuntering, gesticulating, and generally egging each other on. Of more concern is that they're building up a collective head of steam over a situation where they clearly see me as the pariah. It's developing into a rather uncomfortable situation that I'd rather not be at the centre of.

The gaping hole in my attempt to defuse the situation is my inability to say what I need to in French, so I play my trump card and ask Mrs. Bakery to call the gendarme so officers can see for themselves that nothing untoward has occurred, and that this kerfuffle is the result of a simple accident rather than a malicious incident. Hopefully my request for the police will calm the twitchy locals by reassuring them I am happy to remain here until officialdom turns up to sort it all out.

At first Mrs Boulangerie seems irritated by my request but after some over-theatrical muttering to the assembled posse, and a bit of Napoleonic arm-waving, she returns to her bakery to phone the police. In the meantime I take some photographs of the metalwork, the shop, and the bike. It's a largely pointless exercise but it gives the crowd something to be distracted by and proves that my camera still functions.

Quarter of an hour passes before I ask Madam where the gendarmes are whereupon she shuffles uneasily before reversing her earlier claim that she had called the police and telling me that she has phoned the gift shop owner instead. It's clear that I need to change the dynamics of this potentially volatile situation before the odds get worse for me with the arrival of the giftshop owner and any henchmen they may bring. Accordingly, I face the group and instruct them, *'Je suis allez le gendarmes.'* I say it loudly so as to appear more confident than I really feel. Perfect French and grammar aside, hopefully this conveys that I'm going to the police station to sort this out rather than abandoning the situation or running away. They're not at all happy but as I can't back down I stoop down and pick up the bike. Doing so makes me vulnerable, which is a ridiculous situation to be in. The uncomfortable glares and silence that follow me do nothing to lessen my feeling of uneasiness as I climb over the crossbar and pedal slowly away from the situation.

*Voila!* It seems I've called their bluff.

What a situation to find myself in, unbelievable really, something out of nothing. I resist the temptation to look back because I'm sure they're all glaring at me and I don't want to risk anything that may incite them to detain me for presentation to the shop owner or whatever. A couple of streets away I feel like the quarry that's outwitted its tormentors. It's quite a relief, let me tell you. A passing couple (with the first smiling faces of today) direct me to the police station in the very next street.

The uniformed sergeant hears the tale of the collapsing metalwork and his agitated countrymen. Fortunately for me he speaks pretty good English. I tell him that a couple of years ago I retired from the police in England and that I am more than happy to provide him with my name, address, and passport details. The sergeant explains: *The people think you are Roma. You do not look like Roma, but you are not from France and it is festival time, so you are a Roma.* The sergeant is fifty-six; he's retiring soon and he's very happy about this as policing in France, as in England, is not what it was. We discuss how policing has changed since the nineteen seventies when we both put uniforms on for the first time: before we had radios, when policing relied on a wing and a prayer, the Ways and Means Act, and a bucketful of common sense. The sergeant doesn't record my details as he considers what's happened just *'un petit incident'*. So, with a *'Happy Retirement'* from me and *'Bon Courage'* from him, we part company with a handshake and a knowing smile that the metal grille incident is simply the lifeblood of traditional policing. Thankfully it didn't escalate to physical conflict, but another day, another place, other participants, well, who knows? *C'est la vie.*

Once on the higher ground clear of St-Maries-de-la-Mer I stop to look back at the sea, which sparkles in the morning sunlight. A group of anglers standing on the distant breakwater appear as tiny silhouettes against the brilliant silvery-gold Mediterranean: tranquillity has returned to my day. Water lies on both sides, the *Étang-des-Launes* on my right and the Petit Rhône backed by the many lagoons of the Petite

Camargue to the left. The occasional gnarled and twisted tree and a few patches of scrub are all that breaks the flatness here.

Emerging from a roadside reed bed I'm surprised to find myself facing a group of black Camargue bulls. The animals look free to roam at will, which is disconcerting at first but they're not concerned by me and after my initial wariness has faded, I feel the same about them. The situation pleases me no end as I doubt I could outpace the bulls even with my new wheel and the inevitable adrenalin rush should the bulls head my way.

The *'Bac de Sauvage'* ferry is a curious little vessel that carries a maximum of eight cars across the Petit Rhône River. The vessel looks very antiquated, although it's only operated since 1974. There is no charge for me or the bicycle, which is a local policy I very much approve of. The ferry is propelled by paddle wheels and guided from shore to shore by a thick iron hawser, which runs through a large pulley suspended on head-height davits on the starboard side. However primitive the *Bac de Sauvage* boat may appear, the embarkation point is surprisingly modern with its large outdoor LCD screen that lists the loading priorities of the ferry as follows: $1^{st}$: Emergency vehicles. $2^{nd}$: Bicycles. $3^{rd}$: Horses, and $4^{th}$: Other vehicles including cars – but only if there is room. How can anyone not smile at such priorities in today's world?

The ferry runs every half hour except for a ninety-minute break for the crew's lunch. Ninety minutes for lunch, how very French. During the two-hundred-yard journey across the Petit Rhône I lean against the starboard side-rail of the boat looking upstream. The *'Clank-Clank-Clank'* of the steel hawser running noisily through the iron pulley makes a rhythmic antiquated sound as I gaze over the side. It's an absorbing few minutes in an old-fashioned, 'they-don't-do-it-like-this-anymore' sort of way.

The wind picks up clear of the river; occasionally a stronger-than-usual gust tries to knock me off balance. If this continues, I'll have to get the MP3 out: I sense a 'gustometer' afternoon coming my way! There are no bee-eaters sitting on overhead wires today, and no curved-billed waders strutting their stuff in the shallows, and where are the pencil-thin flamingos flying in formation? I reckon they're probably all around me somewhere, out of sight, hunkered down out of the wind.

One of the 'mas' I cycle past is particularly striking: its long-manicured drive lined by whitewashed walls topped with half-round terracotta tiles, bold red tiles against the brilliant white, it all looks very impressive. At the end of the wall stands a 'bottle' – it's a good twenty feet high and made from rendered stone painted white. Ornate ceramic tiles make up the 'label': *Eau de Vie de Poire Williams*. The bottle advertises that fruit spirit (pear brandy) is made here. Later I learn that the Williams Pear is the most popular fruit to distil *Eau de Vie* (water of life) from, although plums and other soft fruits are also used. Both the ceramic 'label' and the farm entrance display a symbol of an anchor overlaid with a heart. I recognise it as the same symbol that I saw yesterday branded on some of the Camargue horses I came across. As if to answer my wishes the road slingshots two hundred and forty degrees, rendering the wind impotent. Cycling instantly becomes easier and so pleasurable with the warm sun on my face and the deep blue sky above.

Although the sea is a few miles from here its presence lurks all around me. Salty tentacles creep silently inland to create saltmarsh, hundreds of acres of it, and when you first look at this landscape it appears natural, but look closer and you'll see the hand of man in a series of brine lagoons that lie between here and the ocean: *'Étang de la ville'*, *'Étang des Caitives'*, and the wonderfully named *'Salins du midi'*, or 'Salt flats of the south'. In places these irregular watery shapes fit together like a jigsaw pieces separated by the merest sliver of sandy ground raised a foot or two proud of the water. These fragile ridged paths form access routes for the salt farmers or *'saulniers'* so they can tend the lagoons and harvest salt, as they've done in the Camargue for at least the last two thousand years.

The most prominent ground-level natural feature are the lagoons – but if only you could look up as I can, at the magnificent herculean sky above. It draws the eye, the master of all before it. It's truly an awesome sight to gaze upon, and then there's the contrast, the contrast between the vast blue sky and pillows of stationary puffy white clouds. Stunning, quite stunning. The immensity of it all takes your breath away. What a place this would be to lie on your back and gaze up at what truly is the wide blue yonder.

Returning to land, the patches of scrub and tall grasses that have featured for so much of the last day and a half have receded, for now at least. And now, for no good reason I should point out, the road has gone back on itself, allowing the wind to make its unwelcome return. The outstretched hand of the breeze is in front of me as I pedal into it. I can feel its large hand on my chest, it's pushing against me, but not in an unfriendly way, just enough to hold me back and remind me who's in charge here.

A few miles on and I'm confronted by another incredible sight. If anything the view at ground level is even more impressive than the sky above, and that's saying something. The scene leaves me quite speechless and being lost for words is not a good state to be in if one day you hope to write a book about the experience. The sky is as bold and impressive as earlier but it no longer demands my full attention, no, the vast sky has been toppled by the stunning sight of Aigues-Mortes. Like a backdrop from the epic film 'Ben Hur', the walls of Aigues-Mortes bar my way across the empty arid landscape ahead. The town of 'Dead Waters' is enclosed within a perfect rectangle of ancient stone walls where crenelated ramparts and circular stone towers complete the impregnable defences. Huge gates, made from wood a good twelve inches thick, are the only way into the town. The stunning medieval scene before me is so imposing and enthralling that it's genuinely difficult to look away. The visual impact of this place, for me at least, surpasses the historical wonders of Avignon and even the wonderful fortifications of Carcassonne, which our family visited years ago.

Opinions vary as to when human settlement actually started in what's now called Aigues-Mortes, but by 791AD King Charlemagne had ordered the construction of the Matafere Tower in nearby swamps to protect fisherman and salt collectors from seaborne attack. Within a few hundred years a thriving town had developed – its real prominence coming during the crusades.

I've pulled up half a mile from the medieval walls where the view ahead is unchanged for a thousand years. It's as if I'm looking at the world through the eyes of a horseman back from the crusades. What a thought.

None of Aigues-Mortes' stone buildings are taller than three storeys, which ensures that nothing of the town protrudes above the protection of its colossal outer walls. After pushing the bike between the heavy wooden gates I find myself in a large open space where a few mature trees provide shade to the throngs of people seated at the outdoor cafés that edge the square. It's lunchtime, the weather's great, and the cafés are enjoying a roaring trade. Aigues-Mortes is a lively town with UNESCO World Heritage status. First impressions are very good; I think I'm going to like this place.

The walls have provided a barrier to intruders for a thousand years. Small gangs of rogues to opposing armies have all been halted, but no wall's going to tame today's wind, it seems, and although I can't feel it inside the town it blows overhead, causing an odd acoustic effect that resonates and whistles above the town in a surprisingly loud and eerie way. It's a very strange sound indeed but it adds greatly to the atmosphere of Aigues-Mortes.

The noon sun makes the air extremely hot inside the town so having pushed the bike for an hour, now seems a good time to join those taking a break at one of the many outdoor cafés here.

A substantial temporary stage stands in the middle of the large open square. Surrounding the stage are scores of tables and hundreds of chairs. The seating arrangements are all jumbled, gloriously haphazard, and full of happy customers; it looks dishevelled in a charmingly rustic-French sort of way.

Shade, lots of shade, is provided by a massive overhead awning stretched between substantial gantries above the stage. The triangular canvas is at least sixty feet long and suspended at its three corners by robust scaffolding that also holds aloft some very complicated-looking stage lighting. Surprisingly the visual conflict between the very ancient and the very technical doesn't look at all out of place here. After finding an empty seat next to the raised stage I settle down for a restful half hour or so. Two mature ladies at the table next to me are shaded by the awning while just a few feet away I bake in the full glare of the sun. Every shaded chair, and there must be a couple of hundred of them, is occupied. Once seated I enjoy watching the contrast between the inactivity of the customers and the energetic scurrying of waiters as I sit back and enjoy a cold beer from a comfy wicker chair.

With absolutely no warning the tranquillity of this peaceful day is shattered when a gust of wind comes from nowhere and lifts the awning high above the stage. The lifting of the canvas is accompanied by a sudden loud *'THWUMP'* as the awning balloons up as if a ripcord has been pulled. Ordinarily I doubt that such an event would shatter the normality of day-to-day life in the square below, but not so today! The billowing-up and the *'THWUMP'* coincide with the emptying of the generous barrelful of rainwater that had pooled in the canvas above the stage. An almighty surprise is a nanosecond away!

Gallons of water cascade from a height of about fifteen feet onto the two ladies seated at the next table to me. The ladies are not just splashed, this is no glancing blow, oh no, this is nothing less than a direct hit on their table. It's a complete deluge. Are they surprised? I would say so. Damp or wet? Submerged would be more accurate. I doubt they would have been wetter had they been keel hauled! In that single, brief, and rather spectacular moment 'ever-so-tranquil' Aigues-Mortes had changed from dead waters to very much alive waters. Waiters, who seconds ago were scurrying with measured purpose have been turbocharged into a hyper-flurry of mopping and apologising. Sincere and well-meaning it may be but the excessive gusto and theatrical aplomb of the waiters' actions adds comedic value to the unfortunate incident.

Both ladies are gently lifted to their feet, and their handbags, the table, and a brace of rattan chairs are dried with a couple of towels. Next, the scattering of broken crockery is put into some semblance of order until somebody realises this is entirely pointless and brushes the pieces into a bin. Thankfully both ladies survive the watery Armageddon uninjured. I watch on as the waiters try to dry the ladies using a variety of napkins and table cloths. Never in a million years is this going to cure the problem; nothing short of a complete change of clothing is needed to solve this one.

An uneasy conflict emerges before me between the waiters, who in all fairness are simply trying to do their best, and the ladies who are visibly uncomfortable at receiving this level of fussy assistance. Too much hands-on attention for their liking, I would say. For my own credibility I must add that I didn't sit passively by or even worse take photographs of this calamity, as seems to be the modern way when misfortune strikes someone. No, I stand up and offer to help but it's clear there's nothing I can do that they haven't already got in hand. I could demolish a second cold beer but now's really not the time to distract the waiters from the water-ladies so I leave them to their task and set off pushing the bike through the narrow streets. Once I've exited by another set of massive gates at the far side of town, I feel a renewed sense of freedom as I set off once more over the open landscape and big skies of the Camargue.

A line of triangular white mounds lie half a mile ahead of me between the *Canal-du-Rhône-à-Sète* and the sea. Even from here I can make out coal-mine-sized conveyor belts set at forty-five degrees against the hills so raw salt can be moved from the sea-level evaporation pans to the summit. Production is on a commercial scale here, that said, I'm not looking out over some bleak industrial landscape, not at all; each saltpan is tinted pink, which makes this pastel-coloured landscape interesting, unique, and strangely beautiful.

To either side of the dusty uneven track a carpet of cotton grass grows all snowy and wispy, each feather-like top swaying happily to and fro in the warm breeze. Intriguing stuff, this cotton grass: to all intents and purposes it's a grass, it looks like a grass, it's called a grass, but it's not a grass, it's a sedge. Why so? Well, the main distinction between grass and sedge is that grasses have hollow cylindrical stems and sedges have solid triangular stems – how on earth does anyone have a fulfilling and rich life without that priceless nugget of information?

Thick clumps of reed border the lagoon edge along with more cotton grass. Beyond this vegetation the wind agitates the surface of the salt pans, larger ripples on the far side, wavelets even, but even choppy water doesn't deter the birds from feeding. Flamingos are a prominent species here, great swathes of them knee deep in brine, heads slowly moving from side to side sieving the water in their rhythmic search for food. Most are resplendent in their rosy pink plumage, which tells me they have reached maturity and are at least three years old. Younger birds, and there are a few here, are pure white.

I've no idea where I'm camping tonight and the wind is starting to make life difficult as it fluctuates in strength and direction. Mostly it's just a strong breeze then without warning I'm forced to half close my eyes as a gust comes from nowhere, rocks the bike and blasts a sprinkling of sharp sandy dust into my face.

The most prominent feature in Le-Grau-de-Roi is the row of tall palm trees lining the Marina boardwalk. Pedalling is a struggle now but I don't know if it's the prevailing coastal westerlies or just that the weather's deteriorating. Back on the wooden boardwalk the wind's whipping the tattered palm fronds almost horizontal, it's a spectacular sight that brings to mind newsreel footage of some fierce Caribbean storm. Sometimes stubborn determination and blind foolishness are but a whisker apart: dismounting from the bike has been inevitable for a while but you've got to give it go, haven't you? That said, it's now time to put my sensible head on and push. Enough is enough, as they say. Fifteen minutes after dismounting I notice my cyclometer's stopped working. I last glanced at it about fifteen miles ago but as I can't be sure I'll have to factor a few extra miles into my records.

Le-Grau-de-Roi sports two stubby piers that jut into the sea. The piers mark the start, and come to think of it the end, of the Canal-du-Rhône-à-Sète, which links to the sea at this very point. An ornate lighthouse on the tip of the right-hand pier is conveniently positioned for me to shelter from the wind and look out over the bay at the battalions of white horses sweeping towards land over the blue-grey waters of the Golfe-d'-Aigues-Mortes.

The futuristic-looking town of Le Grande-Motte lies on the far side of the bay and it is an unusual sight by any measure. The seafront is made up of a line of large angular buildings, roughly triangular in shape but with flat tops and stepped sides. Taken individually, each building looks like a modern version of the Mesoamerican pyramids of Mexico but from where I'm standing, which is good mile away, the waterside buildings merge together and look convincingly like a row of massive cruise liners berthed bows to stern.

Le Grande-Motte does nothing to inspire me closer up. Doubtless the place was strikingly modern in its day, but nowadays the architecture is showing its age and not in a good way. I wonder what the Brazilian architect Oscar Niemeyer would think about his futuristic brainchild if he could see it now.

Twenty minutes on and by some stroke of good fortune I come upon a campsite. It's an unexpected blessing, really, as my legs have had enough. They've put in a good shift today so I take the hint and prop the bike against the reception wall. Thirty days ago, the booking-in process was unfamiliar, whereas now it's very much part of my daily routine, although today's guest form has more significance as it's the last time I'll complete one. As usual checking in brings the familiar questions: Have you come far? Where are you going? Are you alone?

The receptionist warns me that overnight and tomorrow hundred-kilometre winds are expected in Montpellier. The prospect that today is just a taster for what's around the corner gives me something to think about – this may be a good time to take stock: Being in Montpellier on time is non-negotiable but at least the weather warning gives me the opportunity to re-evaluate my plans. The receptionist adds that the news is reporting widespread damage expected from around midnight.

Of course, there's a good chance that damage will be hit and miss so I could well be absolutely fine. My little tent may not fare so well but tonight is my last night of camping, and however fond I've become of my snug little home, in all likelihood I'll never use it again. Harsh, I know, disloyal even, but I have to deal with facts and for all practical purposes I don't need to worry about my tent, not for now at least. The bike – I have no concerns about the bike. Nothing's going to blow the bike away, it's far too heavy for that. It's late afternoon and time's ticking away; scenarios are racing through my mind and I'm prevaricating with myself about decisions that can't be left until tomorrow. It's sorting out priorities and decision time, is it not?

Distance needs to be my overriding priority, eating up as many miles as possible before the storm arrives. Miles covered now are less tomorrow when cycling may be more challenging.

It's time to get the map out, and the reception desk makes a perfect podium: The motorway linking France with southern Spain prevents me from cycling to Montpellier as directly as I'd wish. It looks to be about thirty miles (forty-eight kilometres) from here to the pick-up point and very fortunately I'm meeting the bus just south of the city so I'll avoid the city centre. The first half of the journey to Montpellier is along a road sandwiched between the sea and a large saltwater lake. This road's likely to be very exposed to wind but on the other hand, with water to either side there's little chance of fallen trees or debris blocking my way. Swings and roundabouts, as they say. The lady at reception, like so many I've met, speaks more or less fluent English. She understands my predicament and offers me a refund before I set off to narrow the gap to Montpellier. A concerned expression, with the words, *'Fais attention,'* and, *'Bon courage,'* set me on my way west along the coast road.

An hour after leaving the site I'm on the narrow isthmus of land that I spotted on the map. It's extremely blustery as expected but with the afternoon sun sparkling on the sea to my left it's really quite beautiful here. Every now and again the parting words of the receptionist, *'Fais attention,'* or, *'Be careful,'* encourage me to step up the pace before the storm arrives in force.

To the right the *'Étang de Mauguio'* is a particularly large inland salt lake. Its surface is turbulent and moody today with waves prancing across its waters just as boldly as those I watched from the pierhead lighthouse in Le-Grau-du-Roi. Between these two bodies of water the D59 provides a scenic route that hugs the coast for several miles before merging with the larger road that funnels Montpellier's quarter of a million inhabitants this way whenever they wish to visit the coast. My proximity to the city is emphasised by the frequent sight of aircraft as they take off and land at Montpellier's airport on the far side of the salt lake. After another thirty minutes of huffing and puffing into the wind I cycle into the twin coastal resorts of Canon Plage and Palaves-les-Flots. I'm now only twelve miles from the pick-up point in the suburb of Jean-le-Sec and that'll do me very nicely for today.

There is only ever one chance to make a first impression, and with that in mind it's unfortunate that there is nothing particularly positive I can say about Palaves-les-Flots other than, for my purposes at least, it's very conveniently placed for Montpellier. Admittedly my views are tarnished by a few minor but nevertheless irritating experiences:

Firstly: The campsite fee is twenty-one and a half euros, which is extortionate beyond belief for such a minute pitch, but with no alternative what can I do? The tent is positioned with particular care. Ordinarily I would face the door towards the most pleasant view, but today it's prudent to pitch the tent on an east-west axis to set the most streamlined profile against the prevailing wind. On benign nights I've taken to pegging every second eyelet in the groundsheet and it's been secure enough. Not so tonight, in fact I've double pegged every hole crossed in the 'X' shape to firm up anchorage.

Secondly: As this is my last night in France, I decide to eat out to mark the occasion, not unreasonable after a thousand miles of solo self-propulsion in all weathers, may I suggest.

Later I come upon a restaurant where, as tradition seems to dictate in some cheerless little resorts that take tourists for granted, I am led to a table by a surly waiter whereupon I take a seat as directed and try to read the menu, which somewhat inconveniently is written only in French. How dare they! I ponder silently to myself for endless minutes with nobody taking the slightest interest in either me or in taking my order. I begin writing up my notes to pass the time. A good twenty minutes later it crosses my mind that perhaps I am invisible as no-one in this near empty restaurant has shown any interest whatsoever in making a profit. After closing my notebook and stowing my pencil I sit for several more minutes twiddling my fingers with a vacant and hungry expression plastered across my face. Naturally I give up and leave, although it seems odd that as I walk past the bar the waiter smiles cheerfully and bids me farewell as if this is the way things are done around here. A strange reaction, if you ask me. Anyway the waiter got a quiet evening and maybe that's all that matters. I can understand being ignored had I been curt to the staff or rude about the proud nation of France but given that I have not even mentioned Agincourt or Trafalgar, the lack of interest is bizarre. I am left with an option to find somewhere else to eat in preference to dying of starvation.

Thirdly: I get as far as ordering a fifty-centilitre bottle of red at the next restaurant, so far so good. Then I have the temerity to ask if I can order food in about twenty minutes' time (so I don't lose the thread of my writing, you understand). I am informed rather too firmly for my liking, that such flexibility of not permitted. When the waiter, Jean-Pierre or Claude or whatever he's called tells me this is not allowed, he does so with both hands on his hips and his chin set at what any fool can see is an aloof angle. I counter by pointing out that the restaurant isn't busy, but the waiter plays his trump card and tells me my table is booked. He emphasises the point with an unfortunate gallic snarl that I find quite unnecessary. Not only that but I catch the unmistakable whiff of a fib as there are more than enough unoccupied tables to cater for the whole village and absolutely no reservation signs on any of them. Quite appropriately I feel, I cancel the bottle of red and leave. This involves some personal risk as I have absolutely no idea if there are any other places to eat in Palaves-les-Flots. I am entirely aware that humble pie is not in the least bit nutritious or tasty should I need to return here if it proves to be the only eatery open.

Fortunately for me, only a few minutes on foot brings me to a modest café-restaurant. The place is nothing special but I'm not looking for special and the staff and I quickly establish a mutually satisfactory arrangement whereby they offer some service, some food, and some wine, and I provide some payment. Remarkable; all parties are happy with this and it has not proved a challenge for anyone. This restaurant also permits the whims of a getting-on-a-bit English cyclist who wishes to delay the arrival of his food for half an hour so he can complete his journal. The juxtaposition between the attitude of Jean-Pierre/Claude or whatever he was called and the waiter in this restaurant is astounding, a complete contrast, I am happy to say. Naturally I celebrate my good fortune by upping my order from a half bottle of red to a full one. I also make a mental note to convert my surplus euros into a tip if the food is up to par. In the event, the service was grand, the food tasty, and the tip reasonable.

It's dark as I stroll back to the campsite and halfway back it dawns on me that the wind is against my back and nowhere near as strong as earlier. This is a much more relaxing thought to go to sleep on, and as this more promising prospect for tomorrow is ably assisted by red wine, slumber is quick to arrive.

*Day 31 – Sunday 16th May*

*Department of Herault:*

*Palaves-les-Flots to Montpellier, then an overnight transit of France from Montpellier to Calais docks*

I've just enjoyed my last night in the Vango tent and when my little home's rolled up and loaded onto the bike for the final time it'll feel like waving a good friend off at the railway station. My tent's served me well for thirty nights in a row. It cost just thirty pounds to buy and you know what, that may work out at only a pound a night but it's proved itself to be inexpensive rather than cheap. The wind tried to break it, the rain tried to permeate it, and the cold tried to daunt it but they all came up short. How remarkable is that? My little tent has steadfastly remained up to the task of keeping me more or less snug: In northern France, it insulated me and made sure I stayed the right side of freezing – just about. Later it said 'NO' to the fearsome mistral wind, which challenged us both as it whistled down the Rhône-Saône valley, and on many a night on the second half of my coast to coast adventure the little Vango shielded me from torrential rain. How could anyone ask for more?

When I bought the tent a few weeks before setting off, the packaging gave no clue that entertainment was included, but entertainment comes as standard. Even now, ripples flexing across the tent roof are as fascinating as when I first saw it, then I watch the second act as a sharp gust snaps the material light, and finally the encore when the tension is released with an audible crack. For over half my little adventure gaffer tape has held the frame together and still the tent serves me well. Reluctant though I am to draw myself away from the canopy of entertainment above me, I really do need to get myself sorted. After all, I have a bus to catch.

Outside, enthusiastically windy about sums it up. Given half a chance a gust would have my tent away in a jiffy so I leave the panniers inside as anchors. But this wind is no novice, it's seen such tactics many times on the campsites it's blown across on its way from northern Spain. To make the point, the wind tries to stake its claim by grabbing the outer tent just as I'm trying to collapse it. As a result I have a short tug-of-war against an invisible opponent as I try to fold the tent into a more manageable shape. It is a tussle that makes me smile. This morning the wind has power; it's an out-of-the-ordinary wind for sure, but it is well short of the hundred kilometres an hour predicted. Best of all, it's a warm wind and the sun is out, and I'm still in the south of France and I only have fifteen miles to pedal. That all sounds pretty good to me. The final camping task of my trip is to take out the groundsheet pegs and remove the pannier bag ballast so I can roll and stow the tent. Once done I secure the panniers to the bike and carry out a pitch check one last time.

Once clear of Palaves-les-Flots I realise just how much protection the buildings have given me from the wind. Beyond the town is a flat treeless landscape where nothing prevents the weather from giving me a bit of a battering. I'm sure the wind becomes angrier as I turn northwest and head inland. There's really no need for that kind of attitude, is there? The wind gives it a go but not once does it completely destabilise the bike. Admittedly I am caught unawares once or twice when a particularly strong gust pushes me sideways, but even then, after wobbling from side to side for a few seconds I regain control. It's rather like being at the helm of a ship when the waves are hitting the starboard quarter. Progress is halting and zig-zag for short periods.

Pure white great egrets poke about for food in the dull wind-rippled water next to the road, usually statuesque birds but today their shoulders are hunched over as they shelter to eat behind clumps of stubby reeds. The other birds that have become such a familiar sight in the waterways of the Camargue are nowhere to be seen, hunkered down if they have any sense.

Herault is department thirty-four and it's set deep in Occitania. This prefecture of Montpellier takes its name from the Herault River, which pours into the sea southwest of here having started life ninety miles to the north in the Cevennes mountains, on the high slopes of Mont Aigoual to be precise. Here in Herault I'm pleased to report that the wind has eased notably in the last hour. The change brings much easier cycling, which is just what the doctor ordered – and thirty minutes later it's as if wind had never been invented. Overhead, a motorway sign informs me that Spain, Andorra, and Barcelona are all ahead. Initially the sign concerns me as I really don't have the appetite, and certainly not the time, to negotiate multiple lanes of dual carriageway traffic. Fortunately for me my concerns are put aside a few minutes later when I come to a bridge that takes pedestrians and cyclists over the busy France-Spain-Andorra motorway.

A short time later I arrive at Saint Jean de Vegas to await my bus. This final section involves some tricky navigation and I could well have become lost were it not for the helpful map sent by the bus company with my reservation documents and tickets. In fact, the pick-up point is not a bus stop as I expected, but a sizeable parking area set aside for commercial vehicles and long-distance buses, which is attached to Montpellier motorway services.

I'm three hours early for my bus, which is just fine by me as today is dry and sunny and thanks to the ever-ubiquitous McDonald's I can whittle the time away at an outdoor table, which I share with a paper mug of hot coffee, and some food. Not only that but in an outburst of uncontrolled spending I have just invested five pounds for a copy of the *Sunday Times*! I'll have many hours on the bus and I'm looking forward to catching up on world news. That said, the paper cost more me than I earned for a five-and-a-half-day week in my first job in an old-fashioned ironmongery and saddlery shop in Morpeth, Northumberland. I know time moves on and things change but how can that even be possible?

The European Bike Express arrives from southern Spain and gracefully rolls to a halt a few minutes earlier than expected. The bus has picked up other cyclists along the way and unless someone is cutting it very fine indeed, I'm the only one getting aboard here. The bus looks new and is towing a large curtain-sided trailer that's pretty well the same height as the bus and half as long. Once the side-curtains are pulled back I can see that the trailer contains two rows of bicycle racks, one above the other. All the bikes look to be lightweight high-end machines built for speed – my bike is a great deal chunkier than the others.

The driver asks me to remove the panniers. Once done he flips the bike up like a prancing horse so my velo rests on its rear wheel and its handlebars are secured at head height into the rack for the overnight trip to England. The bus began its return journey to the UK near Barcelona. It's only about a third full now but it will pick up more bicycles and riders as we head north on our journey through the heartlands of France. Both front seats on the upper deck of the bus are unoccupied, which is a bit of a surprise, so unless someone else wants to use one later, there's plenty of room for me to spread out and get comfortable. I know I have a newspaper to pass the time but by bagging the front seat I'll have a good view of the surrounding countryside until nightfall. Eventually I sort myself out in my seat of choice, although once I sit down it takes me several minutes to get my breath back after hauling three pieces of heavy cumbersome luggage up the narrow stairs to the top of the bus, surprisingly, I seem to be unique in having luggage with me.

Now, listen up – I know full well that I've only just clambered onto the bus so I'm the newbie, but I've had a look around and I can't help but notice that I am the only person here equipped with massive panniers and camping equipment. Everyone else, absolutely everyone else, I should repeat in case you missed it, has no luggage, none whatsoever! And, as if that isn't enough to make me suspicious, when I think back to the bike trailer, I remember that all the other passengers are riding sleek lightweight bikes of the go-faster sort. Now, at the risk of sounding judgemental, by glancing behind me I can see that my fellow passengers seem to be the *'look-at-me-don't-I-look-like-Billy-Whizz-in-my-shiny-spray-on-Lycra'* type. You know the sort.

I've stumbled upon a rather shocking revelation, don't you think? These aren't 'bike-adventurers' at all, they're masquerading, fraudulently masquerading as such – nothing more, nothing less. They've been staying in hotels! Now, this may well be my first time on a bike-bus, but if there's a hierarchy amongst passengers (and obviously there needs to be, let me tell you) then it's abundantly clear that true camping-cyclists, such as me, in case I'm ahead of you, must be at the very pinnacle. Even though only five weeks ago I was just a have-a-go novice without much hope, I've come a long way since then, over a thousand miles in fact, so I suffer no shame in being a little smug and feeling a smidgen superior in some ways. I hope that's not wrong of me. Anyway, who cares if it is? Not me, that's for sure; it's important to know your own worth.

The bus and its trailer pull out of Montpellier and trundle off up the northbound carriageway of the N9 motorway. The road is extremely congested and by the time we have passed through Nimes, Avignon, Valence, and Lyon we are running a good three hours behind schedule. This is not ideal as we are still only a quarter of the way to Calais. Today is 'Ascension Sunday', a fellow passenger tells me (without even the merest hint of the deference that my authentic cycle-adventurer status deserves, I should point out). AND – whilst I don't want to go off on one, I do find this sort of attitude rather disappointing in all honesty. Nobody expected him to make an appointment or crawl up the centre aisle to make his point before retreating backwards still on his hands and knees, but some sort of metaphorical 'doffing of his cap' is the least I would expect. Standards really aren't what they were.

Moving on: Ascension Day is a national holiday in France and many other European countries. No doubt the holiday and fine weather have done much to generate the additional traffic, which causes us to crawl along for the first few hours. Once the novelty of watching the delightful

French scenery from my elevated seat has diminished, I use the time well, and by nightfall I have read almost every page of my newspaper.

It's a long-established and well-understood scientific fact that beds are for sleeping in and buses are not. Much to my regret, sleeping in a semi-upright position is a somewhat specialised skill that I have yet to develop, it's the same in aeroplanes, how does anyone even doze when flying is beyond me. Sleep, such as is possible, comes in short uncomfortable stints from around one in the morning, until about five, which is about the time that we enter Paris. We drive into the capital just as dawn bathes the city in a hazy light. To be honest, due to my semi-stuporous state I don't actually recall stopping in Paris, although I know we must have because the bus has scooped up a few more cyclists since I last looked. There's no need for you to concern yourself with them, I'm pretty sure they are all of the lower status sort, I regret to say.

A few hours later the bus pulls up at Calais dock terminal. Hardcore passengers, that is to say, those of us who have travelled overnight from Spain or from the far south of France, including the no-luggage-spray-on-Lycra brigade to be fair, are suffering from chronic sleep deprivation. In my case the effect is wholesale: My brain, together with most of my cognitive functions have been adversely affected. Perhaps this state of torpidity is not quite as severe as I am making out but it's bad enough, let me tell you, and most unpleasant. Think 'man-flu' and then some, and you have a general idea of the level of debility involved. As you can probably deduce, this state of semi-consciousness is absolutely not the time to have one's patience tested. Well, it was bound to happen, wasn't it? Sod's Law or Murphy's Law, I really can't remember, and because I can't think straight right now, I really couldn't care less.

Anyway, the sight and sound of five busloads of excitable, noisy, unkempt, and I have to be honest with you, exceptionally irritating European teenagers occupying the buses parked on all sides of our vehicle, really is the last straw. I do of course realise that my attitude could be viewed as unreasonable, although to be fair I haven't slept in a bed for the last five weeks and I've just overnighted on a moving bus. Yes, I appreciate that just as I have enjoyed an adventure in their country, so these young people should be encouraged to enjoy an adventure in England. Travel to another country is always exciting and joyous and they are entitled to express that, although to be fair not once did I impose myself on the French nation, as these adolescents seem to be doing, by skipping, whooping, and making unwelcome approaches to members of the opposite sex. What is the world coming to?

## Day 32 – Monday 17th May

### England: From Dover docks to my North Devon home, via London

The return crossing to Great Britain takes just under ninety minutes and is as smooth as my outward journey five weeks ago. We berth at Dover at eleven-thirty on the dot, after which I make my way down several decks to unshackle my bike from the metal pipework I tethered it to before leaving Calais. I pass customs unhindered then cycle clear of the port following the coast road towards Dover Priory railway station. The next train departs for London at eleven fifty-two; there is another thirty minutes later, but I'm keen to catch the first train as I'm meeting our daughter Katie in London and we only have ninety minutes together. It's a bit of a rush.

In my haste to gather up my belongings from the bus I forget the brand-new Michelin tyre bought as a spare in Chalon-sur-Saône. The tyre will now be sliding around the floor of the bus trailer on its way north to Middlesbrough. It's a small price to pay to have an extra thirty minutes with Katie, who because of her university commitments I haven't seen for months.

Even if I say so myself, I set an impressive pace cutting through the streets of Dover before gliding at speed into the station entrance – there's less than two minutes to go. Cutting it tight is an understatement and I've yet to buy my ticket.

I hate ticket machines. Parking tickets, train tickets, underground tickets, all of them really. Let's face it, the machines are out to get everyone over fifty, it's as simple as that. The problem's crystal clear: Ticket machines are made to irritate – all of them. In fact, the primary purpose of every automated ticket machine is to irritate; dispensing tickets is secondary. And, they've all been designed by some young bod with a master's degree, probably in 'the history and decline of common sense'. Luckily for me a very pleasant youngster with a knack for such machines (haven't they all) sorts out my ticket as quickly as I could say, 'That -*bleep*- machine,' several times.

Everyone else has boarded the London train – I can see them watching me through carriage windows as I scurry towards them. This is good news because the platform is empty so I can whizz along towards the nearest carriage door. Most helpfully, I spot a guard standing next to the open door. My luck is in, until the exact moment I reach the guard, at which point he signals to the driver and the doors start to close slowly. I am right next to the door, I am right next to the guard, and for a foolish microsecond I assume the guard will pause the closure so I can get aboard. Wrong!

Naturally, I adopt a mournful hound-dog expression and wave my ticket in a forlorn way but this has no impact whatsoever on the guard. Now, inflexibility due to the legitimate health and safety policy of the rail company is one thing and I can take that on the chin. But the guard ignores me; he does, he actually ignores me. I may as well be invisible (rather like that restaurant in France, not that I'm bitter). Had the guard said, 'Sorry, I have no choice, mate,' or whatever, that would have been fine, but looking straight through me as if I'm transparent is just rude, very rude, and rather like the ticket machine, deeply irritating. But it is what it is, as they say, so I make good use of the thirty minutes by purchasing some credit for my phone. At least I can tell Katie that I am running a little late.

After an entirely uneventful journey through the undulating and pretty countryside of Kent the train pulls into Charing Cross Station, freeing me up to push the bike through the crowds of central London to the *'Lord Moon of the Mall'* pub in Whitehall. It was fantastic to grab an hour together and I wish it could have been longer but we both had matters to attend to. Katie had her studies at the university and I had to cycle to Buckingham Palace. We depart in the happy knowledge the whole family will be together again in North Devon a few days from now to celebrate Katie's recent twenty-first birthday.

After leaving the pub I push the bike along Whitehall and into Trafalgar Square where after turning left at Nelson's Column I climb back onto the saddle and cycle under Admiralty Arch. It feels surreal to be cycling in the middle of London and the sensation increases as I pedal slowly down The Mall. St. James' Park is to my left, St. James' Palace and Clarance House are on my right, and the view ahead is funnelled by trees on either side of the road. Buckingham Palace forms the grand centrepiece ahead of me at the end of The Mall, and as I cycle round the two and a half thousand tons of white marble that make up the Queen Victorian memorial, I notice that the Royal Standard is fluttering proudly on the palace roof – Her Majesty is in residence. As usual, a sizeable group of onlookers are gazing through the ornate gilded gates at the vast royal residence. In some ways Buckingham Palace makes the perfect finale to my adventure, a visual highlight *par excellence* to remember the end of my travels by, and a more fitting conclusion to my jolly little adventure than the southbound platform at Exeter St. David's railway station. Naturally an audience at the big house to mark the end of my trip would have been grand. We could have taken tea together, wouldn't that have been pleasant? But who knows, maybe Her Majesty is looking out of one of her windows right now. Maybe she has spotted the guy with the heavy bike and small tent. If so, she's probably thinking, *I hope he's not going to camp outside my place.*

After a few moments of reflection, I turn away from the grandeur of the palace and climb over the crossbar for the last time. I find pedalling down Birdcage Walk surprisingly tranquil considering I'm in the middle of one of the world's great capital cities. Next comes Parliament Square; as always it's a busy place so I dismount and walk my two-wheeled friend south over the river, passing the Houses of Parliament and Big Ben on my right as they look down at the Thames.

Westminster Bridge is the perfect location for gazing downstream at the wonder of central London. Today's skyline view is as captivating as always what with the iconic dome of St. Paul's Cathedral on the north bank with the Gherkin and the Cheese Grater buildings beyond it. Downstream the seventy-two-storey Shard commands the south bank. It's nearing completion now and when finished will stand one thousand and sixteen feet above the Thames and take its place as the tallest building in Britain. Running through all of this and stretching as far as I can see is the silver ribbon of Old Father Thames. My eyes follow the line of glittering water as it tapers past the East End, sweeps to the right, and flows out of view.

Leaving Westminster Bridge I push the bike along Riverside Walk, next the London Eye, then a short hop over Jubilee Gardens brings me to Waterloo Railway Station.

So that's it, I suppose. My little adventure is done and dusted and my bike can have a well-earned rest on the train back to Devon. As for me, my fitness has increased and my weight has decreased, both of which are a fine thing indeed.

\*\*\*

I'll sign off with a few words of appreciation and some of encouragement, if I may. Although I've left saying 'thank you' to my wife until the end of the book I'm more grateful to her than I could ever express.

I've tried to imagine the likely conversation between most couples after nearly forty years of marriage if one of them said, 'I'd like to cycle across France.'

'But you don't cycle, you haven't got a bike, and you're not exactly young, are you?'

'It's about seven or eight hundred miles, I reckon. I should do it in about five weeks…'

But I didn't get the response I expect many husbands would have. My wife supported my idea. How fantastic is that? Obviously, I wouldn't have gone without her blessing and because of her support I had a unique and wonderful experience, which allowed me to explore France and taught me much about myself. I shall always be exceptionally grateful to my wife. I've even forgiven her for creating those bogus weather forecasts.

*\*\*\**

Have you an idea in the back of your mind? Has it lurked there for years? Mine did. I would be delighted to think that reading about a novice who cycled a thousand miles solo has rekindled your idea. If so, there really is only one thing I can say: *Bon courage!*

PLEASE RECOMMEND THIS BOOK
IF YOU ENJOYED IT AND
IF BOUGHT ON AMAZON PLEASE REVIEW IT ONLINE.

# MEMORIUM for TSC

I think it was in late 1969 that I first became acquainted with TSC. We hit it off immediately and quickly became great friends. First, we explored the Northumbrian hills, just the two of us. Later we spent many days on the Lake District fells, then the west coast of Scotland – happy times. Two years later we made our first foray into Europe together and the year after that we explored the continent for several months. Exciting times. Much more recently TSC served me well, as it always had, when I pedalled across France.

After returning home to Devon, TSC (Trangia Storm Cooker) was very keen not to be put out to grass, and some months after we got back from our coast to coast adventure TSC was happy and excited to go to a music festival with our daughter and her husband. Many months later I asked my daughter about TSC coming home only to discover it had been donated to an unknown charity shop. At first it was difficult to accept that my companion of 50 years had gone, but I've had time to think now. TSC was not one to be put into storage so it's for the best that it's gone to a new home. And now that I've reflected, I think it's rather joyous to think that TSC has gone to cook with its new owners high in the uplands of England or even further afield. *'Bon courage'* on your future travels, TSC.

Printed in Great Britain
by Amazon